MANIPURI GRAMMAR

1

MANIPURI GRAMMAR

Chungkham Yashwanta Singh
Department of Linguistics
Manipur University, Imphal

RAJESH PUBLICATIONS
NEW DELHI - 110 002

ISBN (10) : 81-85891-33-8
ISBN (13) : 978-81-85891-33-0

Published by :
Sanjay Gupta
RAJESH PUBLICATIONS
1, Ansari Road, Darya Ganj
New Delhi - 110002
Ph.: 011-23274550

Typesetting by :
Sanjay Enterprises
Delhi - 110002

Printed at :
R.K. Offset Process
Delhi - 110095

First Published in India : 2010
Reprint : 2011
2nd Edition : 2019

Dedicated
In the memory of my loving parents
Chungkham Ongbi Ibeyaima Devi
and
Chungkham Noyonchand Singh

PREFACE

This book is a modest attempt to swift out the gross imposition of the grammatical rules of the other languages to the study of Manipuri language by the so-called Manipuri Sanskrit scholars. The book has ten chapters. The First Chapter discusses about the cultural and linguistics setting of Manipuri language dealing with land and people, language, history, meitei script and review of literature. This language has script, Manipuri is the only one Tibeto-Burman language having script of its own in India.

The Second and Third Chapters deal with Phonological system and Morphological system respectively. Word-formation also becomes the Fourth Chapter dealing with the three strategies of word formation - affixation, compounding and affixo-compounding. The Fifth Chapter discusses about word class and its grammatical constituents. The Sixth Chapter deals with morphophonemics (Lexical and Post-lexical phonological rules). The Seventh Chapter explains about clause structure. The Eighth Chapter deals with sentence processes discussing the three kinds of sentences-negation, interrogative and imperative. The Ninth Chapter discusses about syntactivization explaining about verb 'be', nominalization, complementation, relativization, causativization and reduplication. The book tries to see how the language is used in the society. The Tenth Chapter deals with the social grammar of this language explaining taboo, kinship terminology and terms of address.

Imphal **Ch. Yashawanta Singh**

ACKNOWLEDGEMENT

It is a long desire for me to write a descriptive Grammar of Manipuri in English. Today the dream has come to true and become Manipuri Grammar. For quite a long time there has not been any adequate and scientific study on Manipuri though it (Manipuri, locally known as Meiteilon) is one of the major languages of the Tibeto-Burman sub-family of the Sino-Tibetan family.

For this study I get different helps from different persons and from different institutions in financial support as well as moral boost. I sincerly thank University Grant Commission (UGC), India, for recommending me to Associations of Commonwealth Universities, London for the award of Commonwealth Academic Staff Fellowship for the academic year of 1995-96. I thank British Council for looking after me to solve any problem coming on my way. During my staying in the School Oriental and African Studies (SOAS), University of London, I take up the work of writing this book . I am indebted to John Okell, Department of South East Asia, for his weekly discussion on my writing. I also express my gratitude to David Bennet, Department of Linguistics, SOAS, University of London, for his readiness to help me when I have any problem. I also thank Denwood, SOAS, for his reading of my half completed manuscript.

I am indebted to my colleagues and teachers for their moral support and encouragements. I am really indebted to my wife, Aruna, also for her moral support and help. Finally I wish to acknowledge my debt to my University of Manipur.

Ch. Yashawanta Singh

CONTENTS

ABBREVIATION

abl.	ablative	inst.	instrumental
acc.	accussative	loc.	locative
AObR	action Oriented bound root	NZR	nominalizer
asp.	aspect	neg.	negative
ass.	associative	nom.	nominative
caus.	causative	obj.	object
comd. mk.	command marker	part.	particularization
compl.	completed	pleo	pleonastic
con.	conjunctive	pot.	potenstial
cop.	copula	prog.	progressive
dat.	dative	proh.	prohibitive
def.	definitizer	propo.	proposal
dem.	demonstrative	purs.	purposive
det.	determiner	Q or q. mk.	question marker
dir.	directional	qut.	quotative
dur	durative	reci.	reciprocal
encl	enclitic	ref.	reflexive
end.	endearment	rem.	remote
exp.	experiencer	seq.	sequence
fp	formative particle	un. asp.	unrealized aspect.
gen.	genitive	V.ed	voiced
hon.	honorific	V. less	voiceless

CHAPTER–I

THE CULTURAL AND LINGUISTIC SETTING

1. INTRODUCTION

1.1. Land and People

That Manipur was an ancient Kingdom was reflected in the language having maintained difference in the terms of address — royal's term and commoner's term. Manipur literally means the city of or the land of 'gems'. According to Manipur Historical work, Sanamahi Laikan, the name Manipur was first officially introduced in the early eighteen century during the reign of Hindinised King, Garibniwaj (1709-48).

In the past, Manipuri was known by the neighbouring states by various names; Kathe to the Burmese which term they equally applies to the land as well, Meklee to the Assamese, Moglie to the Cacharis, Cassey to the Shans or those who inhabited the country east of the Ningthi or Khyendwen river, of which term Kathe is a corrupted form. In reciprocal the Manipuries used coining names to identify their neighbouring peoples. To them the Burmese bore four names-according to the regions of their settlement in Burma (now called Myanmar). The Assamese, the Cacharis, the Tripuris and the Chinese were respectively known as Takhao (since they inhabited by the river Dikhu), Mayang, Takhel and Khagi. Here indigenous names are Kangleipak, Poireipak and Meitrabak.

Manipur was one of the routes between South Asia and South East Asia and central Asia. Various, ethnic groups belonging to Southern Mongoloid group, the Tibeto- Burmans, the Indo-Aryans and a sizeable section of Tai (Shans) came to Manipur from pre-historic times down to the present day (Gangmumei Kabui,1991:12). The three major ethnic groups of this state of Manipur - the Meities of the valley, the Nagas and the Kuki-Chin of the surrounding hills are regarded as the descendants of those migrating people. They speak Tebeto-Burman (TB) languages. Officially it is recognised that there are twenty nine dialects in the state; they all belong to Naga group and Kuki-Chin group of TB sub-family.

1.2. Language

Manipuri, locally known as Meiteilon (the Meitei + lon 'language'), is spoken basically in the state of Manipur which is in North-eastern India. It is also spoken in Assam, Tripura, Mizoram, Burma and Bangladesh. More than ten lakhs people speak Manipuri in Manipur. Manipuri is the only medium of communication among the speakers of 29 different mother tongues. Hence it is regarded as lingua franca. Since 20 August 1992 Manipuri becomes the first TB language to receive recognition as a schedule VIII language of India. Before this very date, Manipuri has adopted as the medium of instruction and examination. More and above, Manipur University has Manipuri Department in the P.G and research in literature including folklore and Old Manipuri are continuing. During the British regime (1891-1947) its state language status continued. Deliberation of Darbar (the highest Executive Judiciary and Legislature) were held; judgements of law courts were delivered in the language. Its state language status finds special recognition in the relevant provisions of the Manipur State Court Act 1947 and the Manipur State Constitution Act. 1947.

In the classification of TB languages of the Sino-Tibetan family, Manipuri is placed in Kuki-Chin Proper separately by Grierson-Konow (1903-1928), in Meitei Branch of Kukish Section by Shafer (1955, 1966, 1974), Benedict (1972) placed Manipuri in Kuki-Naga under further from Kuki-Naga. According to Benedict, 'Meitei, the state language, shows significant points of contact with Kachin as well as with Kuki-Naga, though the affinities are prominently with the latter'. In the classification of DeLancey (1987:800) Manipuri is part of a distinct sub-branch in TB which he calls Mikir-Meitei where both the languages Mikir and Meitei are closely related to the Naga and Kuki-Chin sub-branches. But in the opinion of Matisoff (1994) Manipuri is close to the Kuki-Chin Naga branch. By observing these opinions on the whole, these are minor differences.

Manipuri shares genetic features of TB features. Some genetic rather than areal, shared TB features include phonemic tone, SOV word order, agglutinative verb morphology and tendency to reduce disyllabic forms to monosyllabic ones (DeLancey 1987) while Manipuri exhibits many of these features, it is, an a typical language in some ways, that is, pronominal marking on verb, which is considered an original TB trait (Bauman 1975:75, DeLancey 1889) is not present in Manipuri. But still there is nominal pronominal markers which is regarded as remnants of TB pronominal feature. Very specifically, Manipuri has extensive verb morphology, extensive suffix with more limited prefixation. It has no watertight compartment between morphology and syntax: the concept of subject is not so distinct (in other words, subject can be deleted or understood); different word classes are formed by affixation of the respective markers. In words-formation, compounding is more productive.

1.3. History

In the history of Manipur, there were some significant dates which affected language. In the 14th century the valley was divided into small Kingdoms under the rule of distinct groups of people particularly the celebrated seven clan dynasties. They are Khaba, Chenglei, Luwang, Khuman, Moirang, Angom and Ningthouja speaking different dialects. The last representing the Meitei was the most powerful and reigned in the heart of the valley. In the 14th century during the process of state formation, the king of Ningthouja, Nongda Leiren Pakhangba, consolidated the various groups into one, the Meitei. In other words during the process of the state formation all the groups merged into one and became the Meitei. This is reflected in the language. That is, commonly found use of double synonyms, technically known as 'Semantic reduplication' such as **ucek-səwa** 'bird' **pamba - kəy** 'tiger' **ciŋu -lay** 'God' etc. are literarily very effective. Of each phrase, one form belongs to one clan, another form to another clan : **ucek** belongs to Meitei clan, while **səwa** to Moirang clan [see detail in 9.6].

Here it can be remembered what Moravcsik said in his paper' Reduplicative construction' (1978), in semantic reduplication the synonymous words may derive from different languages. Before the end of 17th century, there is no influence of Indo-Aryan languages like Hindi, Bengali and Sanskrit on Manipuri.

In the 18th century during the reign of Maharaj Garibniwaj (1709-1748), the name itself is a sanskritized one, mass conversion of the Meitei from the local religion 'Sanamahi' to Hinduism was taken place under his order. Since the coming of Hinduism, many loan words from Sanskrit, Hindi and Bengali have come into; Bengali script replaced Meitei script in writing, Bengali sounds have started entering Manipuri sound system. Specially religious terms were borrowed, borrowing of kinship terms led to a simplification of kinship terminology (Pramodini Devi: 1990:105).

From this conversion of Hinduism, the birth of dialects of Manipur had started - the birth of Kwatha dialect, Phayeng, Andro, Sekmai and Kakching etc. Two groups of the Meitei population were exiled from the main Manipuri speaking areas in the valley to the surrounding hill areas. These groups are the Lois who resisted conversion to Hinduism and the Yaithibis who did not follow strictly enough the rituals of and rules of Hinduism. They formed those dialects- Kwatha; Sekmai, Andro, and Phayeng. Their dialects are not influenced by Sanskrit nor Hindi nor Bengali. These dialects have been reinforced by geographic and social isolation of these groups. Further more, in an effort to preserve their Meitei identity, the exiled groups have tried to align speech with the written language so that they speaks conservative, older form of Manipuri. Till today, lexically they maintained some of old archaic Manipuri. In the urban area, the language contact between Manipuri and other Indo - Aryan languages is very significant and the process is continuing very significantly (specially use of English words is very prominent).

The Western education had started since when Manipuri was under the British rule(from 1835 to 1947). During this time English medium schools were established in Manipur and became bilingual — Manipuri as well as English. Affairs of the state were also carried out in English. English language is started becoming very important in education. In 1949 Manipur was incorporated into the Indian Union since then Hindi also is becoming important besides English. In course of time importance of English language is increasing more and more, side by side with the growth of Manipuri language and literature many loan words of English are coming into Manipuri.

1.4. Meitei Script*

As regard Manipuri Script, locally know as Meitei Mayek, it is very controversial due to lack of scientific studies. And there are three major questions first, when exactly is it created; secondly, whether it is a own creation or not and thirdly, how many letters are ? All these answers to these questions are not satisfactory, they aren't free from controversy.

For giving answers to the above first and second questions, it is very necessary to incorporate the following three different opinions.

a) The views of Britishers.
b) The views of Indian scholars (Non-Locals) and
c) The views of local scholars.

These are discussed below :

(a) The Views of Britishers are Hudson (1975), Damant (1875), Brown (1873), Dun (1981). Except Hudson, the three others have the same opinion. Grierson quotes Hudson's opinion that local tradition declares that the art of writing was acquired from Chinese who came to Manipur about 1500 A.D. This opinion is totally rejected on the basis that they (Chinese and Manipuri writings) are quite different from each other. Grierson again quotes Damant's opinion that

" .... the old Manipuri alphabet was introduced from Bengal in the reign of Charairongba, who flourished about 1700 A.D. There are no traces of the existence of writing in Manipuri before that time" (Grierson : P21).

Brown and Dun have the same view. In the opinion of Brown, 'The written character of the Manipuris is a modification of the Nagari' (1873 : p94). The same is the view of Dun. In his

* See appendix-I

word 'the Manipuris possess a written character of their own, which seems a modification of the Nagari' (Dun,1981 : P94). Grierson endorsed to the opinion of Damant, Brown and Dun: this is substantiated by showing Manipuri script on page 22 of his (Grierson) Linguistic Survey of India (LSI) Vol III Part III. But he does not express his own view.

(b) Indian Scholars' View : In the line of the Britishers (i.e. Damant, Brown and Dun), the Indian scholars like S.K Chatterjee and Bholanath Tiwari express their opinion that Manipuri script is a modified form of Devanagari or Bengali script. But they did not present appropriate evidence.

(c) Local Scholars' View : In their views also there are two opinions: one is saying that it is their own creation and another is that it is derived from Brahmi (from Devanagari, Bengali and Assami). The first view is supported by books, namely, Cheitharol Kumbaba (The Royal Chronicle), Wakoklon Thilel Salai, Amailon Pukok, scholars like Padma Shree Khelchandra Singh, Shree Wangkheimayum Tomchou Singh and Meitei Mayek Expert committee Report, (1979) etc. The second view is supported by the Manipuri Sanskrit Scholars, namely, Pandit Atombapu Sharma, R.K. Sanahal, L. Ibungohal, Nandalal Sharma, R.K. Jhalajit Singh, Manipuri Sahitja Parishad etc. In this juncture scientific analysis and further studies are felt necessary to answer satisfactorily to these questions.

The first stone inscription in Meitei alphabet was installed by Kyamba, the Meitei King (1467-1508) at Khoibu village in south-east Manipur & the writing of Cheitharol Kumbaba also commenced during his time. These facts at least refute the categorical assertion of G.H. Damant.

The British scholars like Damant (1875) & Hudson (1975) point out that the 'Meitei script' had been developed as late as 16/17th century. On the contrary, W. Y. Singh, a local scholar has pushed back the date as early as 3rd century A.D. (1935:P.19). Unfortunately there is no valid historical evidence to substantiate the view. Learning & production of Meitei manuscript were started during the reign of King Khagemba (1597-1652 A.D) & upto the close of the 17th century, i.e. until the conversion of Hinduism. They cover as varied subject as traditional faith, mythologies, rituals, administrative codes, chronicles, genealogies, description of different hills found in Manipur & also valuable stones, study of clouds, prediction, astrology, description of nature, ballads & other imaginative works of pure literature (Manihar Singh, 1976).

An important point that emerges from the study of the manuscripts is the fact that uptil about the beginning of the 18th century they were completely free from any loan words. In fact loan words from Sanskrit and Bengali languages particularly have been found in manuscripts produced from 1709 onwards. The findings from study of loan words in the old manuscript lead to see the linkages between religion and script (Aggarwal, 1997). Sanatomba Singh (1994), in fixing the date of the creation of Meitei script, based on the inscriptions on stone, coins and written documents; Meitei script may be created as early as during the reign of King Khagemba (1597-1652), by the end of the 16th and beginning of the 17th century.

In naming the letters also different opinions are put forward - one group likes to read as Hindi, another wants to read **kok** for |k|, **səm** for |s|, **lay** for |l| etc. taking from the names of the body parts **kok** 'head' **səm** 'hair' **lay** 'forehead'.

1.5 Review of Literature

Manipuri is notably under described. Existing works can be divided into four categories. First is work of British missionaries or administrators. The most important of which are Primrose (1887, 100 pages) and Pettigrew (1912, 111 pages) who provide useful list of conversational sentences and list of idioms. Pettigrew is specially insightful with regards to the verb morphology.

Grierson (1903) in his LSI, Manipuri is briefly described : vowels, consonants, word categories, syllable, sentence types etc. However, neither of these words is exhaustive in its description ; must of the phonology, morphology, word-formation, morphophonemics and morphosyntax are remained without description. More and above, these works are lack of application of linguistic science.

The second is the works of Manipuri Sanskrit scholars, they applied Sanskrit grammatical principles in the analysis of Manipuri. This is in turn leads to an incorrect analysis of the phonology, morphology and syntax. The major works of this type are : Kalachand Shastri's (1964) 'Manipuri Byakaran Koumudi, Dwijamani Dev Sharma's (1969) 'Meiteilon Byakaran, and Nandalal Sharma's (1976) Meiteilon.

Third is the study of Manipuri by the native speaker linguists. This starts from the late 70s. The first published of primary work is of W. Tomchou (1986) 'Manipuri Grammar, P.C. Thoudam's (1991) T.D.C Remedial Manipuri Grammar and M.S. Ningomba's (1992) 'Meitei Lonmit'. Other works include unpublished works, 35 Master's and M. Phil dissertations and seven Ph.D thesis. They are Madhubalas' Manipuri Grammar (1979), Yashawanta's Some Aspects of Manipuri Syntax (1984), Imoba's Perspectives of Manipuri Lexicography (Problems and Suggestions) (1985), Nonigopal's A Meitei Grammar of Roots and Affixes (1987) and Pramodini's Social Grammar of Meiteilon (1989).

Finally, there is the work of Non-Manipuri linguists writing in English. Bhat and Ningomba's 'A Manual of Manipuri Grammar (1988) unpublished) and Bhat's Grammatical Relations : evidence against their Necessity and Universality (1991) and Inder Singh's Manipuri Phonetic Reader (1975). Since the establishment of Department of Linguistics in Manipur University in 1986, linguistic studies of the language is gradually increasing.

References :

1. O. Bhogeshwar Singh (ed) Sanamahi Laikan (in Manipuri) Imphal, 1973 p.50
2. Gangmumei Kabui, 1991 History of Manipur : Vol. I Pre-colonial Period, National Publishing House, New Delhi.
3. Ch. Yashawanta Singh - 1995 'The Linguistic Situation in Manipur'. In LTBA. Vol. 18:1 Spring.
4. Julius Moravcsik 1978. 'Reduplicative Construction' In Universal of Human Language. Vol. IV ed. by Joseph H. Greenberg. Standford University Press, California.
5. James A. Matisoff 1994. 'Regularity and Variation in Sino-Tibetan'. In Current Issues in Sino-Tibetan Linguistics. Ed Hajime Kitamura et. al Osaka, Japan.
6 G.A. Grierson, 1903. LSI Vol. III. Part III. Ist Edition, Motilal Banarasidas. Delhi.
7. R.Brown . 1874. 'Statistical Account of Manipur' : Ist Publication Reprint, Calcutta.
8. E.W. Dun 1981 'Gazetteer of Manipur'. Delhi p. 26.
9. G.H. Damant, 1875 'Speciment of Manipuri Alphabet' In Proceedings of the Asiatic Society of Bengal ASB, Calcutta.
10. T. C. Hudson 1975 'The Meitheis' Neeraj Publishing House (Reprint) New Delhi.
11. W. Yumjao Singh 1935 Reports on the Archaeological Studies in Manipuri, Imphal.
12. Kailash S. Aggarwal, 1997 'Script and Ethnolinguistic Identity. The Meiteilon Quagmire. In Languages of Tribal and Indigenous People of India. Ed. Anvita Abbi. Motilal Banarsidas, Delhi.
13. Scott DeLancey, 1987 'Sino-Tibetan Languages'. In Bernard Comrie (ed.) The World's Major Languages. Croom Helm. London. 797-810.
14. James J. Bauman, 1975 Pronouns and Pronominal Morphology in TB. (Unpublished) Ph.D dissertation, University of California, Berkeley.

CHAPTER–II
THE PHONOLOGICAL SYSTEM

2.1 Phonology

The phonological system of Manipuri speech contains three major systems of sounds — vowels, consonants and tone — and one minor system of accompanying elements — Juncture. The balance of the phonological structure has to do with the inter-relationships of these elements and systems with one another — the ways in which they are combined to form syllables and pause groups. A brief characterization of each system is provided first. The segments of Manipuri do not show any great phonologically conditioned variation. The sound system of Manipuri consists of 24 consonants and 6 vowels under segmental features while two tones — level and falling — and one juncture are found under supra-segmental feature.

2.2 The Vowel System

It is said that Manipuri has six vowels. They are shown in table 1.

Table 1 : Chart of Vowel Phonemes

	Front	Central	Back
High	i		u
Mid	e	ə	o
Low		a	

Articulatory description of these 6 vowels are given here :

i-	High, front, unrounded vowel
e-	Mid, front unrounded vowel
ə-	Mid, central, unrounded vowel
a-	Low, central, unrounded vowel
o-	Mid, back, rounded vowel
u-	High, back, rounded vowel

On the basis of the following minimal pairs in (1) we can establish different phonemic status of these six vowels.

1.	/i/	pi	'tear (N)'
	/e/	pe	'umbrella'
	/ə/	lən	'wealth'
	/a/	lan	'war'
	/o/	poŋ	'raft'
	/u/	puŋ	'mridanga'

2.2.1 Occurrençe

All the six vowels can occur initially, medially and finally. But initial occurence of /e/ and /a/ are rare in compare with the other remaining vowels. There is no contrast in vowel length.

Initial Occurrence

2.	/i/	in	'fishing net'
		iroy	'buffalo'
		irəy	'current'
	/e/	ensaŋ (yensaŋ)	'curry'
	/ə/	ədu	'that'
		əni	'two'
		əŋaŋ	'child'
	/a/	adə	'there (proximity)
	/o/	ok	'pig'
		otpə	'to torture'
		obə	'to vomit'
	/u/	u	'tree'
		un	'skin'
		ucek	'bird'

Medial Occurrence

3.	/i/	cin	'mouth'
		hik	'louse'
		lik	'neklace'
	/e/	ceŋ	'uncooked rice'
		cek	'brick'
		len	'hail'
	/ə/	səm	'hair'
		təm	'valley'
		məŋ	'dream'
	/a/	may	'face'
		yaw	'sheep'
		hameŋ	'goat'
	/o/	kok	'head'
		pok	'grey hair'
		yot	'iron' (metal)
	/u/	kun	'twenty'
		cum	'wall lizard'
		nuŋ	'stone'

Final occurrence

4.	/i/	yari	'gum' (in the month)
		thəwri	'rope'
		hi	'boat'
	/e/	ce	'paper'
		pe	'umbrella'
		pere	'a kind of can for watering'
	/ə/	pabə	'to read'
		tabə	'to listen'
		pibə	'to give'

/a/	ya	'teeth'
	na	'ear'
	ka	'room'
/o/	mo	'cow or ox' or 'a kind of louse'
	pa-ro	'Read'
	cət-lo	'Go'
/u/	yu	'liquor'
	hu	'poison'
	ku	'coffin'

When a semi-vowel occurs after the vowels /ə/, /a/ , /o/ and /u/ a diphthong like sound is created. as in example (5).

5.			
	əy	əy	I'
		ləy	'flower'
		məy	'fire'
		məytəy	'The Meitei"
	ay	lay	'picture'
		may	'face'
		nay	'pus'
	əw	phəw	'paddy'
		məw	'married woman'
		ləw	'paddy field'
	oy	məkhoy	'they'
		khoy	'bee'
		koy	'beard'
	uy	huy	'dog'
		luy	'a cotten cloth to wear'
	aw	paw	'news'
		thaw	'oil'
		khaw	'bag'

A phonetic feature of the six vowels of Manipuri is shown in the table 2.

	i	e	ə	a	u	o
syllabic	+	+	+	+	+	+
sonorant	+	+	+	+	+	+
consonantal	-	-	-	-	-	-
round	-	-	-	-	+	+
high	+	-	+	-	+	-
back	-	-	+	+	+	+

Table 2 : Phonetic Feature of the Vowel Phonemes.

2.3 The Consonant System

The consonant system makes use of the distinction between aspirate and unaspirate, voiced (v.ed) and voiceless (v. less) only in the case of stops not in other consonats, makes use of the distinction stop, nasal, lateral, fricative and semi-vowel and shows consonants primarily in four positions: bilabial, alveolar, palatal, velar and glottal. Here, below, Manipuri consonant system is given in table 3.

PLACE OF ARTICULATION

		Bilabial		Alveolar		Palatal		Velar		Glottal
		v.less	/v.ed	/v.l ess	/v. ed	/v.l ess	/v.e d	/v.le ss	/v.ed/	
stops	Unaspirate	p	b	t	d	c	J	k	g	
	Aspirate	ph	bh	th	dh		Jh	kh	gh	
Fricatives						s				h
Nasals			m		n				ŋ	
Laterals			l							
Trills			r							
Semi-vowels			w					y		

Table 3 : The Consonant System

A set of 24 Manipuri consonantal phonemes can be established on the basis of the following minimal pairs or overlapping words. Out of these 24 phonemes 7 consonants are borrowed phonemes. They are b, d, g, bh, dh, gh, j, jh, and r. So they are found only in loan words.

2.3.1 Consonant Phonemic contrast

a. Stops : voiceless and voiced

p/b	budhi	'wisdom'
	pu-bə	'to bring'
	bajar	'market'
	pa-bə	'to read'
t/d	ta	'spear'
	dada	'elder brother'
c/j	cura	'a decorative piece for head made of peacock's feather'
	jura	'pair'
k/g	kən-bə	'to save'
	gənja	'hashish'

b. Stop : unaspirate and aspirate

p/ph	pa-bə	'to read'
	pha-bə	'to keep in memory'
b/bh	babu	'gentleman'
	bhari	'huge'
t/th	ta	'spear'
	tha	'moon'
d/dh	dəri	'carpet (rough)
	dhəni	'echo, noise'
j/jh	jəga	'place'
	jhəri	'lace'

k/kh	ka	'room'
	kha	'south'
g/gh	gari	'vehicle'
	ghəri	'watch'

c. Contrast between palatal voiceless stop and palatal voiceless fricative.

c/s	ca	'tea'
	sa	'animal'
	cu	'sugar cane'
	su	'a kind of thread'

d. Constrast between nasals

m	ma	'bug'
n	na	'ear'
ŋ	ŋa	'fish'

e. Constrast between lateral and trill

l/r	ləŋ	'thread'
	rəŋ	'paints'

f. Constrast between semi-vowels

w/y	wa	'bamboo'
	ya	'teeth'

As noted above, /n/ and /l/ are already established as different phonemes by ever minimal pair in the initial position. However, in the final occurrence specially they became a free variation. Under keen observation, what it is found is that either of the two /n/ is found more appropriate in sound sequence. To show it in the examples given below, it is written in this way n/l not l/n.

7.	/i/	in/l	'fishing net'
		cin/l	'mouth' [cinbal 'lips']
		tin/l	'insect'
		lin/l	'snake'
	/e/	turen/l	'river'
		mayren/l	'pumpkin'
		tayren/l	'a kind of tree'
		kawren/l	'a distinguished ox'
		ten/l	'bow and arrow'
		sen/l	'money'
	/ə/	yukhən/l	'curtain'[l/n]
		kaŋkhən/l	'mosquito net' [l/n]
		lən/l	'wealth'
		tən/l	'chappati'
		sən/l	'cow'
	/a/	lan/l	'war'
		tan/l	'timing in music'
		man/l	'wealth security'
		phan/l	'seat'
	/o/	mon/l	'pillow'
		lon/l	'language'
		kon/l	'utensil'

/u/	thun/l	'hip'
	khun/l	'village'
	pun/l	'earthern pot'
	mun	'pubic hair' [/l/ cannot occur]

2.3.2 Distribution

Distributionally, all the consonant phonemes cannot occur in the initial, medial and in the final position, only p, tç, k, ph, th, kh, j, m, n, ŋ, l, s, h, w and y can occur initially.

a. Initial Occurrence

/p/	pa	'eye lash'
	pat	'lake'
	pun	'earthen pot'
/t/	ta	'spear'
	tin/l	'worm or insect'
	təmpak	'valley'
/k/	ka	'room'
	kəy	'tiger'
	kot	'grainary house'
/ph/	phi	'cloth'
	phal	'seat'
	phək	'mat'
/th/	tha	'moon'
	thəro	'lily'
	thəbək	'work'
/kh/	kha	'south'
	khun	'village'
	khəwri	'throat'
/c/	ca	'tea'
	cu	'suger cane'
	cak	'cooked rice'
/j/	jəgoy	'dance'
/m/	ma	'bug'
	məri	'four'
	məcu	'colour'
/n/	na	'ear'
	numit	'sun'
	nəŋ	'you'
/ŋ/	ŋa	'fish'
	ŋəsi	'today'
	ŋək	'neck'
/s/	sa	'animal'
	səm	'hair'
	səruk	'share'
/l/	la	'banana leaf'
	ləm	'place'
	ləmjel	'race'
/h/	ha	'an eatable root'

	hi	'boat'
	həkcaŋ	'body'
/w/	wa	'bamboo'
	wahəy	'word'
	waykhu	'crabe'
/y/	ya	'teeth'
	yoŋ	'monkey'
	yubi	'coconut'

b. Medial Occurrence

Maxium number of consonants can occur medially. They are p, t, k, ph, th, kh, b, d, g, m, n, ŋ, c, s, j, y, r, l and w.

/p/	əpambə	'desire'
	təmpak	'valley'
/t/	ətənbə	'lazy'
	ləyteŋ'	'ornament'
/k/	ləykay	'locality'
	ləykəŋ	'dry land'
/ph/	ləphoy	'banana'
	kəphoy	'pomegranate'
/th/	khonthok	'sound utterance'
	məthək	'above'
/kh/	ləykhom	'mud'
	məkhoy	'they'
/b/	təmbi	'road'
	ləybak	'earth'
/d/	pandəm	'goal'
	cadiŋ	'expenditure'
/g/	teŋgot	'bowl'
	həŋgam	'leaf of mustard plant'
/c/	ləycin	'cloud'
	nacom	'a small bunch of flower to be wore in the ear'
/s/	məsoŋ	'mane'
	ləmsaŋ	'a name of place'
/j/	khəjay	'cheek'
	kəwjeŋ	'grass hopper'
/m/	məmom	'his/her daughter'
	məməy	'tail'
/n/	mənəm	'smell'
	ləynaŋ	'muddy water'
/ŋ/	ləyŋoy	'sand'
	məŋan/l	'light'
/y/	uyuŋ	'pillar'
	məyay	'middle'
/r/	həyraŋgoy	'a kind of fruit'

	ləyrəŋ	'oven'
/l/	ləlonbə	'business man'
	pəlem	'mother'
/w/	əwaŋbə	'height'
	məwoŋ	'his/her nature'
/h/	ləmhaŋ	'open field'
	ləmhuy	'fox'

Final Occurrence

Very limited Manipuri consonants can occur in the final position. They are p, t, k, m, n/l & ŋ.

/p/	həytup	'apple'
	pap	'sin'
/t/	pat	'lake'
	pot	'thing'
/k/	kok	'head'
	məhak	'he'
/m/	səm	'hair'
	leŋjum	'shoulder'
/n/l	lan/l	'war'
	lon/l	'language'
/ŋ/	thoŋ	'bridge'
	loŋ	'a kind of spear having many pointed heads'

Distinctive features of the consonants are given in table 4.

	k	g	kh	gh	c	j	s	jh	t	d	th	dh	p	b	ph	bh	m	n	ŋ	l	w	y	h	r
Syllabic	-	-	-	-	-	-	-	-	-	-	-	-	-	-	-	-	-	-	-	-	-	-	-	-
Sonorant	-	-	-	-	-	-	-	-	-	-	-	-	-	-	-	-	+	+	+	+	+	+	-	+
Consonantal	+	+	+	+	+	+	+	+	+	+	+	+	+	+	+	+	+	+	+	+	+	+	+	+
Anterior	-	-	-	-	-	-	+	+	-	-	-	-	-	-	-	-	+	+	-	+	+	+	-	+
Coronal	-	-	-	-	+	+	+	+	+	+	+	+	-	-	-	-	-	+	-	+	-	+	-	+
Lateral	-	-	-	-	-	-	-	-	-	-	-	-	-	-	-	-	-	-	-	+	-	-	-	-
Nasal	-	-	-	-	-	-	-	-	-	-	-	-	-	-	-	-	+	+	+	-	-	-	-	-
Voice	-	+	-	+	-	+	-	+	-	+	-	+	-	+	-	+	+	+	+	+	+	+	-	-
Spread glottis	-	-	+	+	-	-	+	+	-	-	+	+	-	-	+	+	-	-	-	-	-	-	-	-
Continuant	-	-	-	-	-	-	+	+	-	-	-	-	-	-	-	-	-	-	+	+	+	+	+	+

Table 4 : Distinctive Features of the Consonants

2.3.3 Consonant Cluster

It is generally understood as combination of two consonants within a syllable (intrasyllabic) or in other word. uttarance of two consonant sounds at a time. It differs from consonant sequence which is happened beyond syllable. Consonant cluster is, like many other Tibeto-Burman languages, very rich in initial and medial. Cluster formation is very limited: the second phonemes in the cluster will be by w, y, r and l.

(i). Initial Cluster

It is formed by combination of stops - p, t, k, kh, d + semivowels or l/r .

a. Stops + semivowels or l/r

k+w	>	kw	:	kwa	'bettal nut'
				kwak	'crow'
k+y	>	ky	:	kyamləy	'a kind of tree'
k+l	>	kl	:	klas	'class'
				kləb	'club'
t+r	>	tr	:	tren	'train'
kh+w	>	khw	:	khway	'you people'
				khwaŋ	'waist'
d+w	>	dw	:	ədway-də	'there'
p+r	>	pr	:	prithibi	'mother earth'

b. Fricative + w

s+w	>	sw	:	sway-də	'here'
s+r	>	sr	:	sro-sro	'noises'

(ii) Medial Cluster

a.stop + semivowels or l/r

	p+w	>	pw	:	məwpwa	'her younger brother'
	p+r	>	pr	:	cəmpra	'lemon'
	k+r	>	kr	:	həykru	'amla'
					ləykrək	'making crack in earth'
	kh+r	>	khr	:	cət-khro	'go away {com.mk]
	b+r	>	br	:	ca-bra	'eat-Q.mk'
	th+r	>	thr	:	laŋthrey	'a plant'
	d+r	>	dr	:	ca-dre	'eat-neg.mk'
	g+r	>	gr	:	məŋgra	'sweet potato'
b. b+r	m+r	>	mr	:	ləymram	'a name of place'
	c+r	>	cr	:	ŋakcrow	'a kind of fish'
	j+r	>	jr	:	həyjraŋ	'a kichen knife'
c. s+r	s+r	>	sr	:	cəy-sra	'a name of protagomist in a folk tale'

Manipuri has no final cluster, as other most of the Tibeto-Burman languages specially of the Kuki-Chin group. However, Kanauri can be mentioned as having final cluster among Tibeto-Himalayan languages.

2.3.4 Consonant Sequence

It is already mentioned that sequence is different from cluster. Sequence is that occurence of two or more consonants beyond the syllable while cluster is within the syllable. A number of consonants can have immediate occurrence as given in the following examples.

p: can occur with p, t, k, ph, th, kh, m, n, l, s, n, h and y

p+p	təppə	'slow'
p+t	pətpə	'rotten'

p+c		təpcəbə	'slow'
p+k		təp-kəni	'will be slow'
p+ph		thupphəm	'rest-room' or 'sheltering place'
p+kh		lepkhət-pə	'standing up'
p+m		əkupmən	'charge for roofing'
p+n		kupmənbə	'becoming too small'
p+l		upləkpə	'dip from'
p+s		təpsinbə	'to be added'
p+h		təphənbə [tə-phənbə]	'to make some one a pan'
		nəphənbə [nə-phənbə]	'to cause some one to past'
p+y		kupyan	'to cut minutely'

t: can occur with p, t, k, ph, kh, m, n, ŋ, ç, s, h, l and y, as in the following example.

t+p	:	patpə	'septic' or 'rotten'
t+t	:	phəttəbə	'bad'
t+c	:	cətcəbə	'to go oneself politely'
t+k	:	litkəni	'will wear'
t+ph	:	litphəm	'to pass through (fench)
t+th	:	cithəbə	'forget to pick up'
t+kh	:	cətkhi	'has gone(definite)
t+m	:	khutmaŋ	'the mamer of lost'
t+n	:	litnəbə	'something to wear'
t+ŋ	:	khutŋaŋ	'the manner of speaking'
t+l	:	khutləŋ	'the manner of throwing'
t+s	:	khutsa	'fingers'
t+h	:	tət-hənbə	'to cause something to break'
t+y	:	potyom	'the manner of wraping'or'bundle'

k: has the immediate occurrence of p, t, k, ph, th, kh, m, n, ŋ, ç, h, w and y as in the following examples.

k+p	pokpə	'to be born'
k+t	koktə	'on head'
k+k	məhakki	'his'
k+ph	pokphəm	'birth place'
k+th	lukthəbə	'to bent down'
k+kh	pokkhaybə	'to burst out'
k+m	pikmənbə	'too small'
k+n	laknəbə	'arrange to come'
k+ŋ	pokŋəmdəbə	'unable to be born'
k+l	likla	'dew'
k+s	laksinbə	'to control'
k+c	lokcəp	'gorge'
k+h	lok-hənbə	'to make some one reap the crop'

m: also has the immediate occurrence of the consonants like p, t, k, ph, th, kh, b, d, g, m, n, ŋ, ç, j, s, l, h, and y as in the following examples :

m+p	təmpak	'valley'
m+t	ləmtup	'divided piece of land'
m+k	ləmkoybə	'to travel'
m+ph	(ləmbi)ləmphaŋ	'crossing'
m+th	ləmthuŋphəm	'destination'
m+b	ləmbi	'way or road'
m+d	ləmda	'local name of a month between March and April'
m+g	hamgənbə	'unable to fertilize in the egg or prone to diahhorea'
m+m	ləmmuknəbə	'lost in direction'
m+n	təmnəbə	'having the shadow of horror'
m+ŋ	pumŋaŋ ŋaŋbə	'deep red'
m+c	ləmcət	'character'
m+s	lupsinbə	'to dip into'
m+j	ləmjel	'race'
m+l	ləmlay	'deity or name of a village'
m+h	təm-hənbə	'to make him learn'
m+y	ləmyay	'centre of the passage'

n : can occur in immediate position with other consonants like p, t, ph, th, kh, b, d, g, h, m, n, ŋ, ç, s, h, j and y as in the followings :

n+p	əwunpot	'parents' presentation to their daughter's marriage'
n+t	hentak	'a kind of fermented fish'
n+ph	lanpha	'war prisoner'
n+th	tantha	'a rhythem'
n+kh	kənkhətpə	'to feel stronger & stronger'
n+b	tənbə	'lazy'
n+d	təndən	'fire fly'
n+j	tənja	'chance'
n+g	khəngətpə	'to select'
n+m	lanmi	'army'
n+n	tinnəbə	'to mix with'
n+ŋ	pənŋakpə	'protector'
n+l	pənlanbə	'to pass over a fench'
n+s	tinsinbə	'to add to'
n+h	lanhəwbə	'revolutionary'
n+y	konyay	'iron'

ŋ : has the immediate occurrence of the consonants like p, t, k, ph, th, kh, b, d, g, m, n, ŋ, c, s, j, l, h and y as in the following example :

ŋ+p	khoŋpak	'foot'
ŋ+t	thaŋtup	'date palm'

ŋ+k	əŋkə	'arithmatics'
ŋ+ph	khoŋphəm	'stand'
ŋ+th	pəŋthəbə	'paralyse'
ŋ+kh	kaŋkhən	'mosquito net'
ŋ+b	kaŋbu	'group'
ŋ+d	khoŋdol	'tip of the feet' (tip of the toes)
ŋ+g	koŋgol	'bubble'
ŋ+m	noŋmayjiŋ	'Sunday'
ŋ+n	yoŋnaw	'baby monkey'
ŋ+ŋ	siŋŋut	'a particular weed'
ŋ+c	khoncop	'slang'
ŋ+s	noŋsa	'lion'
ŋ+j	thoŋjaw	'great door'
ŋ+l	siŋli	'nerve'
ŋ+h	kaŋhu	'stick used in polo'
ŋ+w	maŋway-də	'in front of'
ŋ+y	noŋyay	'midnight'

2.4 Syllable

In Manipuri, as in most other TB languages a syllable is vocalic unit or preceded or followed by one or more consonantal margins. In the latter type the vocalic unit constitutes as 'peak' or nucleus of the syllable and all peripheral consonantal or semi-consonantal phonemes as its margin. A syllable may have a zero margin or a simple or complex (cluster) margin or either side of the syllable peak. A syllable can be divided into three parts namely (I) onset (ii) peak and (iii) coda.

Onset, it is the begining of a syllable (it should be a consonant or semi vowels. The sound **y** in **ya** 'teeth and **p** in **pat** are the onset. Like this the begining of **kok** 'head' **thoŋ** 'door' **phək** 'mat', **mi** 'man' etc. are the onset.

Peak is the nucleus of a syllable and it is carried by the vowel not by the consonant. The vowels, say **o** in **kok, a** in **ya, ə** in **phək, i** in **mi** etc. are the peak (nucleus) of the very syllable.

Coda is the very sound which comes after the peak, e.g. **k** in **phək, t** in **pat, ŋ** in **nuŋ** 'stone' coda will be the consonant. In Manipuri, only a peak can be a syllable or a word, for instance, i 'blood' u 'tree' etc.

In every syllable there must be a peak. But there may not be a onset or there may not be a coda in Manipuri syllabic system. There are syllables (being a word) of onset+peak, namely, **ta** 'spear', **la** 'banana leaf', **ya** 'teeth', **na** 'noise', **pa** 'eye lash', **ka** 'room', **ha** 'an eable root', so 'key', **mi** 'man' etc. There are also syllables (being a word) of peak+coda. Examples are **in** 'fishing net', **un** 'ice' etc.

In this language, again syllable can be divided into open and close syllable. Open syllable are those which have no consonant sound after a peak, for instance, **ya** 'teath', **na** 'ear', **ka** 'room' etc, whereas in close syllable, a consonant at least follows the peak, as in example like **cak** 'cook rice', **kok** 'head', **noŋ** 'rain' etc.

2.4.1 Patterns of Syllabic Units

A word level analysis of Manipuri attests the following patterns of syllabic units. (here 'V' represents a syllabic peak and 'C' a syllabic margin (consonants) including an aspirated phonemic unit). In this language there can be one to four phonemic units in a syllable which can occur in their permissible order. There are six monosyllabic patterns and all the six monosyllabic patterns given below can also constitute a syllabic unit of a disyllabic or a polysyllabic word in it.

1. V	i	'blood'
	u	'tree'
2. VC	in	'fishing net'
	un	'ice'
3. CV	li	'cane'
	wa	'bamboo'
4. CCV	kwa	'betal nut'
5. CVC	mit	'eye'
	khun	'village'
6. CCVC	khwaŋ	'waist'
	kwak	'crow'

2.4.2 Syllabic Division

As in other Tibeto-Burman languages, in Manipuri too, the syllabic division depends primarily, on preceding and the following environments of the syllable peak. Other distinctive aspects of the syllabic division in it are juncture or openness of transition and syllabic silence, conditioned by the boundaries of various syllable determined by their structure itself. For instance, in the disyllabic and polysyllabic words like **yumthək** 'roof' **hentak** 'fish paste' **khoŋphəm** 'stand' **pokphəm** 'birth place' **khutsa** 'fingers' **ləmjel** 'race' **ləmınuknəbə** 'lost in direction', the syllable cut falls in between the consonants sequence. Occurring as complex interludes between the preceding and succeding syllables, because the language does not permit- **ndr-**, **-mn-**, **-pt-**, **-tk-**, **-nt-**, **-ml-**, **-kc-**, **-ms-** as onset margins of a syllable. In /ləy-mram/ the cut does not fall in between **-m-** and **-r-**; again the language has not **m** or **n** aspirate so the cut will be /lan-həw-bə/ 'revolutionary' and /təm-hən-bə/ 'to make (him) learn' not in the way */la-nhəw-bə/ or */tə-mhən-bə/.

Since Manipuri is an agglutinative language a number of suffixes can be added to a root, for instance, /ŋaŋ-hən-ləm-dri-ŋəy-də-di-ne-ko/ there are nine syllables and the gloss is 'when (he) is not made (him) speak' /ŋaŋ/ is the root 'speak' and remaining are the suffixes which can be added to any action-related root.

2.5. Juncture

Occurrence of juncture phone in the sense of interruption to the normal transition of sound is normally attested in the form of slight pause occurring between successive segments of syllables, morphemes or any morphological units. In a normal speech behaviour its occurrence is largely conditioned by the tempo of speech; i.e., it can be distinctly perceived in a slow cautions speech but usually eliminated in a quick tempo of it. As such in a normal course of speech the presence or the absence of a juncture phone is not significant.

Interruption in transition between speech elements may be very short or imperceptible, termed as 'close' in linguistic terminology, or of some perceptible duration called 'open' or plus juncture. In terms degree of duration, it is higher in open juncture as compared to the close juncture. For as a principle the characteristic of the juncture, as stated above, is cessation of articulation, for whatever duration it may be, between successive linguistic segments in a speech event, e.g. /ləw-ubə/ 'to plaugh' **phi-subə** 'to wash cloth' **thək-lo** 'drink + comd (Here the cessation has been indicated by a hyphen).

The normal environment for the occurrence of a juncture in Manipuri is occurrence of morpheme boundaries, in other word, it is a syllabic one. Juncture, besides its phonetic features, has a phonemic status as well in which its presence or absence becomes quite significant or contrastive. There, however, it is attested in the form of a clear pause between successive meaningful units or groups of units, controlled by their semantic aspects or breath span, the examples are given below :

1.	hi+honbə	'boat + to roar'
	hihonbə	'sailor'
2.	phi+subə	'cloth+ to wash'
	phisubə	'washer man'
3.	phi+tubə	'cloth + to stitch'
	phituba	'tailor'
4.	phi+lonbə	'cloth + to knite'
	phironbə	'girl who is knitting'
5.	cak+khaybə	'rice + to collect'
	cakkhaybə	'person who is collecting rice'
6.	cak+thoŋbə	'rice + to cook'
	cakthoŋbə	'cook'
7.	cak+nibə	'rice + to alms'
	caknibə	'bagger'
8.	sa+cabə	'meat + to eat'
	sajaba	'non-veg. person'
9.	siŋ+khaybə	'log + to cut'
	siŋkhaybə	'log cutter'
10.	mi+hatpə	'man + to kill'
	mihatpə	'murderer'
11.	ləm+koybə	'place + to travel'
	ləmkoybə	'traveller'
12.	ləŋ+səŋbə	'thread + to dye'
	ləŋsəŋbə	'dyer'
13.	lay+yekpə	'picture+ to paint'
	lakyekpə	'painter'
14.	lay+sabə	'statue + to mould
	laysabə	'sculpture'
15.	ŋa+phabə	'fish + to catch'
	ŋaphabə	'fisherman'
16.	yu+thəkpə	'liquor + drink'
	yuthəkpə	'drunker'
17.	yum+sabə	'house +to build'
	yumsabə	'house builder'

From these instances what it is clear is that first, there is the contrast, secondly, the first unit is a monosyllabic free root substantive and thirdly, when they are becoming compounding they indicate the meaning of profession. It is also very clear that the language has juncture.

2.6 Tone

Manipuri has two tones — level and falling (level is not marked here and falling is marked as`). However, it is not as distinct as in the Chinese and Burmese. It is presumed that tonal feature is gradually loosing. More and above, context also decides the meaning significantly.

Examples are given in minimal pair.

i	'blood'	ka-bə	'to climb'
ì	'thatch'	kà-bə	'over fry'
un	'skin'	ca-bə	'to eat'
ùn	'ice'	cà-bə	'to hang around'
mi	'people'	ta-bɘ	'to hear'
mì	'spider'	tà-bə	'to fall'
kaŋ	'mosquito'	lu-bə	'clear'
kàŋ	'a kind of game'	lù-bə	'deep' or 'difficult question'
khoŋ	'leg'	sa-bə	'to make'
khòŋ	'stream'	sà-bə	'hot'
loŋ	'multiple spear'	law-bə	'to shout'
lòŋ	'a kind of fishing net'	làw-bə	'becoming larger in hole'
thoŋ	'door'	kaw-bə	'to forget'
thòŋ	'bridge'	kàw-bə	'to kick'
		hay-bə	'to say'
		hày-bə	'to swing'
		kaw-bə	'to call'
		kàw-bə	'to short'

Chapter–III
Morphological System

3.1 Roots and Affixes

3.1.1 Root

A root is a form which is not further analysable either in terms of derivational or inflectional morphology. It is that part of a word form that remains when all inflectional and derivational affixes have been removed. A root is the basic part always present in a lexeme. In Manipuri, there are two types of root, viz, free and bound roots.

3.1.1.1 Free Roots

All nouns, in Manipuri, are free roots, for instance, :

mi	'man'	khoŋ	'leg'	məy	'fire'
sa	'ani,al'	səm	'hair'	tha	'moon'
kəy	'tiger'	may	'face'	u	'tree'

However, there are nominal bound roots also. They will be discussed in 3.1.1.2.1.

3.1.1.2 Bound Roots

Bound roots can be broadly classified into two groups, viz (i) nominal bound roots and (ii) verbal bound roots.

3.1.1.2.1 Nominal Bound Roots (NB root)

In this language, limited number of nominal bound roots are available. For convienent in analysing they can be categorized in the following ways :

a. Kinship terms

Examples :

-pa	'father'
-ma	'mother'
-ne	'father's sister'
-ce	'sister'
-buŋ	'brother (elder)'
-bay	'brother-in-law' (elder)
-təyma	'sister-in-law (elder)

Until and unless one of the personal pronominals i-first person. nə second person and mə- third person pronominal is added it does not give a complete meaning, for instance.

i-ma	'my mother'
nə-ce	'your sister'
mə-bung	'his elder brother'

b. Body parts (animal)

Here the third person pronominal marker is prefixed. Examples are given below :

mə-ci	'horn' (its)

mə-məy	'tail' (its)
mə-soŋ	'mane' (its) [məy 'fire']
mə-sa	'body (its) or health'
mə-phəy	'thigh (its)'

c. Miscellenous

The following nominal bound roots are to be prefixed by the third person pronominal marker mə-, otherwise it does not give any meaning.

Examples :

5.	məthəw	'duty (his)'
	məkol	'nest (its)'

3.1.1.2.2 Verbal Roots

All the verbal roots are bound roots. They are more numerous than the nominal ones. Here something has to be clarified, that is, how and why bound roots are categorized as nouns or as verbs. This is a controvercial point among the grammarians.

The first rational argument of categorizing the bound roots as nouns and verbs is that the nominal bound roots, by adding any marker to them , they remain as noun, for instance, (they are given above also) :

6.	-pa	'father'	
	-ce	'sister'	
	-ci	'horn'	
	-məy	'tail'	body part (animal)
	-thəw	'duty'	
	-kol	'nest'	or 'place'

Notice that all the above given roots are to be prefixed pronominal marker and they cannot be added at all by any aspect markers to form verb. So it is very natural and scientific to treat them as nominal bound roots.

On the other hand, bound roots, say, **pa** 'read' **ca** èat', **thək** 'drink' **tum** 'sleep' etc. are all action related roots. They can be derived as pure verb, nominal, adjective and adverb by affixing respective markers. More and above, they cannot be treated as nouns merely because they can be derived as nominals by suffixing nominalizer èating' **-bə~pə [ca-bə** 'to eat', **thək-pə** 'to drink' etc]. There are other types of bound roots also, say, **caw** 'big' **waŋ** 'tall' **ŋəw** white' etc. which can be derived as nominal, verb, adjective and adverb, in the same way as the above mentioned one, by adding respective markers.

Another point is that the first representing by **ca** 'eat' and the second set representing by **caw** 'big' can not be compared to the bound root like **kol** 'nest' and **ce** 'sister' in any case. Naturally, they lie in different side. In lieu of keeping them together as pre-category' or 'zero-category' or 'non-plus-category' root, it will be more convenient to place them separate as 'nominal' and as 'verbal' bound roots based on the nearest sementic boundary.

The verbal bound roots are huge in number. They can be broadly classified into— dynamic (all action oriented roots) and stative roots.

3.1.1.2.2.1 Dynamic Bound Roots

Dynamic bound roots are given below :

ca-	'eat'	cət-	'go
thək-	'drink'	lak-	'come'
tum-	'sleep'	cen	'run'
pok-	'born/burn'	yeŋ	'look'
tha-	'send/plant'	pa-	'read'
phəŋ-	'get'	lot-	'hide'
tak-	'teach'	thəw-	'drive'
təm-	'learn'	ka-	'climb
phəm-	'sit'		

3.1.1.2.2.2 Stative Bound Roots

They are also given below :

caw	'big'	ŋəw	'white'
waŋ	'tall'	mot	'dirty'
nem	'short'	nan	'clean'
saŋ	'long'	mu	'black'
pak	'broad'	sin	'sour'
phə	'good'	kha	'bitter'

Other than these, there are some verbal roots which have zero morpheme of simple aspect. So they express independent meaning and they are ended by vowel i/y. They are given below.

i	'write+asp' [i+y]	si	'die+asp' [si+y]
ki	'afraid+asp [ki+y]	pi	'give+asp' [pi+y]
li	'tell+asp [li+y]	ləy	'have/stay+ asp 'is' [ləy+y]

3.1.2 Affixes

Affixes are bound morpheme which can only occur attached to a root, or stem or word. In Manipuri there are only prefixes and suffixes but not infix. In an agglutinative language like Manipuri, affixes are very important. They take part in the formation of various words and in deriving several word class, namely, verb, noun, adjective and adverb (see **word formation** and **word class chapters**). Besides this, they (only suffixes) are used in forming various sentence types—declarative, negative, interrogative and imperatives. The two types of affixes are discussed below one by one.

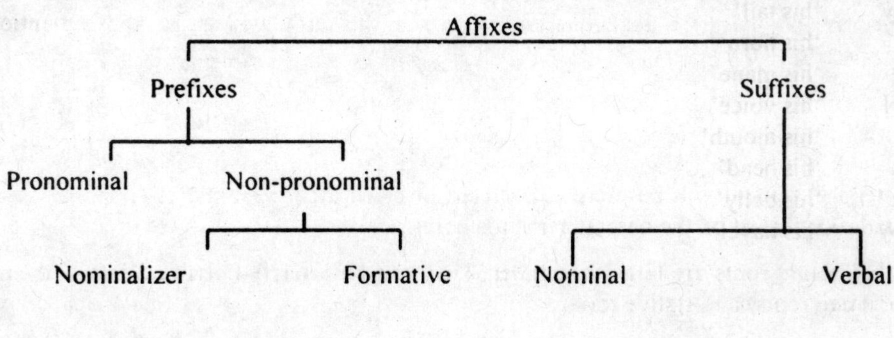

3.1.2.1 Prefixes

Prefixes are very limited in number and they are mostly used in word class formation. Above this , there are also a few prefixes which are used in sentence level : the prefixes can be classed into two (i) Pronominal and (ii) Non pronominal on their grammatical functions.

However, there are also a few prefixes which are used in sentence level. The prefixes used in word level are discussing first.

3.1.2.1.1 Pronominal Prefix

There are three pronominal prefixes they are given in the followings :

I.	i-	' First person' (1P) 'my'
II.	nə-	'Second person' (2P) 'your'
III.	mə-	'Third person' (3P) 'his or her'

Examples :

a.	yum	' house'	i-yum	'my house'
	may	'face'	i-may	'my face'
	lən	'wealth'	i-rən	'my wealth'
	ləm	'place'	i-rəm	'my place'
	ləybak	'country'	i-rəybak	'my country'
b.				
	khoŋ	'leg'	nə-khoŋ	'your leg'
	səm	'hair'	nə-səm	'your hair'
	may	'face'	nə-may	'your face'
	khut	'hand'	nə-khut	'your hand'
c.				
	kok	'head'	mə-kok	'his head'
	pot	'belongings	mə-pot	'his belongings'
	mit	'eye'	mə-mit	'his eye'
	paw	'news'	mə-paw	'his news'

It is noted that the third person prefix **mə-** is the remnant of the proto-Tibeto-Burman verbal pronominal marker. In this language it is retained in the noun only : it can be seen from the inalienable nouns, from body parts, kinship terms etc.

Example :

məkol	'his nest' (refers to animals or bird's nest)
məməy	'his tail'
məci	'his horn'
məsoŋ	'his mane'
məkhol	'his voice'
məcin	'his mouth'
məkək	'his head'
məpuk	'his belly'
məkhoy	'his navel'

3.1.2.1.2 Non-pronominal Prefix

The non-pronominal prefixes are in the followings

a. Nominalizing prefixes - **khu-** and **mə-**
b. Formative prefixes - **ə, i, mə, tə, thə** and **sə.**

a. Nominalizing prefixes : **khu-** and **mə-**

Manipuri has two nominalizing prefixes **khu-** and **mə-** which can nominalize the verbal roots by prefixing. But they are different grammatically and sematically.

1. Prefixation of **khu-** is more preoductive than that of **mə-** (i.e. **khu-** is more appropriate than **mə-**); in the nominalization by **mə-** context plays a significant role : without context prefixation of **mə-** is not found appropriate and its meaning looses also. Example

a.

ca	'eat'	khu-ca	'mode of eating'
tum	'sleep'	khu-tum	'mode of sleeping'
caw	'big'	khu-caw	'the degree of bigness' (sense of very big)
ŋaŋ	'red'	khu-ŋaŋ	'the degree of redness' (sense of very nicely red)

b. Without the context , prefixation of **mə-** looses its meaning (gives another meaning).

mə- ca	'his son/daughter'
mətum	'roundedness'
məthək	'on'
məyi	'lines
məcət	'character'
məpok	'birth'

Consider the following sentences with the context :

1. məhak-ki cak məca-si onthok-nə phəjə-khi-dre
he-gen rice eat-det. very nice -def-neg
'His mode of eating is very bad'

3. məhak-ki yu məthək-tu-nə-di si-ni
he-gen liquor drink-det.-nom.def. die-cop.
'The mode of his drinking will lead him to death.'

2. **khu-** indicates closer meaning to the nature or mode or manner of the action whereas **mə-** refers to one's action since **mə-** is the third person pronominal marker.

a. khu-ca 'the mode of eating'
mə-ca 'the mode of his eating'

b. khu-yeŋ 'the mode of looking'
mə-yeŋ 'the mode of his looking'

c. khu-pa 'the mode of reading'
mə-pa 'the mode of his reading'

d. khu-ta 'the mode of falling'
mə-ta 'the mode of his falling'

3. **khu-** can be prefixed to both action verbal roots as well as stative verbal roots whereas **mə-** is prefixed to action verb only. Consider the following examples :

a. Action verbal roots :

khu-thək	'the mode of drinking'
mə-thək	'the mode of his drinking'
khu-pa	'the mode of reading'
mə-pa	'the mode of his reading'

b. Stative verbal roots:

khu-caw	'the degree of bigness'
*mə-caw	
khu-pik	'the degree of smallness'
*mə-pik	
khu-ŋaŋ	'the degree of redness'
*mə-ŋaŋ	
khu-ŋəw	'the degree of whiteness'
*mə-ŋəw	

b. Formative Prefixes

In Manipuri there are seven formative prefixes ; they are ə-, i-, cə-, tə, thə and se-. They are discussed one by one in the followings :

Prefix ə-

ə- is used to derive (attributive) adjectival form

Example :

saŋbə	'be long'	əsaŋbə	'long'
pikpə	'be small'	əpikpə	'small'
ŋaŋbə	'be red'	əŋaŋbə	'red'
tenbə	'be short'	ətenbə	'short'
tumbə	'to sleep'	ətumbə	'who is sleeping' or 'who has slept'
pabə	'to read'	əpabə	'who is reading' or 'who has read'
cabə	'to eat'	əcabə	'who is eating' or 'who has eaten'

Prefix i-

By prefixing i- to the verbal root it gives the meaning 'anything' in the positive environment and it gives the meaning of a 'little' (not much) in the negative environment. Secondly, it occurs in the sentence level. Thirdly, it reduplicates the verbal roots, Semantically it has different meaning according to its occurrence with differend kinds of verbs. First, it gives the meaning of anything and 'a little' or 'not much' when it occurs with action verbs as in sentences (4) and (5) respectively, while it indicates the meaning 'superlative' it occurs with stative verbs as in sentence 6.

4. məhak-ti i-ca ca-y [positive environment]
he-spec. eat eat-asp.
'He eats anything (tasty or not)'

5. məhak-ti i-ca ca-de [negative environment]
'He does not eat much (a little)'
Sentence 6 and 7 give the 'superalative meaning'

6. məhak-nə iwaŋ waŋ-ŋi
he-nom. tall tall-asp.
'He is the tallest one among them'

7. yuməsi-nə i-phə phə-jəy
house det.-nom. nice nice-asp.
'This house is the most beautiful one'

The verbal roots can also reduplicate thrice when it (i-) is prefixed to stative verb and semantically it gives the meaning of plurality or general not superlative meaning

Example

8. ləykon-du-də sat-pə ləy-siŋ-du iŋaŋ iŋaŋ ŋaŋ-ŋi
garden-det-loc. bloom-NZR flower-pl.det. red red red-asp.
'The flowers blooming in that garden are generally red.'

The three prefixes i- , **pəŋ-** and **puŋ-** have similar meaning ; it is very difficult to make a semantic demarcation among them. The prefix **pəŋ-** is basically derived from **pəŋ-bə** 'to be fool 'or to be blunt'; by this prefixation the verb incorporates the meaning of the 'doing something without a purpose' or 'having no clear stand'. the other prefix **puŋ-** is basically derived from **puŋ-bə** 'having many branches or bushes' or literarily it indicates the meaning of 'having no clear stand or idea'.

Prefix **pəŋ-**

pəŋ- can be prefixed to the action verbs and it adds the meaning of 'a lot' plus 'without a purpose' or 'without a clear stand'. Consider the following sentences :

9. məhak-ti hawbə haw-tə-bə pəŋ-ca ca-y
he spec tasty taste-neg.-NZR -eat eat-asp.
'He eats a lot whether it is tasty or not'

10. məhak-ti əyuk-təgi pəŋ-cət cət-li
he- spec. morning - from -go go-asp.
'He starts going from the morning to anywhere'
(goes without a purpose)

A particle **-də~tə** 'only' is very appropriate in suffixation to along with the prefix (pəŋ+V+də), as in the followings.

a. .... pəŋ-ca-də ca-y ' only eats a lot'

b. .... **pəŋ-cət-tə cətli** ' only goes wihout a purpose'
(goes anywhere)
c. .... **pəŋ-tum-də tum-mi** 'only sleeps a lot'

They **(pəŋ-ca-də ca-y, pəŋ-cət-tə cət-li, pəŋ-tum-də tum-mi)** function in the construction as a modifier to the verbs. In case the particle **-də~-tə** occurs in the negative environment the additional meaning of 'without a purpose' or 'without a clear stand' has lost, as in the following sentences :

11. məhakti pəŋ-ca-də ca-de
he-spec. eat eat-neg.
'He does not eat much'
(He is very conscious of his meal in its quality)

12. məhak curup pəŋ-thək-tə thək-te
he cigarett smoke smoke-neg.
'He does not smoke much'
(smokes at a very specific time)

pəŋ- can also be prefixed to the stative verb along with the particular **-də~ tə** 'only' which is preferred to be suffixed in the positive environment, not in the negative one. as in (13) and (14) respectively.

13. u-du pəŋ - waŋ-də waŋ-ŋi
tree-det tall-only tall-asp
'The tree is very tall'
(the tree is becoming very tall)

*14. u-du pəŋ-waŋ-də waŋ-de

15. u-du pəŋ-wəŋ waŋ-de
'The tree is not much tall'

Sentence (14) is not acceptable because the particle **-də~ -tə** cannot occur with **pəŋ-** in the negative environment. In negative environment without **-də~-tə** is generally used as in sentence (15) and (16).

16. phurit ədu pəŋ-mu mu-de
shirt that-black black-neg.
'The shirt is not much dark'.

Prefix **puŋ-**

puŋ- is very similar with **pəŋ-** semantically: **puŋ-** occurs with action verbs in the positive environment not in negative environment, as in (17) and (18) respectively.

17. məhak yu puŋ-thək thək-y
he liquor drink drink-asp.
'He takes liquor a lot' (without any control)

*18. məhak yu puŋ-thək thək-te

The particle-**də~-tə** 'only' can also be occurred with **puŋ-(puŋ+V+də)**, as in sentence (19)

19. **məhak yu puŋ-thək-tə thək-y**
'He takes liquor a lot' (without any controll).

The prefix **puŋ-** can also be occurred with the stative verb in the positive environment but it is not appropriate to occur in negative environment (**peŋ-** replaced it (**puŋ-**) in the negative environment).

20. **ləwbuk ədu-di puŋ-səŋ səŋ-ŋi**
field that-def. green green-asp.
'The paddy field looks very green'.

21. **ləykon ədu ləy əŋaŋbə-nə puŋ-ŋaŋ ŋaŋ-ŋi**
garden that flower red-nom. red red-asp.
'The garden is almost red with the red flowers'

pəŋ- is often used than **puŋ-** in negative environment:

22. a ..... pəŋ-caw caw-de 'it is not very big'
b .... pəŋ-pik pik-te 'it is not very small'
c. .... pən-ŋaŋ ŋaŋ-de 'it is not very red'.

It is very interesting that there is a verb **hiŋbə** 'to exist' or 'to live' but when it is prefixed by **i-** or **puŋ-** or **pəŋ-** a different cannotation is expressed : the basic meaning is not completely lost. Prefixation of **i-** or **puŋ-** to the very verb **hiŋ** gives the meaning 'the work is not yet completed', as in sentence (23)

a. i+] hiŋ hiŋ-ŋi
puŋ+]

23. luhoŋ-bə-di həyeŋ-də ŋay-re ədugə thəbək-ti i-/puŋ-hiŋ-ŋi
marriage-def.tomorrow on-asp but work-def. exist
'Marriage is very close but works are not yet completed'

But by prefixation of **puŋ-** to the very verb denotes the meaning of 'just pulling on' a reply to 'how do you live on', as in sentence 24.

24. **pəŋ-hiŋ hiŋ-li**
'Just pulling on'

These are the fact that prefixes **i-**, **pəŋ-** and **puŋ-** have different cannotation as they occurred with.

Prefix cə-

cə- is an unproductive prefix and is used with certain verbs ; it gives an additional meaning as 'very'

Example :

25. a. əsi-də-di pambi-siŋ-si kuŋ-ŋi
here-loc.-spec. plant-pl.-det. close-asp.
'Here the plants are close to each other'

b. əsi-də-di pambi-siŋ-si cə-guŋ-nəy
'Here the plants are very close to each other'.

26. a. ka əsi məm-mi
room this dark-asp.
'This room is dark'

b. waphəm əsi cə-məmnəy
issue this confusion-asp.
'This issue is very confusing'.

27. a. ka əsi laŋ-ŋi
room this noisy-asp.
'This room is noisy'

b. ka əsi cə-raŋ-nəy
'This room is too noisy'

28. a. nupa-məca əsi mot-li
boy this dirty-asp
'This boy is dirty'

b. nupa əma əsi cə-motnəy
'This boy is very dirty'

The prefix is also often used in reduplication followed by an auxiliary verb **law**, as in the following sentences :

29. tebəl əsi cə-nəp cə-nəp law-wi
table this sticky sticky aux.-asp.
'This table is found very sticky'

30. cak əsi cə-bet cə-be law-wi [pet-pə' soft']
rice this soft soft aux. asp.
'This rice is found very soft'.
(not properly cooked).

Prefix tə-

This **tə-** is grammatically very specific that it occurs with stative verbs only. They are **nəw** 'tender', **nal** ' smooth'/ clean, **noy** 'fat', **ŋaŋ** 'red', **lu** 'transparent/clear/clean', **yaŋ** 'light', **iŋ** 'cold', **naŋ** ' slippery', **seŋ** 'clear' etc.

31. ŋəsi-di ətiya əsi tərutəru-y
today -spec. sky this clear clear-asp.
'Today the sky is very clear'.

32. məhak-ki məcinbal əsi tə-ŋaŋ tə-ŋaŋ-ŋi
she-gen lip this red red-asp
'Her lips are very reddish'

Prefix **suk**

It is called negative polarity item (NPI) because it is used only in negative environment only. Its prefixation forces the root to reduplicate (see for detail in VII.2.).

Example :

33. məhak yu suk-thək thək-te
he liquor drink-neg.
'He never takes liquor'
(He does not take liquor at all)

Prefix khəŋ-

It gives the meaning of 'suddenly'. It reduplicates the verbal root and can occur in both the environments.

Examples :

34. məhak gari khəŋ -thəw thəw-wi
he-nom. vehicle -drive drive-Asp
'He suddenly drives the vehicle'

35. məhak gari khəŋ-thəw thəw-de [de-neg]
'He does not drives the vehicle suddenly'

This prefix **khəŋ-** can be prefixed to both the verbs — action as well as stative.

Examples :

36. a. .... khəŋ-nuŋ nuŋ-si '.......... suddenly love..'
b. .... khəŋ-waŋ waŋ-ŋi '........ suddenly brcomming tall..."
c. .... khəŋ-caw caw-wi '........ suddenly becoming large...'
d. .. .. khəŋ-ŋaŋ ŋaŋ-ŋi ' .... suddenly becoming red.'

Now it is seen that the prefixes can be categorized into two — the prefixes **i-**(pronominal), **mə-**, **khu-** and **ə-** do not make the verb to occur in reduplication while the other prefixes **suk-**, **khəŋ-** . **pəŋ**, **puŋ-** , **i-**, **tə-** and **cə-** grammatically make the verb to occur in reduplication.

3.1.2.2 Suffixes

Suffixes in this language are numerous and they play important role, for example various sentence types can be constructed by suffixation of respective markers and various suffixes can be added one after another, by which the meaning is also added. For convenient in analysis, they can be grouped into two : (i) nominal suffixes and (ii) verbal suffixes.

3.1.2.2.1 Nominal Suffixes

Suffixes which can be added to nouns only are grouped as Nominal suffixes which include the followings.

a. Case Suffixes (see for detail in 5.6)

Nomentive	-nə
Accusative	-pu/bu
Genitive	-gi/ki
Instrumental	də-tə
Ablative	-dəgi
Associative	-gə kə

b. Number (see for ditail in 5.4)

There are two plural suffixes i.e. **-siŋ** and **-khoy**. They are used differently :- **siŋ** is added to animate (birds and animals) and inanimate objects whiule **-khoy** is added to personal pronouns and proper - nouns to make plural.

Examples :

a. Addition of -siŋ

I. Animate (bird and animal)

ŋanu	'duck'	ŋanu-siŋ	'ducks'
sendraŋ	'sparrow'	seŋdraŋ-siŋ	'sparrows'
kwak	'crow'	kwak-siŋ	'crows'

II Inanimate objects

wa	'bamboo'	wa-siŋ	'bamboos'
thoŋ	'door'	thoŋ-siŋ	'doors'
upu	'box'	upu-siŋ	'boxes'

b. Addition of -khoy

I. Personal pronoun

əy	'I'	əykhoy	'we'
nəŋ	'you'	nəkhoy	'you (pl)'
məhak	'he'	məkhoy	'they'

II. Proper noun

tomba	'Tomba'	tomba-khoy	'Tomba and others'
jon	'John'	jon-khoy	'John and others'

c. Gender Suffixes (see for detail in Gender 5.3)

-a	'indicates male'		
-i	'indicates female'		
yeŋba	'cock'	yenbi	'hen'
əphəba	'good'	əphəbi	'good' (female) etc.

(əphəbə can be used both to male and female)

d. Connectives:

There are three connective suffixes. They are **-ne** 'and' **-gə** 'with' and **-su** ' also' **-ne** :'and' occurs twice with the noun. derived noun, proper noum etc.

Examples :

37. əy-gi huy-ne həwdoŋ-ne ləy
I-gen dog-con. cat-con have
'I have a dog and a cat'

38. məhak-ki thəbək-ti ca-bə-ne tumbə-ne əsi-dəni
he-gen work-part. eat-NZR-con sleep -NZR -con this -only -cop
'His duty is only to sleep and to eat'

39. tomba-ne cawba-ne kəythel cət-khre
Tomba-con Chaoba-con market go-asp
'Tomba and Chaoba have gone to market'

-gə 'with'

It has another allomorph **-kə** (**-kə** occurs after voiceless consonants whereas **-gə** elsewhere). It can occur with every noun occurred in the structure.

Example :

-gə occurring 'once' :

40 məhak tomba-gə skul cət-li
he Tomba-with school go-asp
'He goes to school with Tomba'

-gə occurring twice or thrice :

41. məhak tomba-gə cawba-gə skul cət-li
he-with Tomba-with Chaoba-with school go-asp
'He, Tomba and Chaoba go to school'

Here in such structure **-gə** indicates the meaning of 'identifying' or 'specified', as in the given sentences.

-su 'also'

This suffix also, like **-gə**, can occur twice or 'thrice' in a 'construction'.

42. məhak-su cət-khre
he also go-asp
'He also has gone'

43. məhak-su tomba-su skul cət-khre
He also and Tomba also have gone to school'

44. məhak-su tomba-su chaoba-su skul cət-khre
'He also, Tomba also and Chaoba also have gone to school'.

e. Interrogative

One pecularity of this language is that interrogative is formed by addition of interrogative suffix - **ra~ la** (only the Yes/No question). This suffix can be added to noun, pronoun, proper noun and derived nouns (see for detail in 8.2).

f. Particles

ti~di 'definitive' or 'particularization'

45. tomba-di lak-te
Tomba-def come-neg
'The very Tomba does not come'

-du~ tu 'determiner'

46. məhak-tu lak-te
'He does not come

47. əy-gi huy-du si-khre
I gen. dog-det. die-asp
'The very my dog has died'

-si : 'determiner'

48. məhak-si phət-te
he-det good-neg
'He is not good'

-mək : 'self' (emphatic)

49. məhak-mək lak-y
He - self come-asp
'He himself come'

50. məsi haibə-mək ya-re
this say-NZR only agree-asp
'This can be said' (emphatic)

-də ~tə 'only' or 'exclusive'

51. tomba-də məphəm-si-də lak-y
Tomba -only place -det-loc. come -asp
'Only Tomba comes here'

-təmək : 'only (emphatic)

52. tomba-təmək məphəm-si-də lak-y
'Only Tomba comes here'

-gidəmək ~ kidəmək : 'for only' or 'only for'

53. əy-nə layrik-tu tomba-gidəmək pu-rək-pə-ni
I-nom. book-det. Tomba-only for bring-dir-NZR-cop
'I bring the book for Tomba only'

naw 'diminutive'

It is used in word formation for indicating 'small'

Example :

huy+ naw	>	huynaw	'puppy'
dog-small			
sən + naw	>	sənnaw	'calf'
cow-small			
thoŋ+naw	>	thoŋnaw	'window'
door-small			

-muk :

It is used for the meaning of 'like', again' and 'about depending on its occurrence with the noun.

Example for 'like' :

54. **mǝhak-ti tomba-muk kǝl-li**
he-def Tomba-like strong-asp.
'He is as strong as Tomba'
(He is very strong like Tomba)

Example for 'again' :

55. **nǝŋ hǝyeŋ-muk lak-u [-muk > ǝmuk ' again']**
you tomorrow - again come-comd.
'Come tonmorrow again'

Example for 'about' :

56. **turel ǝdu ǝsi-dǝgi kilomitǝr mǝŋa-muk lap-pi**
river that here-from km. five- about far-asp
'The river is about 5 kms. from here.'

3.1.2.2.2 Verbal Suffixes

In such type of agglutinative language the number of verbal suffixes are more than that of the nominal suffixes. This also clearly shows the real characteristics of being an agglutinative language. The verbal suffixes are listed below :

1. Aspect
2. Mood
3. Negative suffixes
4. Imperative suffixes
5. Deitic suffixes
6. Intentive suffix
7. Suggestive
8. Concessive
9. Adverbial
10. Nominalizing
11. Copula
12. Directional
13. Towards the goal
14. Suffixes of destruction
15. Reciprocal
16. Together
17. Excessive
18. Causative
19. Reflexive
20. Honorific
21. Endearment
22. Superiority
23. Sufix - **kum**
24. Suffix - **lǝm**
25. Reported suffix **-ne** as well as copula

1. Aspect Suffixes (see for detail in 5.9.2)

-y is a simple aspect marker. It has many allomorphs. They are **-y ~ li~mi~pi~ŋi ~wi~ni.**

-ri is a progressive aspect marker expressing 'the action is continuing'. It has another allomorph **-li.**

-re is a perfect maker indicating the action is completed. It has allomorphs (i.e. **re~ le~ŋe~me.**

- gǝni~ kǝni is an unrealized or irrealis aspect, it indicates the action is to be profermed in the next moment.

2. Mood

In this language, there is one suffix - **niŋ** which indicates 'desire' or 'wish'. It is generally added to dynamic verbs ; certain stative verbs like **waŋ** 'tall', **noy** 'fat', **caw** 'big', **poŋ** 'proud' **ŋew** 'to be white' etc. also take this suffix.

Example :

sinema yeŋ-niŋ-ŋi
cinema see -wish-asp

'(I) wish to see a film'
əy waŋ-niŋ-ŋi
I tall-wish-asp
'I wish to be tall'

This suffix has specific linear order : it is frequently preceded by certain suffixes, like, directional **-thok**, reciprocal **-nə**, causative **-hən**, reflexive **-jə**, benefactive **-bi**, start **-khət**, auxilary **-həw** .

Examples : [V+X+wish+asp]

a. pi-thok-niŋ-ŋi 'wish to give out'
give -dir-wish-asp
b. phu-nə-niŋ-ŋi 'wish to beat each other'
beat-reci-wish-asp
c. ca-hən-niŋ-ŋi 'wish to cause him to eat'
d. sem-jə-niŋ-ŋi 'wish to make it myself'
e. thoŋ-bi-niŋ-ŋi 'wish to cook for (him)'
f. ca-khət-niŋ-ŋi 'wish to start eating'
g. ca-haw-niŋ-ŋi 'wish to continue eating'
(wish to start eating)

However, certain suffix like, causative **-hən**, auxiliary **-həw** can also precede the mood marker **-niŋ**. At the same time a slight difference in meaning is created, as in the following examples.

a. ca-niŋ-hən-li 'wish to cause him to eat'
(to create an atmosphere to cause him to eat)
b. ca-niŋ-həw-ri 'wish to continue eating'
(want to continue the on-going - action of eating since he is still hungry)

Generally the mood marker **-niŋ** is followed by the aspect markers.

3. Negative Suffixes

There are four negative suffixes. They are **-te ~ -de, -roy ~ -loy, -gum~ -kum** and **-nu**. There is also a morphological negative suffix **-tə~də**. (see for detail in Negative).

4. Imperative Suffixes

There are some command suffixes. They are **-o ~ mo ~ po, ŋo, -u ~ -mu ~ -pu ~ -ŋu ~ -yu, ro ~ -lo** and **-ru ~ -lu**, request is formed by adding honorific marker **-bi ~ -pi** (see for detail in Imperative).

5. Deitic Suffixes

There are four deitic suffixes. They are **-rə -ru, -rək** and **-khi**. They are used for indicating the location or orientation of an event or state. There are three different semantic parameters which help to differentiate one from the other. They are (i) motion or orientation of the event (ii) place of occurrence of the event and relative positions of these two (event preceding or following the motion or orientation). They are discussed below :

-rə

It indicates event towards the speaker, performing the event at the speaker's place and event follows the motion. It has allomorphs : **-r-** assimilates compietly to the preceding consonant when that consonant is **m, ŋ or p** and that consonant is **k** then **r** is deleted, only **ə** is maintained. The simple aspect suffix **y** is suffixed finally.

ca-rəy	'came here and ate'
thi-rəy	'came here and searched'
thoŋ-ŋəy	'came here and cooked'
phəm-məy	'came here and sat'
kəp-pəy	'came here and cried'
thək-əy	'came here and drank'

-ro

It has the same semantic parameter of suffix **-rə** but it **(-ro)** is a command suffix and it has allomorph also-**ro lo. -ro** occur after vowels while **-lo** after consonants (see for detail in Imperative).

ca-ro	'come here and eat'
phu-ro	'come here and beat'
thək-lo	'come here and drink'
thoŋ-lo	'come here and cook'

-ru

It is a command suffix. It is very much opposite to **-ro** in the semantic parameter : it denotes event away from the speaker, performing the event at some other place but here also event follows the motion like **-ro**. It **(-ru)** has allomorph **-ru~ -lu~ -ru** occurs after vowels while **lu** after consonants (see for detail in Imperative) Examples :

ca-ru	'go there and eat'
phu-ru	'go there and beat'
thək-lu	'go there and drink'
thoŋ-lu	'go there and cook'

-ru+y (ruy)

This becomes a declarative suffix expressing a simple statement (**y** is a simple aspect suffix). It has the same semantic parameters of **-ru**, very much opposite to **-rəy** e.g event follows the motion. It has allomorph **-ruy ~ -luy**, same is the phological of **-ru ~ -lu** : Examples :

ca-ruy	'went there and ate'
phu-ruy	'went there and beat'
thək-luy	'went there and drank'
thoŋ-luy	'went there and cooked'

-rək

It denotes that motion is towards the speaker, performed the action away from the speaker's place and the event precedes the motion. It has allomorphs and can be explain phonological rules in two ways : they are alternative : (i) the consonant **r** of this suffix **rək** assimilates compltely to the preceding consonant when that consonant is **m, ŋ**, or **p**.

Applying rule (ii) :

r > m/-m
r > ŋ/-ŋ
r > p/-p

phəm-mək-y	'came by sitting (as on a bus)/ sat sometime (somewhere else) and came here'
lep-pək-y	'came by standing (as on a bus)/ stopped sometime (somewhere on the way) and came here' or 'decided and came'
thoŋ-ŋək-y	'Cooked there and came here'

(iii) **r-** occures after vowels while after consonants, **-rək~ -lək**. example :.

ca-rək-y	'ate there and came here'
koy-rək-y	'visited some place there and came here'
yeŋ-lək-y	'looked something there and came here'
thək-lək-y	'drank there and came here'
cam-lək-y	'washed there and came here'
tum-lək-y	'slept sometime there and came here'
lep-lək-y	'came standing (as on a bus)/ stopped ' there sometime and came here'

-khi

It can indicate two meanings (I) expressing action completed with defeniteness not giving any deitic sense and (II) action completed plus deitic sense of performing the event at the speaker's place and went away, here event precedes the motion. It has no allomorph.

Example :

tum-khi	'slept + definite'
ca-khi	'ate + definite'
thək-khi	'drank + definite'
cət-khi	'went + definite'

That the deitic meaning of 'went away' and 'event precedes motion' depend on the context or linguistic situation; they are additional. Father has the knowledge of his son's going out but at the moment of his son's going out he (father) is not there. So he enquired to his wife 'Has he (son) taken his meal? 'Reply to this question is : **məhak cak cakhi** 'He had taken his meal' and went'. In every situation three parameters are accompanied, they are action completed, it is definite and the action is performed at the speaker's place or in front of the speaker.

6. Intentive Suffix -ge

It gives an intentive meaning, the action is not yet performed and to be performed in the later moment. It has allomorph **-ge ~-ke** : **-ge** occurs after vowels and voiced consonants while **-ke** after voiceless consonents. Examples:

57. a) əy ca-ge 'Let me eat' (intentive not suggestive)
b) əykhoy ciŋ ka-ge 'Let us climb hill' (intentive not suggestive)
c) əy səŋ gom thək-ke 'Let me drink milk' (intentive not suggestive)

7. Suggestive Suffix -si

It is a suggestive suffix and performed the action in the next moment. Example :

58. a) əykhoy cət-si 'Let us go'
b) əykhoy sajel khəra təw-si
we exercise some do-
'Let's do some exercise'

8. Concessive Suffix -sənu

It also makes benefective meaning also.

59. a) nuŋay-nə panbə oy-sənu
'happily live be-
'Wish you a happy life'

b) məhak cak yam-nə ca-səmu
he rice much eat
'Let him eat more'
thək-sənu 'Let him drink'
ca-sənu 'Let him climb'
pa-sənu 'Let him read'

9. Adverbial Suffix

The adverbial suffix is -nə in this language. It can be added to stative as well as dynamic/action verbs.

Examples :

a. Stative verbs

waŋ 'high'	waŋ-nə	'highly'
təp 'slow'	tap-nə	'slowly'
poŋ 'proud'	poŋ-nə	'proudly'
ten 'short'	ten-nə	'shortly'

b. Action verbs

kəp 'cry'	kəp-nə	'cryingly'
nik 'smile'	nok-nə	'smilingly'
cen 'run'	cen-nə	'running (by)'
sək 'sing'	sək-nə	'singing (by)'

There are some peculiar adverbial suffixes, i.e **- drəŋ, -driŋ, -drit, -dorŋ, -pək, -rok, -səŋ, -sin, -sit, -srok, -suk, throk** etc. which force the verbal root to reduplicate. They are used in order to intensify the meaning. They are not productive ; certain stative verbs take these suffixes (their suffixation to the stative verbs is very specific).

Examples :

waŋ 'tall'
waŋ-drəŋ waŋ-ŋi '(It) is very tall'
cum 'straight'
cum-driŋ cum-mi '(It) is very straight'
pa 'thin'

pa-drit pa-y '(It) is very thin'
saŋ 'long'
saŋ-droŋ saŋ-ŋi '(It) is very long'
khoy 'winding' (not straight)
koy-drik khoy '(It) is very winding'
khu 'narrow'
khu-drik khu-y '(It) is very narrow'
tum 'round'
tum-pək tum-mi '(It) is very round'
ŋəw 'white'
ŋəw-rok ŋəw-wi '(It) is very white'
ŋaŋ 'red'
ŋəŋ-səŋ ŋaŋ-ŋi '(It) is very red'
mu 'black'
mu-sin mu-y '(It) isvery black'
kut 'dent'
kut-sit kut-li '(It) is very badly dent'
ŋəw 'white'
ŋəw-srok ŋəw-wi '(It) is very white'
caw 'big'
caw-throk caw-wi '(It) is very big'
law 'loose' (large)
law-throk-law-wi '(It) is very loose
(the hole is becoming larger)
mu 'black'
mu-suk-mu-y '(It) is very black'

The suffix **-trik** can be suffixed to the following stative verbs

Examples :

səŋ 'green'
səŋ-trik səŋ-ŋi '(It) is very green'
tum 'pointed'
tum-trik tum-mi '(It) is very pointed'
hən 'new'
hən-trik- həl-li '(It) is very new'
ten 'short'
ten-trik tel-li '(It) is very short'
mun 'ripe'
mun-trik mul-li '(It) is very ripe'

10. Nominalizing Suffix

The nominalizing suffix in this language is **-bə~ -pə** (**-bə** after vowels and voice consonants whereas **-pə** after voiceless consonants). It is added immediately to the verbal roots.

Examples :

ca	'eat'	ca-bə	'to eat'
thək	'drink'	thək-pə	'to drink'

thoŋ	'cook'	thoŋ-bə	'to cook'
tum	'sleep'	tum-bə	'to sleep'
cət	'go'	cət-pə	'to go'
pi	'give'	pi-bə	'to give'

The nominalizer **-bə~pə** can be used for derivation by adding after the aspectual marker i.e. progressive suffix **-ri~ -li** , definitive **-khi** , durative **-rə~lə** and deitic marker i.e. **-lək** indicating from a distance, **-lu** indicating to a distance. The word so derived is grammatically used as adjectival.

Examples :

thək-pə	'to drink'
thək-li-bə mi	'the person who is drinking'
thək-khi-bə mi	'the person who had drunk and left'
thək-lə-bə mi	'the person who had drunk'
thək-lək-pə mi	'the person who came after drinking'
thək-lu-bə mi	'the person who went and drank'

This suffix **-bə~pə** is used in relativization also (see in 9.4).

11. Copula

In this language copula is a suffix **-ni**. It is used in equational sentences and can be suffixed to noun, pronoun and propernoun.

12. Directional

There are four types of directional suffixes i.e. **-sin** 'inwards', **-thok** 'outward', **-khə** 'upward' and **-thə** 'downward'.

a. Suffix :- sin

The suffix **-sin** 'inward' has two other allomorphs **-cin~ jin** (very often in spoken these are used : **-sən~cən~jən** respectively).

The allomorph **-jin** occurs when the initial of a verbal base is an aspirated sound (i.e. kh, ph, th, h, s) and the final one is a vowel or voiced sound.

Example :

thəm-jin-bə	'to put inside'
hum-jin-bə	'to keep inside'
thaŋ-jin-bə	'to put insdie'
phu-jin-bə	'to hit inside'
khəŋ-jin-bə	'to know for future'
khu-jin-bə	'to become narrow'
pha-jin-bə	'to lighten'

The allomorph **-cin** occurs when the initial of the verbal base is an aspirated sound as in the allomorph **-jin** and when the final sound is a voiceless one (the latter phonological condition is different from the case of **-jin**).

Examples :

thək-cin-bə	**'to drink (inside)'**
thak-cin-bə	**'to drop (inside)' (to put salt in the curry)**
hap-cin-bə	**'to put (inside)'**
phot-cin-bə	**'to stitch together (inside)'**
hot-cin-bə	**'to run inside'**
huk-cin-bə	**'to put into the mouth'**

The allomorph -sin occurs elsewhere.

Examples :

pu-sin-bə	**'to bring inside'**
pi-sin-bə	**'to give (inside)'**
ca-sin-bə	**'to eat (inside)'**
i-sin-bə	**'to write something for record'**
lot-sin-bə	**'to hide inside'**
ləw-sin-bə	**'to take inside'**
lak-sin-bə	**'to control'**
kəŋ-sin-bə	**'to become dry'**

b. Suffix :-thok

The suffix -thok 'out' has two othere allomorphs i.e. -dok~thok. Their distribution are the same as that of the allomorphs of the suffix -sin 'inside', that is, the phonological condition of -dok is similar with that of -jin, -tok similar with -cin and -thok similar with that of -sin.

Examples of –thok :

pa-thok-pə	**'to read out'**
pay-thok-pə	**'to fly out'**
pu-thok-pə	**'to carry out'**
pi-thok-pə	**'to give out'**
cen-thok-pə	**'to run out'**
coŋ-thok-pə	**'to jump out'**

Examples of –dok :

tha-dok-pə	**'to sent out'**
thaŋ-dok-pə	**'to move out by lifting up'**
khun-dok-pə	**'to pick out'**
sin-dok-pə	**'to replace'**
haŋ-dok-pə	**'to open out'**
sum-dok-pə	**'to squeez out'**
pheŋ-dok-pə	**'to clean'**
həy-dok-pə	**'to pour out'**

Examples of –tok :

thap-tok-pə	**'to make a far away'**
sət-tok-pə	**'to draw out'**
sat-tok-pə	**'to blossom'**
khəp-tok-pə	**'to winnow away'**

khət-tok-pə	**'to evade by striking'**
hut-tok-pə	**'to bore' (to make a hole)**
phat-tok-pə	**'to open (in the drainage)'**

The suffix -thok can give the meaning of 'finish completely' or 'emphasis' in the following verbs

ca-thok-pə	**'to eat something completely'**
thək-tok-pə	**'to drink something completely'**
tum-thok-pə	**'to sleep' (started already)'**
phut-tok-pə	**'to boil whole thing completely'**
hat-tok-pə	**'to kill' (emphasis).**

c. Suffix :- khət

This suffix **-khət** 'up' has two another allomorphs i.e **-kət~gət**. Their distribution are the same as that of the allomorphs of the suffix -sin 'inside', that is, the phonological condition of the occurrence of **-khət** is similar with that of **-sin**, **-gət** is similar with that of **-jin** and **-kət** is similar with that of **-cin**.

Examples of –khət :

ka-khət-pə	**'to climb up'**
cət-khət-pə	**'to go up' (in the hill)**
pu-khət-pə	**'to carry upward'**
pay-khət-pə	**'to fly up'**
cen-khət-pə	**'to run up' (in the hill)**
lon-khət-pə	**'to pile up'**

Examples for – **gət** :

thon-gət-pə	**'to resurface up'**
khun-gət-pə	**'to pick up'**
hun-gət-pə	**'to throw up'**
thaŋ-gət-pə	**'to lift up'**
phun-gət-pə	**'to choke up'**

Examples for – **kət** :

phuk-kət-pə	**'to pull up'**
hap-kət-pə	**'to add up' (to put more up)**
set-kət-pə	**'to pull upward' or 'to start wearing'**
thet-kət-pə	**'to put something up'**
khik-kət-pə	**'to sprinkle upward'**

There are certain verbal roots, such as **ca**-'eat', **pa**'read', **cət**- 'go', **cen**- 'run', **thəw**- 'drive', **thoŋ** 'cook' gives the meaning of the 'start' or 'ahead'. Consider the following examples

Examples :

a.	**ca-ro**	**'Eat'**
	eat-comd.	
	ca-khət-lo	**'Start eating'**
b.	**pa-ro**	**'Read'**
	read-comd.	

pa-khət-lo 'Start reading'

c. cel-lo 'Run'
run-comd.
cel-khət-lo 'Run ahead'

d. thəw-ro 'Drive'
drive-comd.
thəw-gət-lo 'Drive ahead'

e. thoŋ-lo 'Cook it'
cook-comd.
thoŋ-gət-lo 'Start cooking

f. thi-ro 'Search it'
search -comd.
thi-gət-lo 'Start searching'

d. Suffix : -thə

This suffix -thə gives the meaning of 'downward'. It has no allomorph.

Examples :

cen-thə-bə 'to run down'
pu-thə-bə 'to carry downward'
khət-thə-bə 'to drop'
hun-thə-bə 'to throw downward'
ləw-thə-bə 'to take down'
thəw-thə-bə 'to drive downward'
pay-thə-bə 'to fly down'
hay-thə-bə 'to fell down'

This suffix also gives the meaning of 'continue' when it is suffixed to certain verbal roots such as **pa-**' read', **cət** 'go' i 'write' **thək** 'drink' **thəw-**' drive' etc.

pa-thə-bə ' to continue reading'
cət-thə-bə ' to continue or ' to go on'
i-thə-bə 'to continue writing'
thək-thə-bə 'to continue drinking'
thəw-thə-bə 'to continue driving'

Directional suffixes

1. jin = dok = gət
2. cin = tok =kət
3. sin = thok = khət

Similarity of their occurrence in the phonologically conditioned environment.

13. Towards the Goal

The meaning of 'towards the goal' is expressed by the suffix **-rə** which has many allomorphs, such as, **lə-~ rə~ mə~ŋə ~pə-** (level tone). The conditioning factors of these allomorphs are same as that of the allomorphs, perfect aspect suffix **le~re**. This suffix is always followed by aspect suffix.

Examples of – **rə** :

ca-rəy	**'came and ate'**
tum-mə-y	**'came and slept'**
kəp-pə-y	**'came and cried'**
thoŋ-ŋəy	**'came and cooked'**
thək-ləy	**'came and drank'**

It is an interesting point here that when **-rə** goes with simple aspect suufix **-y** it is very significant that the tone is level indicating towards the goal. But when it (**-rə**) occurs with the unrealized aspect suffix **-gəni~ kəni**, indicating the same meaning (towards the goal), the tone is in the falling

Example of - **rə** :

ca-rə-gəni	**'will come and eat'**
kəp-lə-gəni	**'will come and cry'**
thək-lə-gəni	**'will come and drink'**
pa-rə-gəni	**'will come and read'**
tak-lə-gəni	**'will come and teach'**

When this suffix **-rə** (level tone) occurs with unrealized aspect suffix **-gəni** or with associative suffix **gə** it (**-rə**) indicates the meaning of 'durative'

Examples of **-rə** (Durative meaning with **-gəni**) :

ca-rə-gəni	**'will eat'**	**(within a short duration)**
thoŋ-lə-gəni	**'will cook'**	**(within a short duration)**
thək-lə-gəni	**'will drink'**	**(,,,,,,,,,,)**
kəp-pə-gəni	**'will cry'**	**(,,,,,,,,,,,,,,,,,,,,,,,,,,,,,,,,,,,,,,)**

Examples of **rə** (Durative meaning, with **-gə**) :

ca-rə-gə	**'after eating'**
thoŋ-rə-gə	**'after cooking'**
yeŋ-lə-gə	**'after seeing'**
kəp-pə-gə	**'after crying or by crying'**

As in the sentences

məhak ca-rə-gə cət-khre
he eat-dur.-asso. go-asp
'After eating he has gone'

məhak əsi-də ŋayhak tum-lə-gə məyum-də hən-khre
he here sometime sleep -dur-asso his-house-loc. return-asp
'After sleeping here for some time he has gone back'

14. Suffixes of Destruction

There are three suffixes in Manipuri which indicate the meaning of destruction or break. They are **-khay** , **-thət** and - **thək.**

a. Suffix : - khay

This suffix **-khay** has two other allomorphs, such as **-kay ~ gay**. They occur under phonological condition. This gives the meaning of 'break into pieces'.

The allomorph **-gay** occurs after a verbal root (dyanamic) that begins with an aspirated stop, like **th, ph**, and **kh** or with a fricative, like s and **h** and ends with a voiced sound.

Examples :

theŋ-gay-bə 'to collide and break'
thom-gay-bə 'to hit and break'
phu-gay-bə 'to beat and break'
se-gay-bə 'to tear and break'
su-gay-bə 'to pound and break'
ho-gay-bə 'to scratch and break'
həŋ-gay-bə 'to prick and break'

The other allomorph **-kay** occurs with a few roots (dyanamic) with begin with an aspirated stop or a fricative and ends with a voiceless stop (k, t, p).

Examples :

phək-kay-bə 'to pull out' (break into two pices)
sik-kay-bə 'to pinch and break'

It has also the extended meaning of 'open', when it occurs with the verb **sat** 'blossom', **sat-kay-bə** 'to blossom' (in full blossom), it indicates the degree of blossom of a flower.

The another allomorph **-khay** occurs elsewhere .Consider the following examples:

Examples :

met-khay-bə 'to press and break into'
tək-khay-bə 'to grind and break into'
təm-khay-bə 'to make level and break'
(to break and make level)
ləy-khay-bə 'to twist and break'
kap-khay-bə 'to shoot and break (into pieces)
ləŋ-khay-bə 'to throw and break (into pieces)
cəp-khay-bə 'to crust'

It is an interesting point that the modern youths use this suffix **-khay** very often and incorporates a different meaning of 'high headed' or 'contempt'. Here the meaning of 'break' is neglected . Consider the following examples :

a. muk-pə 'to challenge'
muk-khay-bə'to challenge' (with a feeling of contempt)

b. yeŋ-bə 'to see'
yeŋ-khay-bə 'to see' (with a feeling of contempt)

c. phəm-bə 'to sit'
phəm-gay-bə 'to sit' (with a feeling of contempt)
(with any other whether this place is proper or not)

b. Suffix : - thət

This suffix **-thət** has two other allomorphs, as **-dət~tət**. They occur under certain phonological conditions : **-thət occurs in the same phonological environment as -khay occurs, in the same way, -gay has same environment of dət and -tət has also the same environment of -kay.**

Examples of the allomorph **–thət** :

cəp-thət-pə **'to cut and break into'**
cik-thət-pə **'to bite and break into'**
tək-thət-pə **'to rub and break '**
ləy-thət-pə **'to twist and break'**

Examples of the allomorph **–dət** :

phoy-dət-pə **'to fetch and break'**
thom-dət-pə **'to hit for break'**
su-dət-pə **'to pound and press' (not to come up)**
soy-dət-pə **'to cut' (emphatic)**

Examples of **– tət** :

phək-tət-pə **'to fetch and break'**
phuk-tət-pə **'to pull out and break**
sik-tət-pə **'to scratch and break'**
hut-tət-pə **'to bore and break'**
se-tət-pə **'to tear and break'**

c. Suffix : – thek :

Like the above suffixes of destruction it (**thek**) has two other allomorphs **-te~dek**. They have the same phonological condition in their occurrence. The occurrence of **thek** is similar with that of **-khay, -tek** is similar with that of **-kay** while **-dek** is similar with that of **-gay**.

Examples of **–thek** :

ciŋ-thek-pə **'to pull and break'**
nəm-thek-pə **'to press and break'**
ləy-thek-pə **'to twist and break'**
nən-thek-pə **'to press from the above and break'**
(broken because of pressure from the above)

Examples of the allomorph **– deķ** :

thu-dek-pə **'to twist and break'**
(He twists and breaks the plant)
su-dek-pə **'to pound and break'**
thom-dek-pə **'to hit and break'**
phu-dek-pə **'to beat and break'**
kham-dek-pə **'to spoil and break'**

Examples of the allomorph **– tek** :

phuk-tek-pə **'to pull out and break'**
(He pulls out and spoils the plant)

sik-tek-pə 'to pinch and spoils the plant'
(killing of)

This suffix **-thek** has the extended meaning of 'defeated in debate' when it **(-thek)** is used with the verbal root **pay** - 'hold' (but not use in this sense). Consider the following sentence.

60. məhak-nə wa ədu hay-rək-pə-də əy-nə hek pay-thek-pə-ni
he speech det. say-dir-NZR- I nom at say -NZR-cop.
When he said so many things I replied exactly to the point .

(When he mentioned the particular situation I exactly pointed the situation, Then I felt that my counter argument defeated him in the debate).

Here it is a point that these suffixes of destruction say, **-khay, -thəy** and **-thek** have different meaning since they are near to the verbal root (in other word it can be said that they are derived from the verbal roots say, **khay** cut with a knife, **kay** 'break into pieces'; **thət** 'break into pieces by pulling'.

15. Reciprocal

In this language the reciprocal suffix is **-nə.** It is used with the dyanamic (action) verbs, such as . **phu** 'beat', **kaw** 'kick' **pi** 'give', **pha** 'catch' **cəy** rebuke', **yeŋ** 'look', **kəw** 'call', **həŋ** ' ask', **ca** 'eat', **mun** 'snatch', **hun**' throw', **law** 'shout', **u** 'see' etc.

Examples :

phu-nə-bə 'to fight with each other'
beat-rec-NZR
kaw-nə-bə 'to kick with each other'
pi-nə-bə 'to give with each other'
pha-nə-bə 'to catch with each other'
law-nə-bə 'to shout with each other'

16. Together

'Together', in this language, is expressed by a suffix **-min**. It can be used with the reciprocal suffix **-nə** and it is used with dyanamic verbs.

Examples :

ca-min-nə-bə 'to eat together'
thək-min-nə-bə 'to drink together'
tu-min-nə-bə 'to sleep together'
pa-min-nə-bə 'to read together'
phəm-min-nə-bə 'to sit together'

Here is a sentence :

məkhoy cak ca-min-nə-ri
they rice eat-tog-rec.-asp.
'They are eating together'

17. Excessive Suffix -mən

The suffix for denoting excess is **-mən** or **məl**. It is used with dynamic as well as stative verbs.

Examples :

ca-mən-bə	'to eat excessively'
thək-mən-bə	'to drink excessively'
tum-mən-bə	'to sleep excessively'
pa-mən-nə	'to read excessively'
lum-mən-bə	'too heavy'
caw-mən-bə	'too big'

18. Causative Suffix

In this language, causative is formed by suffixation of **-hən~ həl** to the verb (see for detail in 9.5). It is used with both dyanamic and stative verbs, i.e. **ca** 'eat' **cen** 'run', **waŋ** 'tall, **ŋaŋ** 'red' etc.

1. əy-nə tomba-bu cel-həl-li
   I-nom Tomba -acc. run-cau-asp
   'I make Tomba run'
2. məhak-nə tebəl ədu waŋ-həl-li
   he-nom table det high-cau-asp
   'He makes the table high'

Other examples are :

kəp-hən-bə	'to make cry'
phu-hən-bə	'to make beat'
sa-hən-bə	'to make warm'

19. Reflexive Suffix

The reflexive suffix in Manipuri is -cə which has another allomorph -jə. They occur under phonological condition :-cə occurs after a voiceless unaspirated stop (p, t, k,) and the other allomorph -jə occurs after vowels and voiced consonants.

Occurance of -cə

thək-cə-bə	'to drink oneself'
kəp-cə-bə	'to cry oneself'
cət-cə-bə	'to go oneself'

Occurrence of -jə

ca-jə-bə	'to eat oneself'
i-jə-bə	'to write oneself'
phu-jə-bə	'to beat oneself'
thoŋ-jə-bə	'to cook for oneself'
ləw-jə-bə	'to take for oneself'
phəm-jə-bə	'to sit oneself'

As in the sentence :

61. məhak-nə layrik ədu ləw-jə-y
    he-nom. book det take -ref. - asp.
    'He himself takes the book'

62. əŋaŋ məca ədu-nə cak ca-jə-y
kid det-nom rice eat-ref. -asp
'The kid himself takes his meal'

When this suffix -cə occurs with the intentive suffix **-ge~ke** expresses polite, as in the following sentences.

63. əy isinŋ khəra thək-cə-ge
I water some drink
'Let me drink some water'

64. əy cak khərə ca-jə-ge
I rice some eat
'Let me take some food'

65. əy cət-cə-rə-ge
I go
'Let me go'

20. Honorific Suffix -bi

This suffix **-bi** has another allomorph **-pi**. They occur under phonological conditions : **-bi** occurs after vowels and voiced consonants while **-pi** occurs elsewhere.

(1) When it (**-bi**) is followed by command marker, say, **-o, -u, -lo, -lu** etc., it indicates the meaning of the 'request' and **-bi** functions as a "honorific marker", as in the following sentences.

66. cak ca-bi-ro 'Please have your meal'
rice eat

67. ca thək-pi-yu 'Please take your tea'
tea drink

68. tomba-gi yum-də khəra cət-pi-ru
Tomba-gen house-loc some go
'Please pay a visit to Tomba'

69. tebəl-dəgi layrik ədu pi-bi-rək-u
table -from book det give-
'Please pass me the book from the table'

(ii) But when it (-bi) is followed by the intentive suffix **-ge~ke**, it gives the meaning of a 'challenge tone' or 'contempt tone', as in the following sentences :

70. (əy) mayren əsi ca-bi-ge
I pumkin det eat
'Let me eat this pumkin' (challenging)

71. isiŋ jək əsi-mə thək-pi-ge
water jug det-one drink-
'Let me drink this jug of water' (challenging)

72. (əy) ka-si-də cəŋ-bi-ge
I room-det-loc enter-
'Let me enter this room' (challenging)

(iii) when it (-bi) is followed by aspect markers (-y, -ri , -le and -gəni) it expresses the meaning of "benefactive".

73. məhak-nə əy-gi ka ədu way sit-pi-re
he-nom I gen room det sweep
'He has swept my room for me'

74. məhak-nə əhəl ədu-gi cithi pa-bi-re
he-nom old det-gi letter read
'He has read the old man's letter for him (old man)'.

75. məhak-nə lay ədu phəklaŋ-də nəp-pi-re
he-nom picture det wall-loc paste
'He has pasted the picture on the wall (for me)'

21. Endearment

There are two suffixes for indicating 'endearment'. They are -ko and -co ; the suffix -ko is always preceded by command markers and the suffix -co is also preceded by command markers but it (-co) has an additional meaning of 'proximity' (away from the speaker). i.e with the command marker -ru 'command' (away from the speaker)'.

Suffix - ko

76. nəŋ niŋthinə səŋgom thək-u-ko
you nicely milk drink-com-end.
'Drink the milk nicely' (to the baby)

77. nəŋ yum-də həl-lo-ko
you house-loc return-com-end.
'Go back '

Sentences with - co

78. nəkhoy-gi cece-də pi-ru-co
you-gen elder sister -loc give -com-end
'Give this to your sister'

79. nəŋ para pa-ru-co
you lesson read -comd-end.
'Read your lessons' (not here)

80. nəŋ məkhoy-gə sannə-ru-co
you they -asso play -comd. end
'You go and play with them'

22. Habitual

The suffix for habitual is -kən which has another allomorph -gən. The allomorph -kən occurs voiceless unaspirated stop (p, t, k) and -gən occurs elsewhere. It has two different meanings : when the referent is an animate it indicates the 'habitual' meaning and when the referent is inanimate, it expresses 'natural process' or 'uneven recurrence of an event'.

The suffix **-kən** is used with certain verbal roots, (related with human being) like **ca** 'eat' **thək** 'drink' **nok** 'laugh' **kaw** 'forget' **law** 'shout', **saw** 'angry', **tum** 'sleep', **u-** 'see', **phu** 'beat', etc. for expressing 'habitual meaning'.

Examples :

81.a. tomba ŋa ca-y
Tomba fish eat -asp
'Tomba eats fish'

b. tomba ŋa ca-gəl-li
'Tomba eats fish habitually'

82. a. əŋaŋ əsi kəp-pi
baby det cry-asp
'The baby cries'

b. əŋaŋ əsi kəp-kəl-li
'The baby cries habitually'

83. a. ənaŋ əsi nok-y
baby det smile-asp.
'The baby smiles'

b. əŋaŋ əsi nok-kəl-li
'The baby smiles habitually'

For expressing 'natural process' the suffix **-kən** occurs with the verbal root, like, **cak** 'burn', **caw** 'big', **sa** 'hot' **iŋ** 'cold', **pum** 'rotten', etc.

Examples :

84. petrol-di məy cak-kəl-li
petrol -def fire burn-
'Petrol is highly inflamable naturally'

85. kalen-də yensaŋ pum-gəl-li
summer -loc. curry rotten-
'In summer curry is naturally gets rotten'

86. nasik pambi-si yam-nə thunə caw-gəl-li
Eucalyptus plant-det very quickly big-
'The eucalyptus plant is naturally very quick in growth'

22. Superiority

The suffix for superiority is **-hət** which is used with certain verbal roots, such as, **cəy** 'scold' or 'chide', **nəm** 'supress' law 'shout' **ka** 'burn' **nəy** 'stir' **ca** 'eat' **thum** 'submerge' etc.

Examples :

87. məpu-nə minay-siŋ-bu tu-hət-li
owner-nom servant -pl-acc. exploit -asp
'The owners are exploiting the servant'

88. əŋaŋ-bu cəy-hət-kə-nu

child-acc. chide -sup-unrea -prohi
'Don't chide the child' (scolding in a rude manner)

89. nəŋ-nə məhak-pu nəm-hət-pə ŋəm-loy
you-nom he -acc suppress can -neg
'You cannot supress him'

90. məhak wabə-nə məmay əsi ka-hət-le
he poor-nom one's face det burn - sup-asp.
'He is in abject poverty'

23. Suffix -kum

This suffix **-kum** has another allomorph **-gum** (**-kum** occurs after voiceless consonants while **-gum** elsewhere). It has multiple meaning depending on its occurrence : broardly it has two meanings (i) when it is added to dyanamic verb along with proposal suffix -si, it becomes 'let' negative marker (see in 8.1.2)

91. 'əykhoy yu thək-kum-si
We liquor drink-
'Let's not drink liquor'

(ii) When it is added to noun (**mi** 'man', **sa** 'animal' **ŋa** 'fish' etc.) or derived noun (**ca-bə** 'to eat', **thakpə** 'to drink' etc.) it gives the meaning of 'like' depending on its occurrence with.

a. -kum 'like' or 'similar'

huy-gum 'like dog' phurit-kum 'like shirt'

sa-gum 'like animal' ucek-kum 'like bird'

ŋa-gum 'like fish' phək-kum 'like mat'

ləycil-gum 'like cloud' nəp-kum 'like mucus'

pele-gum 'like Pele'

(iii) When it is used with stative verbs, say, **ŋaŋ** 'red', **sa.** 'hot', **ten** 'short', **saŋ** 'long', **kən** 'hard', **pet** 'soft', **kha** 'bitter', **thum** 'sweet' etc. it gives the meaning of 'appear' or 'seem'.

Example :

92. məhak-ki phurit-tu ŋaŋ-gum təw-wi
he -gen shirt -det red - do-asp
'His shirt seems red'

93. thəwri-du ten-gum təw-wi
rope-det short - do-asp
'The rope seems short'

94. hidak ədu thum-gum təw-wi
tablet det sweet do -asp
'That tablet tastes slightly sweet'

(iv) It may express additional meaning of 'doubt' or 'seems', as in following sentences:

95. məhak cak ca-khi-gum təw-re
he rice eat-def.- do-asp
'He seems to have taken his meal' (but not sure)

96. tomba skul cət-khi-gum təw-re
Tomba school go-def. do-asp.
'Tomba seems to have gone to school'

97. kot-tu ŋaŋ-gum təw-wi
coat-det red do-asp
'The coat seems red (but not sure)

(v) When it is added to numerals, like, **təruk** 'six', **təra** 'ten', **kun** 'twenty', **niphu** 'forty', **cammə** 'hundred' etc. it indicates 'about' and is followed by **-bə.**

Example :

98. əyŋon-də lupa cəni-gumbə yaw-ri
i(obj) -loc rupee 200 have-asp
'I have about Rs. 200 with me'

99. komla kun-gumbə thumok-tə ləy
orange 20 basket-loc have
'There are about 20 oranges in the basket'

This suffix **-gum** can also be preceded by **-rək** 'times' in forming **məŋa-rək-kumbə** 'about five times', **təret-rək-kumbə** 'about seven times', **niphu-rək-kumbə** 'about forty times' etc.

24. Suffix -ləm

It is a suffix indicating that the action is already completed and is followed by the aspect markers, i.e. simple aspect **-y**, progressive **-li**, perfect **-le** and irrealis (unrealized) **-gəni**. This suffix **-ləm** has other allomorphs **-rəm~ŋəm~pəm**. The phomological condition of their occurrence is same with that of the aspect markers **-li** and **-le**. When it **(-ləm)** is followed by the aspect i.e. simple **-y** progressive **-li** and perfective **-le** it **(ləm)** expresses the action is already completed looking from the speech.

Examples :

ca-rəm-li 'had eaten' (continuing at the time of his arrival)

thək-ləm-mi 'had drunk' (continuing at the time of his arrival)

ca-rəm-le 'had eaten' (had taken already)

thoŋ-ləm-le 'had cooked' (had cooked already)

But when it is followd by irrealis aspect (unrealized) **-gəni** it gives the meaning of 'doubt' as in the following examples :

100. məhak cak thoŋ-ləm-gəni
he rice cook-compl. -unreal.
'He might be cooking (now)
(but it is not certain)

101. mәhak ca thәk-lәm-gәni
he tea drink-compl. -unreal.
'He might be taking tea' (now)
(but it is not certain)

25. Reported Suffix -ne

This suffix **-ne** has two grammatical functions: one as a 'conjunction and another as a copula plus expressing 'emphasis.

a. As a Conjunction

102. tomba-ne cawbә-ne iroy-ri
Tomba and Chaoba swim-asp
'Tomba and Chaoba are swiming'

103. cabә-ne tum-bә-ne yaribә mәkhәy mәtәm nay-yu
to eat -and to sleep -and at least in time keep asp
'Be regular at least in eating and sleeping'

b. As a Copula

104. a. mәhak oja-ni
he teacher-cop.
'He is a teacher'

b. mәhak oja-ne
'He is a teacher (emphasis)

105. a. mәhak skul cәt-pә-ni
he school go -NZR -cop
'He goes to school'
(His going is to the school)

b. mәhak skul cәt-pә-ne
'He goes to school' (emphasis)
(His going is to the school)

106. a. mәhak thәbәk әdu tәw-bә-ni
he-nom work det do-NZR-cop
'He does the work'
('the work is done by him')

b. mәhak-nә thәbәk әdu tәw-bә-ne
'He does the work'(emphasis)
(The work is done by him)

It is known from the above discussion that the role of affixes (prefixes and suffixes) in this language is very significant. The number of suffixes is also numerous. The affixes very forcefully proved that this language is an agglutinative one.

Possible order of verbal suffixes :

Verbal roots	Causative	Honorific	Auxiliary	Deitic	Nominalizer	Aspect of different sentence marker

CHAPTER–IV

WORD-FORMATION

4.1 Word-Formation

Word-formation is a collective term for the set of processes by which lexical items are derived from or related to, other lexical items. In its most general sense, the term refers to the whole process of morphological variation in the constitution of words, i.e. including the two main division of Inflection (word variations signalling grammatical relationship) and Derivation (word variations signalling relationships). In a restricted sense, word-formation refers to the latter process only.

In English and in many other languages, the principal devices for forming words are compounding and derivation, though other devices exit. The study of word-formation is often referred to as derivational morphology; this is in general quite distinct from inflectional morphology. In most languages, word-formation processes constitute the most striking examples of partially productive processes. In the 1960s, there were attempts to integrate word formation into syntax, but these attempts were not very successful, and most current frameworks handle word-formation by lexical rules contained within the lexicon, though some approachs postualate a distinct component of the grammar to deal with word-formation.

4.2 Derivational Processes

Natural languages are found to use two main types of strategies in order to derive composite words from simpler constituents. The two stategies are Affixation and Compounding. These two processes differ from one another by the fact that in the case of compounding, two or more linguistic elements (roots or words) are combined to form a new words, whereas in the case of affixation, a dependents element (affix) is attached to an independent one.

In another way, affixation differs from compounding. In the case of composit words derived through affixation, it is found not necessary to establish underlying structures which are different from the structures that actually occur in the derived words. But in the case of composit words involving the process of compounding, it is found possible or even necessary to establish very rich underlying structures, of which only a very small truncated part is overly shown by the composite words.

4.2.1 Affixation

Manipuri uses these two processes — affixation and compounding — in its words-formation. New word forming through affixation is not so rich in the language. In this language, new words can be formed through affixation, specifically by prefixation to a bound root. (action related are all bound roots see, Root)[1]. For our convenience in the study of word-formation through affixation, it can be devided into two: (1) derivation from bound roots and (2) derivation from free roots.

---

1. In Manipuri, there are two bound roots -free and bound. All the nominals are free (but there are some exception) they are called as substantives and the bounds are called as 'Zero category' or 'Pre-category' to which by addition of respective markers we can derive such as verb, adjective, adverb and nouns.

4.2.1.1 Derivation from Bound Roots

By affixation (prefix or suffix) to a bound root new words belonging to kinds of word class can be formed.

a) $Root_b$ + Aspects/Moods > V

ca+y	>	ca-y [eat + simple asp]
thək+ri	>	thək-li [drink+progressive] 'drinking'
pa+re	>	pa-re ['read+perfect] 'has read'
cət+kəni	>	cət-kəni [go+irrealis] 'will go'
ta+ro	>	ta-ro [listen +comd.mk] 'Listen'
pak+y	>	pak-y 'wide + asp'
ŋəw+y	>	ŋəw+y 'white + asp'
pik+y	>	pik-y 'small + asp'
tha+y	>	tha-y 'thick + asp'
waŋ+y	>	waŋ-ŋi 'tall + asp'
pa+y	>	pa-y 'thin + asp'

(b) Root +Nominalizer > Nominal Form

ca+bə	>	ca-bə 'to eat'	
cət+pə	>	cət-pə 'to go'	
thoŋ+bə	>	thoŋ-bə	'to cook'

(c) [Adj.mk +[Root + NZR] Adjective

or

Adj + Nominal > Adj form. (Attributive Adj.)

ə+pabə	>	əpabə 'thin' əpabə phi 'a thin cloth'	
ə+phəŋbə	>		'available'
		əphəŋbə	pot-siŋ 'the available things
ə+waŋbə	>	əwaŋbə	'tall'
		əwaŋbə u	'the tall tree'
ə+caybə	>	əcaybə	'spread'
		əcaybə səmlaŋ 'the spread hair'	

(d) b Root+Adv.mk. > Adverb

təpə +nə	>	təpə-nə	'slowly
kəp+nə	>	kəp-nə	'crying'
tən+nə	>	tən-nə	'lazily'

(e) There are three nominalized pronominal markers, namely i- for 1st person, nə- for 2nd person and mə- for 3rd person. Without these pronominal markers some very closed kin-terms can not indicates a complete sense (in other words they are just like bound roots). They are given below :

ma	'mother'
pa	'father'
ben	'grand mother'
pu	'grand father'

ne		'fathers sister'
ce		'elder sister'

These kin-terms are all bound roots (they cannot indicate these meanings), just for our convenience, the referent terms are given in the gloss respectively. By the prefixation of the respective pronominal markers they become independent kinship term as in the following illustration :

	ma		i-ma	'my mother'
	pa		i-pa	'my father'
	ben	>	i-ben	'my grand mother'
i +	pu		i-pu	'my grand father'
1st person	ne		i-ne	'my father's sister'
(singular)	ce		i-ce	'my elder sister'
	ma		nə-ma	'yours mother'
	pa		nə-pa	'yours father'
	ben	>	nə-ben	'yours grand mother'
nə+	pu		nə-pu	'yours grand father'
2nd person	ne		nə-ne	'yours father's sister'
(singular)	ce		nə-ce	'yours elder sister'
	ma		mə-ma	'his mother'
	pa		mə-pa	'his father'
	ben		mə-ben	'his grand mother'
mə+	pu	>	mə-pu	'his grand father'
3rd person	ne		mə-ne	'his father's sister'
(singular)	ce		mə-ce	'his elder sister'

4.2.1.1.2 Derivation by Prefixation of Non-Pronominal Marker mə

There are some words derived by prefixing this marker mə- to certain roots which, rather irregularly, denotes abstract entities or even concrete.objects that have resulted from the events. The examples are given below :

(a) Abstract :

ŋal	'bright'	mə-ŋal	'light'
pok	'bron'	mə-pok	'birth'
lep	'stand'	mə-rep	'height', depth'
haw	'tasty'	mə-haw	'taste'
ləy	'turn'	mə-rəy	'trick, argument'
cət	'go'	mə-cət	'character'

(b) Conerete :

pəy	'keeping together in a place'	mə-pəy	'heap'
pun	'bind'	mə-pun	'bundle'
phəm	'sit'	mə-phəm	'place'

i	'write'	mə-yi	'mark'
paŋ	'help'	mə-paŋ	'friend'

4.2.1.3 Prefixation of Khu

This prefix **khu-** is productive and can be prefixed to any action oriented bound roots. Then it indicates 'the manner' or 'the way of,' or 'the nature', as in the following examples :

pa	'read'	khu-pa	'the nature of his reading'
ca	'eat'	khu-ca	'the nature of his eating'
thək	'drink	khu-thək	'the nature of his drinking'
tum	'sleep'	khu-tum	'the nature of his sleeping'
cen	'run'	khu-cen	'the nature of his running'
yek	'draw'	khu-yek	'the nature of his painting'
si	'die'	khu-si	'the nature of his death'
ŋaŋ	'speak'	khu-ŋaŋ	'the nature of his speaking'
yeŋ	'look'	khu-yeŋ	'the nature of his looking'
yon	'sell'	khu-yon	'the nature of his selling'
pi	'give'	khu-pi	'the nature of his giving'
lep	'stand'	khu-lep	'the nature of his standing'
sa	'make'	khu-sa	'the nature of his making'

There are some professional terms in which the ending of each terms can indicate gender, that is, ended by **ə** denotes male while ended by **i** denotes the female, as in the following examples :

cəphusabə (M)	'potter'	cəphusabi (F)
phisabə (M)	'weaver'	phisabi (F)
phisabə (M)	'washer	phisabi (F)
luciŋbə (M)	'leader'	luciŋbi (F)
maybə (M)	'priest'	maybi (F)
isəysəkpə (M)	'singer'	isəysəkpi (F)
potyonbə (M)	'seller'	potyonbi (F)
jagoysabə (M)	'dancer'	jəgoysabi (F)

In such pairs of words, one might regard the feminine (F) form as being derived through affixation, i.e by the addition of a feminine marker **i**. On the whole, it can be said that word-formation through the process of affixation is limited in this language. The process of compounding in the word-formation is very rich.

4.2.2 Compounding

A compound word is usually understood to be the result of fixed combination of two or more free forms, or words that have an otherwise independent existence. In Manipuri it may be also the combination of one free form plus one bound root. Compounding is usually subdivided according to the form class of the resultant compound : that is compound nouns, compound adjectives etc. It may also be subdivided according to the semantic criteria into Exocentric and Endocentric. Another type of compound found in Manipuri is coordinate compound.

4.2.2.1. Endocentric Comounds

4.2.2.1.1 Right-headed Compounds

In the right headed compounds, both the constituent elements are generally found to be nominal bases. The two nouns functioning as the constituent elements of this right headed compounds might be related with one another either by the possessive suffix **-gi~ -ki** or by one of several bases that are not actually related in the final composite word. Ample examples are given below :

Possessive relation :

u-gi	məhəy	'fruit of tree'	>	u-həy	'fruit'
khoŋ-gi	məsa	'branch of leg'	>	khoŋsa	'toe'
məy-gi	məri	'string of flame'	>	məyri	'flame'
u-gi	məna	'leaf of tree'	>	una	'leaf'
ləy-gi	məna	'leaf of flower	>	ləyna	'petal'

There is another type of possessive relationship that of directional, as in the following examples :

phi-gi　　məpan　　>　　phi-ban　　'lace'
cloth-gen　　broder
'side of the cloth'
yum-gi　　məthək　　>　　yumthək　　'roof'
house-gen　　top
'top of the house'
mit-ki　　məpan　　>　　mitpan　　'eyelid'
eye-gen
'broder of the eye'
ləy-gi　　məton　　>　　ləyton　　'tip of the tongue'
flower-gen top/tip
'top of the tongue'
khut-sa-gi　　məyay　　>　　khuyay　　'middle finger'
finger-gen middle
middle of the finger'
khoŋ-gi　　məton　　>　　khoŋdon　　'tip of the toe'
leg-gen top/tip
tip of the leg

Verbal Relation

ləw　　u-bə　　mi　　>　　ləwmi　　'cultivator' or farmer
paddy field　　to cultivale　　person
'a person to cultivate the field'
mi-nə　　sabə　　laŋ　　>　　miraŋ　　'cobweb'
spider-nom.　　to make　　snare
'snare made by spider'
məy-dəgi　　thokpə　　mərik　　>　　məyrik　　'spark'
fire-from coming out pieces

'pieces coming out from fire'
i-nə kup-pə yum > iyum 'thatch house
thatch-inst. covered house
'thatch covered house'
huy-gi oybə məkon > huykon 'kennel'
dog-gen being nest

Here it can be said that in these directional compounds, the second elements are generally a verbal root. Further we can have more compound words. For our convenient in the study we can categorize into some groups depending upon the kind of endings that these verbal-Nouns take in the underlying structures.

I. Resultatives (ending with the nominalizer **-bə/-pə**)

ciŋ-də ləy-bə mi > ciŋmi 'tribal people'
hill-loc live people
(ciŋ-gi mi 'hill's men')
'men living in the hills'
təm-də ləy-bə mi > təmmi 'valley people'
Valley-loc live people
(təm-gi mi 'valley's men')
'men living in the valley'
thum yawbə məhi > thumhi 'saline'
salt containing liquid
(saltwater)
(thum -gi mə-hi 'liquid of salt')
'liquid containing salt'

II Purposives (ending with **nə+bə**)

yum sa-nəbə məphəm > yumphəm 'housing site'
house build for site
'site for building house'
(yum-gi məphəm 'site of house')
pot yon-nəbə mə-phəm > potyonphəm 'stall'
goods sell forplace
həy thanəbə məkon > həykon 'òrchard'
fruit plant forplace/nest
(place of growing fruits)
(həy-gi məkon) 'placing fruit'
mə-həy təm-nəbə məkon > məhəykon 'school'
study learn for place
'place for studying' (educational institute)
ləy -thanəbə məkon > ləykon 'garden'
flower plant for place
'place for growing flowers'
(ləy-gi məkon 'place of flower')
sa phunəbə cəy > sajəy 'whip'
animal beat for stick

'stick for beating animal'
(sa-gi cəy ' stick of animal')
phi hap-nəbə luk > phiruk 'basket for keeping cloth'
cloth keek for basket
'basket for keeping cloth'
(phi-gi luk ' basket of cloth')

III. Relationals (ending with **bə+gi**)

thəw təw-bəgi məwoŋ > thəwwoŋ 'method'
work do of manner
'manner of doing work'
ceŋ cam-bəgi məhi > ceŋhi 'id'
rice wash of liquid
'liquid of washing rice'
khoŋ-nə cət-pəgi mərəm > khoŋləm 'foot path'
leg-inst go of path
'path of walking by foot'
sa-nə cət-pəgi mərəm > sarəm 'animal's way'
animal-nom. go of path
'path of animal's walking'

There are some compound words in which the verb in the middle relates the two nouns. In other words it is a kind of compound word made of combination of three roots. The examples are given below :

mi thuŋ-nəbə səŋ > mithuŋsəŋ 'sheltering house'
people arrive for house
'house for staying by travellers'
khut-nə subəgi məmən > khutsumən 'wage'
hand-inst work of price
price for working by hand'
həy yon-bə məphəm > kəyonphəm 'fruit stall'
fruit sell to place
'place for selling fruits'
phi yonbə məphəm > phyonphəm 'cloth centre'
cloth sell-to place
'place for selling cloth'
laynə yeŋnəbə məphən > lay-yeŋphəm 'hospital'
disease see for place
'place of desease treathment'
lay niŋ-nəbə məphəm > layniŋphəm 'prayer centre'
God pray for place
'place for praying god'

There are some compound nouns which are made of noun-plus-noun. The examples are given below :

ləy-gi məhi > ləyhi 'nector'
flower-gen liquid

'liquid of flower'
khoy-gi məhi > khoyhi 'honey'
bee-gen liquid
'liquid of bee'
noŋ-gi mərik > noŋlik 'rain drop'
rain-gen drop
'drops of rain'

There are some compound nouns also which are the composite of noun-plus-action oriented bound root. The examples are given below :

laybu niŋbə > layniŋ 'prayer'or 'religion'
God pray
'praying the god'
ləŋ-nə taybə > ləŋday 'seam'
thread-inst to stitch
ləm-də sibə > ləmsi 'death in other's place' (wild death)
outside-loc to die
'death on the road' (not in the house)

There are some other right-headed compounds having the noun (substantive) root **phəm** < **məphəm** 'place' as the second constituent element and an action oriented bound root as the first element. It is very interesting that **phəm** is very productive : it (**phəm**) can form many new compounds with the combination of any other action oriented bound roots.

Example :

ləy-nəbə məphəm > ləyphəm 'accomodation'
live for place
'place for staying'
lot-nəbə məphəm > lotphəm 'hiding place'
hide for place
'place for hiding'
ca-nəbə məphəm > caphəm 'dinning room'
eat for place
'place for eating'
thəknəbə məphəm > thəkphəm 'tea-stall'
drink for place
'place for drinking'
thoŋ-nəbə məphəm > thoŋphəm 'kitchen'
cook for place
'place for cooking'

Noted that **phəm** can compose with many others action oriented bound roots, viz **tum** 'sleep', **ŋay** 'wait', **lip** 'stand' **cen** 'run', **pa** 'read', **pok** 'born', **coŋ** 'jump', **sanə** 'play' **həw** 'grow', **yok** 'bear', **lek** 'stay', **law** 'shout', **yeŋ** 'look' etc. It is, no doubt, very productive for the formation of right -hearded compound. Further **məphəm** can form new right-headed compound with noun, as in the following examples :

məy həw-nəbə məphəm > məyphəm 'fire place'
fire grow for place

'place for burning fire'
sa theŋ-nəgədəbə məphəm > sa-phəm 'dangerous place'
animal meet for
'place for facing animal'
lan theŋnəgədəbə məphəm > lanphəm 'battle place'
war face for
'place for war'
lay-gi məphəm > layphəm 'worshipping place'
God-gen for
'place for worshipping God'
ləw-gi məphəm > ləwphəm 'paddy field'
field-gen
'place where paddy fields are'

4.2.2.1.2 Left Headed Compounds

In the left headed compounds the second constituent element as the head, is a noun. We can see here different types of left headed compound.

I. Some compound are formed by reversing the order of the underlying structure and simultaneously root of the first element is retained as in the following examples :

ətoppə mi > mitop 'stranger'
'strange person'
ənəwbə mi > minəw 'new person' (new settler)
'new person'
əpakpə ləm > ləmpak 'play ground'
broad land
ərumbə pot > potlum 'load'
'heavy object'
əhawbə ləy > ləyhaw 'manure'
tasty earth
əŋaŋbə ləy > ləyŋaŋ 'stiky mud from hills'
red earth
əŋaŋbə phi > phiŋaŋ 'red cloth'
red cloth
əsibə tha > thasi 'new moon'
dead moon
əyuŋbə u > uyuŋ 'post'
erected tree
əsaŋbə wa > wasaŋ 'the whole bamboo'
long bamboo
əŋəwbə khun > khunəw 'new village'
new village

II. In some compound, the relationship is preferably that of purpose, as in the following examples :

ca-nəbə ləw > ləwca 'estate'
eat for paddy field

'paddy field for eating'
set-nəbə phi > phijet 'dress'
wear for cloth
'cloth for wearing'
thaŋ-nəbə məy > thaŋməy 'lamp'
carry for fire
'fire for carrying'
su-nəbə cəy > cəysu 'walking stick'
hit for stick
'stick for hitting ground'å

III. There are some directional left headed compounds. Example:

məkha thəŋbə ya > yakha 'lower teeth'
lower be teeth
'tooth in the lower gum'
məthək thəŋbə ya > yathək 'upper teeth'
upper be teeth
məmaŋ thəŋbə khoŋ > khumaŋ 'fore leg'
front be leg
'leg which is in the front'
məmaŋ thəŋbə ya > yamaŋ 'front teeth'
front be teeth
'tooth which is in the front'

IV. There are also some other left headed compounds in which <u>oy</u> 'be' relates the noun with adverb as in the following examples :

məmay oybə phi > phimay 'right side of
face be cloth the cloth (face of the cloth)
'face which is of cloth'
len oybə phi > phiren best cloth'
best be cloth
'best which is of cloth' 'loth which is the best'
len oybə niŋthow > niŋthəwren 'Emperor'
best be the king
'greatest which is of king' > 'king of the kings'

V. There is also another type of left headed compound in which the two constituent elements are related by possessive suffix **-gi/-ki**, as shown in the following examples :

wa-gi pəl > wapəl 'place where bamboos grow'
bamboo-gen fench
'the fench of bamboo'
ləypak-ki pəl > ləypəl 'fench made of mud'
earth-gen fench
'the fench of mud'
tha-gi məməy > thaməy 'the last part of the month'
month-gen tail
'the tail of the month'
u-gi məpak > upak 'plank'

tree-gen plank
'plank of the wood'

4.2.2.2 Exocentric Compound

A type of compound word in which one element modifies or restricts the other and the whole denotes an entity which is a hyponym of an unexpresed semantic head. In other words, composite words which neither of the two constituent elements function as the head. These compounds are generally made of a noun and an action oriented bound root. Since neither of them can function as the head there is a need to introduce a count element such as **pot** 'thing or object', **mi** 'man', **məphəm** 'place' etc, as the head for these compounds.

They are categorized into two types — purposive and resultatives, depending upon the type of relationship that exists between the constituent elements. Examples are given below :

(a) Purposive

kaŋ khənnəbə pot > kaŋkhən 'mosquito net'
mosquito prevent to thing
'thing for preventing mosquito'

may khənnəbə pot > maykhən 'a kind of partition' (or kind of curtain)
face prevent to
'thing not to be seen by other'

naw sumnəbə pot > nawsum 'cradle'
small lull to
'thing for keeping the child to sleep'

mon-də khumnəbə pot > moŋkhum 'pillow case'
pillow-loc cover to
'thing for covering pillow'

khujeŋ-də sinəbə pot > khuji 'bracelet'
arm-loc wear-to
'thing for wearing in arm'

khoŋ-da sinəbə pot > khoŋji 'bangle' (for leg)
leg-loc wear to
'thing for wearing to the leg'

(b) Resultatives

nəm-də pobə pot > nəmbo 'bundle (lɔad)'
back-loc carry to
'thing that is carried on the back'

ləy-dəgi səwbə tin > ləysəw 'white ant'
earth-from grow -worn

səŋ-dəgi təpthəbə məphəm > səŋtəp 'shade (of the house)
house -from to extend place
'shade extended from the house

6 phəy supnəbə phi > phəyjup 'quilt or duvet'
thai to cover cloth

'cloth for covering thai'

There are some other exocentric compound in which the noun **mi** 'man' is functioning as a covert head the verb is in the nominal form by suffixation of nominalizer **-bə/-pə** in the covert, as in the following examples :

phi sabə mi > phisabə 'weaver'
cloth to weave man
man who weaves cloth'

puŋ yəybə mi > puŋyəybə 'drummer'
drum to beat man
'man who beats the drum'

yum sa-bə mi > yumsabə 'builder'
house to build
'man who builds house'

u subə mi > usubə 'carpenter'
wood to work
'man who works on plank'

thoŋ sabə mi > thoŋsabə 'bridge builder'
bridge to build
'man who builds bridge'

nuŋ subə mi > nuŋsubə 'mason'
stone to work
'man who works on stone'

There are some other exocentric compound words inwhich **nupi** 'woman' act as the cover head (traditionally woman specialised in these works), as in the following examples :

la yon-bə nupi > layonbi 'banana-leaf seller'
banana leaf to sell woman
'woman who sells banana leaf'

kwa yonbə nupi > kwayonbi 'pan seller'
betal nut to sell
'woman who sells pan'
(betalnut with leaf)

naw loybə nupi > nawroybi 'midwife'
small to care
'woman who tends to the baby'

phi yonbə nupi > phiyonbi 'cloth seller'
cloth to sell
'woman who sells cloth'

There are also a few compounds having the object like **pot** 'thing' as the covert head in which also the verb is in the nominal form by the suffixation of the nominalizer **-bə/-pə**, as in the following examples :

muk cabə pot > mukcabi 'blotting paper'
ink to eat thing
'thing which eats ink'

məy kapthokpə pot > məykappi 'fire crakker'
fire to spark out

'thing which sparks fire'
səm phajin-nəbə pot > səmphabi 'hair-cliff/pin'
hair bind for
'thing which binds hair'
məy-də ianbə tin > məyranbi 'moth'
fire-loc to die
'insect which dies in fire'
u-da taŋbə pambi > utaŋbi 'parasitic plant'
tree-loc to depend plant
'plant that depends upon tree'
u-də kabə ŋa > ukabi 'a kind of local fish'
tree-la to clibe fish
'fish that climbs tree'

4.2.2.3 Coordinate Compound

In this type of compound both the elements, functions jointly as heads which are generally of two different nouns joined together through the associative suffix **-gə/-kə** (this **-gə/-kə** can be treated as conjunction) there are other conjunctions also functioning like this suffix (-gə/-kə). They are **-ne, əməsuŋ, əmədi**, (see in Conjunction 5.1.2)

Example :

yum-gə kəygə > yum-kəy 'estate or property'
house and granary
ləw-gə iŋkhol-gə > ləwŋiŋkhol 'property or estate'
'paddy field and (house) plote'
sa-gə sən-gə > sa-sən 'cattle'
'animal and cow'
cak-kə isiŋ-gə > cak-isiŋ 'meal'
'rice and water
məca-gə məsu-gə > cəca-məcu 'issues'
(his) son and (his) grand-child

Other conjunctions that joined the two nouns are **-ne, əmadi and əmasuŋ**. Examples :

sa -ne sən-ne]
sa əmədi sən] > sa-sən 'cattle'
sa əmasuŋ sən]

4.2.2.4 Form-Class Compound

Very briefly here it can be analysed the process of compounding depending on form class. Here underlying structures are not shown. They are discussed below:

I. [Noun+Noun] > Noun

məy + phəm (məphəm) > məyphəm 'fire place'
fire place

lan + phəm > lanphəm 'battle'
war place
sa + sən > sasən 'cattle'
animal cow

II. [Noun + Verbal -Noun] or [nominal form becoming by suffixation of nominalizer -bə/-pə to the Action Oriented bound Roots (A-O bRoot)]

u + su-bə > usubə 'carpenter'
tree work NZR

III. [adjective + Noun] > Noun

əpakpə + ləm > ləmpak 'playing ground'
wide place

VI. [Noun + Adjective] > Noun

ya + thək (< məthək) > yathək 'upper teeth'
tooth above (upper)

V. [Noun + A-O bRoot+ Noun] > Noun

mi + thuŋ +səŋ
man + arrive +house > mithuŋsəŋ 'Accomodation'
(very low price accumodation)

pot + yon +phəm(<məphəm)
thing + sell + place > potyonphəm 'market'

VI. [Noun +A-O.bRoot] > Adjective

ləm + koy > ləmkoy 'travel'
place tour ⎤ ləmkoy wari 'travellock'
travel ⎦ story

4.2.2.5 Extended Compound

It has been seen that most of the compounds are of the dia-syllable in nature or of two roots. But there are a few compounds which is overtly presence of three or more roots.

Example :

I. Of three roots :

mi +thuŋ +səŋ > mithuŋsəŋ 'dharmasala'
man arrive house
pot +yon +phəm > potyonphəm 'market'
thing sell place
wa +roy +pot > waroypot 'finalisation for marriage'
word finalise thing

II. Of four roots :

məhəy + təm + phəm +səŋ
education learn place house > məhəytəmphəmsəŋ 'Educational institution (school/college)'

4.2.3. Affixo-Compounding

There is a very complicated process of word formaton involving in this language. There is a few words which are formed by involving the two process of word-formation — affixation and compounding. Hence this is named affixo-compounding. This can be explained here in the following :

ə	'prefix'
sa	'make'
mən -(<məmən)	'price'
əsamən	'the price of making'

Step for formation

I.	(ə + sa)	>	əsa-	
II.	(əsa+mən)	>	əsamən	'price of making'

One important thing is that the middle elements will indicate 'the price of the action' and remain in all the words. The examples are given below :

ətumən	'stitching charge'
əsamən	'making charge'
əsemmən	'repairing charge'
əwamən	
ənommən	'wage'
əsumən	
əpumən	'porter charge'
əpamən	'reading charge'
ətakmən	'tuition fee'
əkhoymən	'ploughing charge'
əsinmən	'coppying charge'

What it is known from this is that in compare with affixation, compounding is more prominent in this language. Historically also compounding is more profoundly used in the old Manipuri literatures. More and above, semantic reduplication also plays in its word-formation for instance, **thəwdunuŋ** 'stone' [**thəwdu** 'stone' and **nuŋ** 'stone'). In aesthetic sense this (semantic - reduplication)is more beautiful.

Now-a-days there are lots of new coined words, and the coined words are very forceful and very natural. This is felt by the speakers. We can cite here some examples, such as **wahəndok** 'meaning' (**wa** 'word' and **həndok** 'translate'), **wakhəmlon** 'philosophy' (**wakhən** 'thought' and

lon 'language'), **yawonloy** 'revolutionary' (**yawon** 'change' and **loy** 'person'),**məhəyroy** 'student' (**məhəy** 'studies' or 'education' and **roy** 'person'), **məhəykol** 'school or college' 'educational institute' (**məhəy** 'studies and kol 'place') etc. We can conclude with the words of Matthew (1991) in word formation, we are concerned not only with grammatical process of derivation but also with the creative derivation (formation) of new words that follow existing patterns.

CHAPTER–V
WORD CLASS AND ITS GRAMMATICAL CONSTITUENTS

5.1 Word Class

In Manipuri , word class is not so distinct, except the noun. The form of the entity cannot show the class of the word : the respective word class is formed by addition of the respective markers; they are derived from the verbal bound root (VbRoot). Illustrations are given below :

Rule I. Formation of verb

VbRoot + asp/Mod ➜ Verb
cət + li ➜ cətli ' is going'
thək +le ➜ thək-le' has drunk

Rule II. Formation of Verbal Noun :

VbRoot + NZR ➜ V Noun
ca + bə ➜ cabə 'to eat' or 'eating'
thoŋ + bə ➜ thoŋbə 'to cook' or 'cooking'

Rule III. Formation of Adjective
(specially from the monosyllabic root)

{FP+ [VbRoot + NZR] } ➜ Adjective
ə + thoŋ + bə ➜ əthoŋbə 'cooked food'
ə + si + bə ➜ əsibə 'dead something'

There are other forms of adjective which has no formative particle (FP) ə-, only the NZR **-bə ~ pə** is suffixed. They are :

phəjə+bə	➜	phəjəbə nupimaca nice girl	'nice girl'
nuŋŋay + bə	➜	nuŋŋaybə mi happy man	'happy man'
niŋkhay+bə	➜	niŋkhaybə torban broken bank	'broken bank'
wanthə+bə	➜	wanthəbə nupi collapsed woman	'collapsed woman'

Rule IV. Formation of Adverb

VbR oot + Adverb ➜ Adverb
kəp + nə ➜ kəp-nə 'cryingly'
pa + nə ➜ pa-nə 'by reading'
təp + nə ➜ təpnə 'slowly'

5.2. Noun and its Categories

In Manipuri, a noun can be defined as a form which takes affixes like demostrative suffix (**si** or **-du**), personification suffix (**- mək**), identifier suffix (**-ne**), isolating suffix (**-təŋ ~ dəŋ**) plural suffix (**-siŋ ~ khov**), a case suffixes etc. A noun may be prefixed by a pronominal prefix which indicates the possessor of the prefixed noun. The constituents and their order are as follows

N+ Number + Dem. Suf.+ case mk + {identi Suf. only}

yum +siŋ-si + case mk + [ne / dəŋ / təŋ]
house -pl-det
'only for these houses'

5.2.1 Types of Noun

On the basis of the sentence, Manipuri Noun can be classified into three : (a) Simple noun (b) Derived noun and (c) Compound noun. They are discussed one by one in the followings :

5.2.1 a. Simple Noun

Noun which can stand alone without any prefixation neither any suffixation, for instance, **mi** 'man' **nupi** 'woman' **sa** 'animal' **səgol** 'horse' **layrik** 'book' **yum** 'house' **isiŋ** 'water' **tha** 'moon' etc.

5.2.2 Derived Noun

There are many nouns which are formed by affixation. They are called derived noun. In other words, in Manipuri many nouns are formed by prefixation to the VbRoot or by suffixation to the VbRoot.

They can be classified into two. They are discussed below :

a. By prefixation **mə** - and **khu** - to the VbRoot :

[mə- / khu-] + VbRoot

mə + ca eat	➜ məca	'the manner of one's eating'
mə+ pok born	➜ məpok	'birth'
khu+thək	➜ khu-thək	'the manner of one's drink'
khu+nok	➜ khunok	'the manner of one's laughing'

b. By siffixation of the NZR-bə~pə to the VbRoot :

ca+bə	➜ cabə	'to eat' or 'eating'
thək +pə	➜ thəkpə	'to drink ' or 'drinking'
ye' +pə	➜ yekpə	'to paint' or 'painting'
pa +bə	➜ pabə	'to read' or 'reading'

5.2.3 Compound Noun

There are nouns which are formed by combination of two or more nouns. They are treated as compound nouns. They are given below :

I. Noun + Noun > Noun

cak + səŋ rice shade	➜ caksəŋ	'kitchen'
yot + cəy iron stick	➜ yotcəy	'iron rod'
sən + lup cow herd	➜ sənlup	'a herd of cows'
way +məy husk fire	➜ wayməy	'fire from bruning of husk'

II. Noun + Vbroot ➜ Noun

wa + həŋ word ask	➜ wahəŋ	'question'
wa + rep word stand	➜ warep	'decision'
paw + khum news -answer	➜ pawkhum	'answer'

III. Noun + Augmentative

huy +jaw (<əcəwbə 'big) dog +big	➜ huyjaw	'big dog'
i+caw water+big	➜ icaw	'flood'
yum+jaw house-big	➜ yumjaw	'big house'
ka+jaw room+big	➜ kajaw	'big room'

IV. Noun+Dimi (nutive) [naw 'small']

huy+naw dog+	➜ huynaw	'puppy'
sən+naw cow	➜ sənnaw	'calf'
yen+naw hen	➜ yennaw	'chicken'
thoŋ+naw door	➜ thoŋnaw	'window'

5.3 Gender

There is no grammatical gender in Manipuri. Human and animate nouns are referred to as masculine or feminine on the basis of natural sex. For human being, the suffix **-a** indicates 'male' while **-i** 'female'. Consider the following examples :

nupa	'man'	nupi	'woman'
hənuba	'old man'	hənubi	'old woman'
phisuba	'washer man'	phisubi	'washer woman'
isəy səkpa	'male singer'	isəy səkpi	'female singer'
əpokpa	'father	əpokpi	'mother'
huranba	'thief (male)'	huranbi	'thief (woman)'

In the same way, the two suffixes **-a** and **-i** are used to the bird also to indicate male and female respectively, for example.

yenba	'cock'	yenbi	'hen'

In the case of animal nouns, the lexical item **labə** 'male' and **əmom** 'female' are used for denoting the natural sex. Illustrations are given below :

sən labə	'ox'	sən əmom	'cow'
huy labə	'dog' (m)	huy əmom	'bitch'
həwdoŋ labə	'cat' (m)	həwdoŋ əmom	'cat' (f)

There are also some opposite words which are used for denoting natural sex. They are given below :

ipa	'my father'	ima	'my mother'
ice	'my sister' (elder)	ibay	'my brother-in-law (elder)
khura	'uncle'	indon	'anty'
mamma	'mother's brother'	ine	'mothers brother's wife' or 'father's sister'

5.4 Number

Manipuri has two numbers only : singular and plural ; there is no grammatical agreement in number. Singular is not marked overtly while plural is marked by a suffix **-siŋ** or **-khoy**.

a. Addition of -siŋ

əŋaŋ	'child'	əŋsŋ-siŋ	'children'
nupi	'woman'	nupi-siŋ	'women'
nupa	'man'	nupa-siŋ	'men'
huy	'dog'	huy-siŋ	'dogs'
sən	'cow'	sən-siŋ	'cows'

The plural suffix **-siŋ** can be added to any nouns .

b. Addition of -khoy

It is used specially to personal pronouns for forming plural, as in the followings :

əy	'I'	əykhoy	'we'
nəŋ	'you'	nəkhoy	'you' (pl)

məhak	'he'	məkhoy	'they'

This suffix -khoy can also be added to proper nouns to indicate plurality, e.g. John and his groups. Here is the illustration :

tomba	'Tomba'	tomba-khoy	'Tomba and his group'
sila	'Sheela'	sila-khoy	'Sheela and her group'

Other than these, there is a lexical item, **məyam** 'many' which is generally used in the formation of plural. This word is very productive: it can occur with any noun. Consider the following examples :

əŋaŋ	'child'	əŋaŋ məyam	'many children'
mi	'man' (person)	mi məyam	'many people'
huy	'dog'	huy məyam	'many dogs'
sa	'animal'	sa məyam	'many animals'

There are some, other words which indicate collective e.g. **səŋgu** 'herd' **məpəy** / **cəbun** 'heap' **məpun** 'bundle' etc.

(a) səŋgu

sən səŋgu əma	'a herd of cattle'
mi səŋgu əma	'a group of people'
ucek səŋgu əma	'a flock of birds'

(b) cəbun 'heap' or 'group'

ləy məpun əma	'a bunch of flower'
ucek cəbun əma	'a flock of birds'

(c) məpun 'bundle'

cu məpun əma	'a bundle of sugar cane'
siŋ məpun əma	'a bunde of fire wood'

5.5 Numeral

Unlike most other south-east Asian languages, Manipuri does not have at all a system of noun classifiers, a neighbouring language, Mizo also does not have a semantically based system of noun classifiers. Numerals in Manipuri are adjectives and they follow the noun. Manipuri numerals can be sub-classified as follows :

a. Cardinals
b. Ordinals
c. Aggregative
d. Functionals
e. Multiplicatives
f. Approximatives

They are discussed one by one in the followings :-

5.5.1 Cardinals

The numerals to 10 are composed of a numerical stem and a prefix

əmə	1	kun	20
əni	2	kunmathoy	21
əhum	3	kunməri	24

məri	4	kuntəra	30
məŋa	5	niphu	40
təruk	6	yaŋkhei	50
təret	7	humphu	60
nipan	8	humphutəra	70
mapəl	9	məriphu	80
təra	10	məriphutəra	90
təra mathoy	11	cama	100
təra məri	14	cani	200
təramapəl	19	lisiŋəma	1000

The prefix ə- has an established Proto-Tibeto-Burman ancestory but is not used productively in the synchronic grammar of Manipuri. The numerals 1, 2 and 3 consist of the attributive prefix ə- and the roots **ma** '1', **ni** '2' and **hum** '3'. After the decimal the prefix ə- is deleted, only the roots **ma, ni and hum** occurs, for instance təra **ma**thoy '11', təranithoy '12' and təra**hum**doy '13' ; **kunmathoy** '21', **kunnithoy** '22' and kun**hum**doy '23' and so on. The prefix like **mə** in **məri** '4' and **məŋa** '5' ; and **tə** in **təruk** '6', **təret** '7' and **təra** '10' are not treated as prefix, because without them (**mə** and **tə**) they cannot occur as opposite to **əma, əni** and **əhum.**

The numerals 11, 12, 13 consist of **təra** '10' and **thoy** 'exceed', 'excel' : thus eleven is **təra+ma** '1' and thoy 'exceed'. This **thoy** is used for every decimal of 11-13, 21-23, 31-33 so on and so forth (to 91-93 also). The **thoy** is dropped for the numerals from 14 to19, 24 to 29, 34 to 39, 44 to 49 and so on. The even numbers 40, 60 ans 80 are formed through muliplication of juxtaposed numbers, following a vigesimal system : thus **niphu** '40' is **ni** '2' times phu 'beat' (multiply) '20'; **humphu** '60' is **hum** '3' times 20 and **məriphu** '80' is **məri** '4' times '20'.

The numbers like 30, 50, 70 and 90 are an addition or/and division of two juxtaposed numerals. Thus **kunthera** '30' is kun '20' plus **təra** '10' (t of təra is aspirated by phonological condition of 'n'); **yaŋkhəy** '50' is half ; **humphutəra** '70' which is **hum** '3' times '20' **təra** '10' and **məriphutəra** '90' : '4' times 20 plus **təra** '10'.

In 40-90 the multiplier comes before the added number but in 100 and upwards the multiplier comes after the added number. Thus **cani** '200' from **cə** or **ca** '100' and **ni** '2' and **cahum** '300' from **cə** or **ca** '100' hum '3'.

The numerals follow the noun and there is no grammatical agreement between the noun and numeral in any construction, as in the following examples :

1. əŋaŋ əma sanə-ri
   kid one play -prog.
   'A kid is playing'

2. əŋaŋ məri sanə-ri.
   'Four kids are playing'

Notice that there is no inflection for number to the noun **əŋaŋ** 'kid' and to the verb **sanə-ri** 'playing + progressive' (which remains same as in sentence (1) and (2). Another grammatical point is that the numerals follow the noun.

5.5.2 Ordinal Numerals

Ordinals are formed by suffixing **-subə** to the cardinal, but in exception for the 'first' there is a separate word, i.e. **'əhanbə'** ; in other word ***əma-subə** is not used for the 'first'. The ordinal numerals are given below :

əhanbə	'First'	məri-subə	'Fourth'
əni-subə	'Second'	kun-subə	'20th'
əhum-subə	'Third'	cama-subə	'Hundredth'

Regarding the word order of the ordinal numeral, it is just opposite to the that of numerals, i.e. it preceds the noun, as in the examples

əhanbə cena	'the first page'
əni-subə əŋaŋ	'the second child'
kunmathoysubə satabdi	'the 21st century'

5.5.3 Aggregative Numerals

In oder to express the meaning ' two together or both', 'three together' or 'all the three' etc. the suffix-**mək** is added to the cardinal numerals, as in the followings :

əŋaŋ məŋa-mək 'all the five kids'
kid five
nupi təra-mək 'all the 10 women'
woman ten
nipa pumnəmək 'all the men'
man all
sa punnəmək 'all the animals'
animal all

5.5.4 Fractional Numerals

In the formation of Manipuri fractional numerals, there is a word with genitive suffix **-gi** between the two cardical numerals i.e. **thok-pə-gi** 'by (thok 'comming out'; **pə** 'NZR' ; **-gi** Genetive) any more suffix is used. Regarding the order the bigger number will preceeds the smaller number in the following examples :

əhum thok-pə-gi əni '2/3'
three two
məŋa thok-pə-gi əma '1/5'
five one
təra thok-pə-gi məri '4/10'
ten four

Besides these, there are lexicalized fractional numerals, they are :

məpum	'the whole'
təŋkhay	'half'
məsuŋ	'quater'

5.5.5 Multiplicative Numerals

For this formation a suffix-**rək** is added after the cardinal forms of the numerals.

Examples :

əma-rək or əmu-rək	'once'
əni-rək one-	'two times'
məŋa-rək five-	'five times'
nipal-rək eight-	'eight times'
cama-rək hundred-	'hundred times'

5.5.6. Approximative Numerals

'About X-numeral' is said in Manipuri by using a form **cawrak-nə to followed by the item** for the specific numeral.

Examples :

cawrak-nə mi tərа about man ten	'about ten men'
cawrak-nə layrik yaŋkhəy about book fifty	'about fifty books'

Without the form **cawrak-nə**, it can be also said by suffixing **-muk** to the specific numeral e.g.

mi məŋa-muk man five-	'about five men'
ŋa cama- muk fish hundred-	'about hundred fish'

In another way, both the form **cawrak-nə** and the suffix **-muk** occur simultaneously, as in the following examples :

cawrak-nə əŋaŋ tərа-muk about child ten - about	'round about ten children'
cawrak-nə lanmi lising-muk about soldier thousand-	'round about one thousand soldiers'

This word order is not rigid, the noun əŋaŋ or **lanmi** can occur in the initial position ; for instance :

əŋaŋ cawrak-nə tərа-muk 'round about ten children'
lanmi cawrak-nə lisiŋmuk 'round about one thousand soldiers'

5.5.7 Measurements

There are certain ways of measuring specific things, areas etc. in Manipuri measurement system can be studied under the following heads :

(1) liquid (2) grain (3) solid (4) breadth (5) length etc.

5.5.7.1 Liquid

In Manipuri, there are two forms i.e. **khuya** 'one palm' or 'a handful' and **khujok** 'two palms hold together'. They are better used in literature, say, in lyrics these two forms of measurements are very appropriate in using with 'water' and ' uncooked rice' the phrases are

a.	isiŋ khuya əma	'a quantity of water contained in a palm'
	isiŋ khujok əma	'a quantity of water contained in two palms'
b.	ceŋ khuya əma	'a quantity of rice contained in a palm'
	ceŋ khujok əma	'a quantity of rice contained in two palms hold together'

5.5.7.2 Grain

The Manipuri used four types of baskets for measuring grain. They are (i) **meruk** 'a small basket which contains a small quantity', (it may contain 500g to 1000g.). There are also various smaller size of **meruk** used in selling various grains. (ii) **laytəŋ** 'a basket which has a wide mouth and short," it may contain 8 Kg. to 10Kg. (of paddy) (laytəŋ is half of **likhay**) (iii) **likhay** 'it contains at least 10 kg. to 20 kg. (cf paddy) (iv) The biggest one is **səŋbay**, it is two times of **likhay, səŋbay** is very much used in selling and buying of paddy. All the four are made of bamboo.

5.5.7.3 Solid (for Measuring Gold and Silver)

cəŋniŋ, sənkhay, səṇ and **mohor** (tula) are the solid measurement of Manipuri, (cəŋniŋ is the smallest unit while **mohor** is the bigger unit, so they are kept in the order). They are used for measuring gold and silver specially.

5.5.7.4 Length and Breadth

For measuring a small size breadth, Manipuris used the units, such as

khubi	'thumb' (breadth of)
khubak	'palm' (breadth of)
khudol	'figertip' (breadth of)

For measuring longer length the Manipuri uses various forms of units. (I) **huy** it means the length indicated by the thumb and the first finger spread horizontally (ii) **kap** 'length indicated by the thumb and the second or third or fourth fingers spread horizontally '(iii) **ləm** 'length indicated by spreading of two hands or arms horizontally 'nowadays the measurements are replaced by foot and metre etc.

5.5.7.5 System of Unit

The followings are the system of unit used by the Manipuris.

əma	1
təra	10
ca	100
lisiŋ	1000
lisiŋ təra	10000 etc.

CASE

5.6 Case

Case is a grammatical category which is established on two counts, (1) syntatic correlation between the substantives and the verb, and (2) between two subtantives in a syntactic unit (applicable to genitive only). Morpho- semanticaly the following types of syntactic correlation of post position, have been established.

5.6.1 Case Markers

In Manipuri there are eigth case markers including vocative case. Of the eight case markers, nominative, accusative and locative case markers are not completely obligatory. Eight case markers are given here :

1.	Nominative	-nə
2.	Accusative	-bu~pu
3.	Instrumental	-nə
4.	Locative	-də
5.	Genitive	-gi~ki
6.	Ablative	-dəgi~təgi
7.	associative	-gə~kə
8.	Vocatives	-o!

It is to be noted that the question of ergetivity does not arise in this language though Mizo is an ergetive language. Because transitive or intransitive verbs do not force the subject to have or not the nominative marker **-nə**. In other words, the subject can occur with or without **-nə** in a transitive sentence or in intransitive sentence. Consider the following sentences :

1. məhak / -nə cət-li
   he nom. go -asp
   'He goes'
2. məkah / -nə sa cay
   he nom. meat eat-asp
   'He takes meat'

Sentences with the nominative marker **-nə** irrespective of transitive or intransitive verb denotes the meaning of specifier (specified the noun among the others whereas sentences without nominative marker **-nə** simply express the habitual meaning.

5.6.1.1 Nominative Marker -nə

Nominative marker in this language is **-nə** and is not found obligatory. Nominative marker **-nə** is used in various meanings, as in the followings :

I. As an agent

3.	məhal-nə	tombə/bu	phuy
	he-nom.	Tomba-accu.	beat-asp
	'He beats Tomba'		
*4.	məhak tomba/bu phuy		

II. As a specifier

5. mөhak-nө ca thөk-y, tomba-nө kophi thөk-y
he-nom. tea drink-asp Tomba-nom. coffee drink-asp
'He drinks tea and Tomba drinks coffee'.

6. mөhak ca thөk-y , tomba kophi thөk-y

Sentence (3) indicates that while others are drinking soft drink or spirit 'he' is taking tea and Tomba is taking coffee. In contrast to this meaning sentence (6) says the habitual meaning, that is, he takes tea not coffee and Tomba takes coffee not tea. -nө (of mөhak-nө) in this sentence also gives the meaning of 'specifier (specified the noun) i.e. 'he' not 'any other' is taller than Tomba. In other syntactic position, say, in object position -nө can occur with the accusative marker, the meaning here also is 'specifer', as in sentence (8).

7 a. өy-gidi thoybi-bu-nө pam-mi
I-gen. parti Thoibi-accu.spe. like-asp
'I like Thoibi (not others)'

b. өy-di thoybi-nө pam-mi
'I like Thoibi (not others)'

The meaning of the sentences is that among the girls 'I' like Thoibi most (I select Thoibi among the girls). Another is that sentence (7b) is more commonly used, (without genitive -gi in the subject as well as without accusative -bu in the object).

III. Use in comparative construction

8. mөhak tomba-dөgi hen-nө waŋ - ŋi
he-nom. Tomba-from/abl. excess-adv tall-asp
'He is taller than Tomba'

5.6.1.2 Accusative bu~pu

The accusative marker -bu ~pu is not completely optional : it can be deleted. However, occurrence of the accusative marker is more commonly used.

9. өy ma-bu/mөhak-pu nuŋsi
I he-accu. love-asp
'I love him'

10. mөkhoy mөma-bu lunө tөw-wi
they their -mother-accu. care do-asp.
'they take care of their mother'

11. өy thoybi-bu pam-mi
I Thoibi-accu. like-asp
'I like Thoibi'

Accusatic marker makes the object noun more specific than the object noun without the accusative marker -bu. It is to be noted that bu is often occured with indirect objects (proper noun and personal pronoun) as in (9, 10, and 11) but not with direct objects, as in sentence (12) and (13).

12. məhak ca thək-y
he tea drink -asp
'He takes tea'

13. tomba səyreŋ pa-y
Tomba poem read -asp
'Tomba reads poem.'

In case **-bu** is added to direct objects, namely, **ca** 'tea', **səyreŋ** 'poem' etc. it gives very unusual meaning and it is ungrammatical (semantically unacceptable)

* 14. məhak ca-bu thək-y
he tea drink-asp

* 15. tomba səyreŋ-bu pa-y
Tomba poem read-asp

These two sentences are ungrammatical because the semantic boundary existing between the speaker and addressee is completely confused. There is the perception that 'tea' is 'to drink' and 'poem' is to read. But when this marker is added, a surprising question has emerged against our preception : Is tea to drink ? or 'Is poem to read' ?

5.6.1.3 Instrumental Case -nə

The instrumentality of an object with reference to an action is expressed by instrumental case **-nə** which is homophonous to nominative marker, adverb marker **-nə** and comparative marker. The primary function of this marker is to indicate the instrument that the agent uses while carrying out an activity. The following sentences are the examples :

16. a. əy siŋjəŋ-nə wa yal-li
I axe -inst. bamboo cut -asp
'I cut the bamboo with an axe'

b. məhak-nə noŋməy-nə kəy hat-li
he -nom. gum-inst tiger kill-asp
'He kills a tiger with a gum'

c. meri-nə pensil-nə cithi əma i
Mary -nom. pencil-inst. letter one write-asp
'Mary writes a letter with a pencil'

As an extension, this marker **-nə** can also indicate the cause of certain states like -mental and physical states etc. Consider the following examples :

17. a. məhak layhəw-nə na-re
he fever-inst. ill -asp.

b. məhak nuŋsibə-nə ŋaw-re
he happy-inst mad-asp
'He is mad with love'

c. John məkhoŋ-nə moyraŋ-də cət-li
John his leg-inst Moirang-loc. go-asp
'John goes to Moirang by walking'

This suffix -nə can also be used in indicating 17(a), the medium through which activities like cooking, painting etc. and (b) the material used for making certain object or construction purposes. Consider the following examples :

A. Medium :

18. a. i-ma-nə isiŋ-mənil-nə paknəm-du niŋthinə
my-mother-nom. water-vapour-inst pastry-det well
mul-həl-le
cook-caus-asp
'My mother makes the pastry well cook by steam'

b. məhak cəru-nə cak thoŋ-ŋi
she/he straw-inst rice cook-asp
'She cooked the rice by burning straw'

c. məhak-nə əsəŋbə məcu-nə ka-du təy
he -nom. green colour-inst room-det painted
'He painted the room with green colour/paint'

B. Material :

19. a cəphusabə-nə ləykhom-nə cəphu say
potter -nom. mud-inst. pot make-asp
'The potter makes (earthen) pot with mud'

b. məhak-nə i-nə kup-pə yum əma say
he-nom. thatch-inst. being roof house one build-asp
'He makes a thatch house' (house being covered with thatch)

c. məhak-nə wanə iŋkhol səmbəl khay
he-nom. bamboo garden fence make-asp
'He fenced the garden with bamboo'

This case marker -nə is also used for denoting means of activity, as in the follwing examples.

20. a. əy kar-nə yunibhersity cət-li
I car-inst. university go-asp
'I go to university by car'

b. həwjik-ti sen-nə mi ləybə yay
'now-def. money-inst. people buy-NZR can
'Nowadays money can buy any person'

5.6.1.4 Locative Case

The place of location of an object or event is expressed by locative case-də. It has other important function also. They are given below one by one :-

(i) Indication of location of an object or event or place

21 a. layrik ədu tebəl-də ləy
book det. table-loc. be
'The book is on the table'

b. məkhoy sendra-də cət-khre
they Sendra-loc. go-asp
'They have gone to Sendra

(ii) The indication of time :

22 a. əy puŋ təra-də nuŋti-gi laybreri-də yəw-rək-y
I o'clock ten -loc. everyday library-loc. reach-dir-asp
'Everyday I reach library at 10 o'clock'

b. əy-nə ca-ri-ŋəy-də məhak lak-y
I-nom. eat asp -while-loc. he come -asp
'While I am eating he comes'

c. tomba niŋthəwkabə-də imphal-də thuŋ-lə-gəni
Tomba Monday-loc. Imphal-loc. arrive-asp
'Tomba will arrive Imphal on Monday'

(iii) The indication of beneficiery or experiencer

23. a. əy-nə tomba-də lupa kun pi
I-nom. Tomba-loc. rupee 20 give-asp
'I give Rs 20 to Tomba'

b. əyŋon-də thəbək əsi-də təw-bi-rəm-mu
I-Obj-loc. work this-only do-hon. -dir-comd-
'Please do this work only for me'

c. tupi əsi əŋaŋ-də cil-li
cap this child-loc. very-adv. tight-asp.
'This cap is very tight to the child'

(iv) The indication of the cause or purpose :

24. a. pulis-nə phubə də nəha-du si-khre
Police nom. beat NZR.-loc. youth-det die-asp
'Because of Police beating the youth has died'

b. yen-saŋ-napi phə-hən-bə-də har dərkar oy
Vegetable good-caus-NZR-loc. manure need be
'Manure is neeeded in growing vegetable properly'

(v) The indication of the possessor of an object or property

25 a. əŋon-də əphəbə layrik əma ləy
I-obj.-loc. good book one have
'I have a good book'

b. məhak tanə-bə-də yam-nə phay
he consult -NZR or very good -asp
'He is very good in consultation'

It is found that the locative marker **-də** is used in various functions including the indication of beneficiary. The language does accept the use of certain post position with locative marker, namely, **məthak-tə** 'on' **mənuŋ-də** 'in' or 'inside' **məpan-də** 'outside', **məkha-də** 'under' **nakən-də** 'beside' it is obligatory that the case marker should be suffixed to the post position. Consider the following pairs :

26 a. phurit ədu upu mənuŋ-də ləy
shirt det almira inside-loc. be
'That shirt is in the almira'

b. məhak ka-gi məpan-də lep-pi
he room-gen outside-loc. stand -asp
'He stands outside the room'

5.6.1.5 Genitive

The basic function of the genitive case is to indicate the relationship between two substabtives in which the preceding substantive acts as a qualifier of the succeeding one. But in this language the use of it is extended.

First, the genitive suffix **-gi ~ -ki** is used to indicate the possessor of an object :

əy-gi layrik 'my book'
I-gen. book
məhak-ki səgol 'his horse'
he-gen horse
yum-gi məmaŋ 'the front of the house'
house-gen. front
u-gi məsa 'the branch of the tree'
tree -gen branch

As in the sentence

27. a. məsi əy-gi layrik-ni
this I-gen. book-be
'This is my book'

b. əy-gi nupi əsi-də lak-le
I-gen. wife here-loc. come -asp.
'My wife has come here'

(ii) It is also used for denoting the beneficiary of an action .

28. a. əy-nə məsi thoybi-gi ləy
I-nom. this thoibi-gen buy-asp.
'I buy it for Thoibi'

b. məhak ləypak-ki khəl-li
he country-gen. think-asp.
'He thinks for the country'

Here in these two sentences 28 (a) and (b) that the genitive case is to indicate the relationship between two substantives is not overtly shown. In 28 (a) the demostrative pronoun **məsi** 'this' optionally precedes noun Thoibi +genitive. When **məsi** follows **Thoibi Gen**. then the relationship between the two substantives is shown in the surface structure also. That is also grammatical. But in sentence 28 (b) a noun is completely understood in the language, the understood noun is **mərəm/phibəm** 'condition'.

(iii) This suffix can also be used for denoting the purpose of action. For this a suffix **-dəmək** can be suffixed to the genitive marker. This is optional. as in the following examples :

29. a. mitiŋ-gi-dəmək mi yam til-le
meeting-gen-for people very gather-asp.
'Many people have gathered for the meeting'

b. əy parikha-gi-dəmək layrik pa-ri
I exam-gen-for book read-asp
'I am preparing for the exam'.

5.6.1.6 Ablative

The ablative marker -dəgi~ təgi is used to express separation, expulsion, source and direction of movement from one to another .

(i) Indication of separation

30. a. Iŋ 1986-tə mənipuri-dəgi liŋguistics khaydok-le
1986-loc. Manipuri-abl. linguistics separate-asp.
'In 1986 Lnguistics is separated from Manipuri Department'

b. niŋthəm-tha-də u-dəgi una yaynə kel-li
winter month-loc. tręe-abl. leave many fall-asp
In winter many leaves fall from the tree'

(ii) Indication of direction of Movement

31. əgəs-tə əy ləndən-dəgi imphal-də həl-lə-gəni
August loc. I London-abl. Imphal -loc./ return-dir-aspt.
'In August I will return to Imphal from London'

(iii) Indication of the source of transfer of material object or idea.

32. a. əy jon-dəgi wari yam-nə ta-re
I John-abl. story many hear-asp.
'I have heard many stories from John'

b. əy-nə dilon-dəgi layrik yam-nə ləy
I-nom Dillon-abl.. book many buy-asp.
'I buy many books from Dillon'

5.6.1.7. Associative Case

The associative marker is used to denote that the action has been performed in conjunction with another person. Whether one or both members of the conjunction may be marked by this marker.

33. a. məhak tombə-gə ŋa phabə turen-də cət-khre
he Tomba-asso fish catch river -loc. go-asp
'He went with Tomba to the river to catch fish'

b. John-gə məkhoy əni ləmpak-tə sanə-ri
John-asso. they two ground-loc. play-asp
'John with two (other they) boys are playing in the ground'

5.6.1.8 Vocative Case

There are two types of vocative markers in Manipuri. One is employed for calling a person from a distance, another for addressing. For distance calling, **o** or **ho** precedes the noun but in addressing the last sound - vowel or consonant of the name of the person is lengthened.

O~ ho bem '(calling)'
Bem
O~ ho i-ma '(calling)'
'My mother !'

i-ma ! (addressing)
'my mother'.
bem (addressing)
'Bem !'

5.6.2 Implicational Uses

One interesting point here is that both the nominative and accusative can be suffixed to the same noun simultaneously (N+bu+nə) and the change of sequence of the suffixation, i.e. (N+nə+bu) denotes a different meaning. Consider the following sentences :

(i) Noun+bu+nə

34. əy -nə jon-bu-nə ghəri pi-re ədugə tombə-bu-nə phurit pi-ri
I-nom. John-acc.-nom. watch give-asp and Tomba-acc.-nom. shirt give -asp
'I have given watch to John and shirt to Tomba'

This sequence N+bu+nə as in (34) gives the meaning of 'distributiveness'. This meaning of distributiveness can also be seen in causative construction.

35. A-bu-nə thəbək əma təw-həl-le ədugə B-bu-nə ətoppə əma təw-həl-le
A -accu.-nom. work one do-caus, asp.and B-accu.-nom.another one do-caus.-asp
'I have made A do one work while B do another work'

(ii) Noun + nə+bu

The above 'distributive' meaning is completely lost in this sequence N+nə+bu which gives a negative sense and syntactically it occurs in interrogative construction. Consider the following sentences :

36. əy-nə-bu məsi təw-gədra
I-nom.-acc. this do-pot.-Q.m
'Should I do such type of thing ?'

37. məhak-nə-bu layrik əsi pa-gə-dra
he-nom.-acc. book det read-pot. Q.m.
'Should he read this type of book ?'

When it is analysed from the pragmatic point of view it portraits an unthinkable situation, as in (36) and (37). This sequence can also occur in conditional clause and the meaning that it expresses is the impression of a person that already had in the mind is more ascertained by his work (taken from the past action).

Example :

38 ma-nə-bu glas cam-lə-di ə-dum kay-re
he -nom. acc. glass wash-dur-if as it break-asp.
'If he washes the glass naturally it will be found bróken'

5.6.3 Double Case Marking

This refers to the appearance of more than one case marker to a single noun where the sequence of case markers does represent a single case role. But this (double case marking) is very limited, that is, genitive - **gi**+**locative-də (gi-də)** which indicates locative case role only. Consider the following sentences

39. a. əy-gi-də lak-u
I-gen. -loc. come -comd mk.
'Come to my place'

b. əy jon-gi-də həyeŋ cət-kəni
I John-gen. loc. tomorrow go -asp
'Tomorrow I will go to John's place'

əy-gi-də in sentence 37 (a) is derived from

əy-gi yum-də / ka-də
I-gen house-loc. / room -loc.
I-gen some place +**loc.**
əy-gi-də

jon-gi-də in 39 (b) is derived in the same way from

jon-gi yum-də/ka-də
John-gen house-loc./ room-loc.

It can be explained in such a way that the noun following the genitive marker in this construction is obviously a **place** or **location** that is understood and only the locative marker is remained ; that marker is added to the genitive -added -noun.

5.6.4 The Nature of Case Roles

It would be very proper to examine very briefly the theoretical basis for postulating of case roles before going direct to Manipuri case roles. It is not a recent one to have differences between the concept of case roles and case markers. In India, the great Sanskrit grammarian, Panini, had made use of it, **vibhakti** 'as a set of termination' that is, case markers while **Karaka** 'as syntactic relationship with other constituents of the syntactic unit', that is, case roles. In the Europe, related aspects of sentence structure were discussed under the heading of 'Valency theory' or 'dependence theory'.

The contemporary linguists did not give much attention to his idea of case roles as distinct from case markers. But when Fillmore succeeded in connecting it up with the concept of 'Deep structure' then many linguists had started giving attention to. His claim is that case roles are better suited for deep structure representation than grammatical categories like subject, direct object, indirect object, etc. or sentence constituents like noun phrase, verb phrase etc. In order to bring out the basic aspects of meaning in natural languages, it has been felt necessary to utilize two distinct grammatical processes, namely Idealization and Disambiguation, while analysing the underlying structure of sentences.

5.6.4.1 Idealization

It involves the disregarding of some of the subtle meaning differences that exist between certain sets of sentences. The meaning differences would be indicated by differences in the case markers that are actually being used in those sentences. In view of the fact that these case markers distinctions are to be disregarded in order to establish the core meaning of sentences, the actual relationship between these abstract case roles and their concrete case marker representations turn out to be rather irregular. Consider the following pairs of sentences :

40. a. kati-**nə** kək-si nətrədi phi-si loy-nə segay-gəni
scissor -inst. cut -propo. otherwise cloth-det. completely tear -asp.
'Let us cut the cloth with scissors otherwise it will be torn'

b. kati-**də** kək-si nətrədi phi-si loynə segay-gəni
'Let us cut the colth with scissors otherwise it will be torn'

41. a. kar-**nə** cət-si , thap-pi
car-inst. go-propo. far asp
'Let us go by car, it is far'

b. kar-**də** cət-si , thap-pi
car-inst. go-propo. far asp
'Let us go by car, it is far'

42. a . əlu məku-du thaŋ-nə khok-u
potato cover-det. knife-inst. peel-comd mk
'Peel the potato with the knife'

b. əlu məku-du thaŋ-də khok-u
'Peel the potato with the knife'

43. a . yetum-nə phot-lə-nu , kon-nə phot-lo
needle-inst. stitch -dur.-proh. sewing machine -inst. stitch-comd.mk
'Don't stitch with the needle but stitch with the sewing machine'

b. yetum-nə phot-lə-nu , kon-də phot-lo
'Don't stitch with the needle but stitch with the sewing mechine'

44. a. pəysa-du khut-nə pay-yu
money-det hand -inst. hold-comd.mk.
'Hold the money with the hand' [in]

b. pəysa-du khut-tə pay-yu
'Hold the money with the hand' [in]

The above paired sentences (40-43) can be normally considered as the paraphrases of one another. There is no basic core meaning different between (a) and (b) sentences. But to a lingist he can explain the differences between (a) and (b) in terms of case roles : the nouns (+**nə**) in (a) are functionaing as instrumental case roles while nouns (+**də**) in (b) are functioning as locative case role. Further it can be explained in another way also, that nouns (+**nə**) in sentences (a) are near agent's place (speaker's or addressee's place i.e. within his arms length) whereas nouns (+**də**) in sentences (b) are away from the speaker's place (i.e. beyond his arm's length) he has to go there. This cannot be a fixed one and this may not be applied. This may be within the agent's arms length. The **car** in (40a) may be there or not and the **needle** in (42) may or may not be there.

5.6.4.2 Disambiguation

Opposite to the previous one, Idealization, there is the second grammatical process to analyse the subtle meaning difference in the analysis of case roles. That is disambiguation which explains that there is certain case role distinctions even when there is no corresponding case marker distinction in the language. In other words, the same case marker performs different case roles in different contexts. Consider the following uses of the locative case marker :

45. a. əy-gi huy əŋəwbə-du memi-də yon-khre
I-gen. dog white-det Memi -loc. sell -asp.
'I have sold my white dog to Memi'

b. əy-gi huy əŋəwbə-du memi-də pi-khre
I-gen. dog white-det Memi -loc. give-asp.
'I have given my white dog to Memi'

c. əy-gi huy əŋəwbə-du memi-də khoŋ-ŋi
I-gen. dog white-det Memi -loc. bark-asp.
'My white dig barks to Memi'

It is seen that the same marker **-də** is occurring 'with different verbs and the locative case marker - **də** is assigned different case roles. That is, the marker - **də** in 45 (a) indicates that Memi is the goal or destination of selling of my white dog', in 45 (b) it denotes that 'Memi' is the beneficiary of receiving of 'my white dog' and in 45 (c) it indicates that Memi 'is the experiencer of the barking of my dog'.

Such a postulations of case role distinctions in the absence of corresponding case marker distinctions in a given language might be considered as involving the process of disambiguation.

5.6.5 Dependence of Verbs

The case roles that can occur in a given sentence is primarily depended on the kind of verb or predicate used in the sentence. For this explaination, four sets of verbs are given here, showing minimum number of case roles involved.

5.6.5.1 Object Assigned Case Role

The verbs like **pak-y** 'is wide', **waŋ-ŋi** 'is tall', **khoy** 'is curve', **phəjəy** 'is nice' etc. need only a single case role, namely, object, as in the following sentences

46. a. ləmpak ədu pak-y
ground that wide -asp.
'That ground is wide'

b. u-du waŋ-ŋi
tree -det tall-asp.
'The tree is tall'

c. ləyyi-du khoy
line-det. curve-asp.
'The line is curve'

The nouns in the sentences, viz. **ləmpak**' ground, **u** 'tree' and **ləyyi** 'line' are assigned object case role.

5.6.5.2 Agent Assigned Case Role

The verbs like **nok-y** 'laugh', **kəp-pi** 'cry', **lep-pi** 'stand' etc. need a single case role, namely, agent, as in the following sentences :

47. a. məkhoy həwnə nok-y
they loudly laught -asp
'They laught loudly'

b. əŋaŋ-du kuynə kəp-le
child-det. longtime cry -asp.
'The child has been crying for a long time'

c. məhak kuynə lep-pi
he long time stand -asp.
'He stands for a long time'

Here the nouns **məkhoy** 'they, **əŋaŋ-du** 'the child' ; **məhak** 'he' are assigned the Agent case role ; they are the agent performing the action of laught, 'cry' and 'stand' respectively. Notice that there is no need to refer to any additional objects or individuals in these 45 and 46 sentences in order to properly understand the situation that they describe.

5.6.5.3 Two Assigned Case Roles

The verbs like **yek-y** 'paint' **yeŋ-ŋi** 'see' **thoŋ-ŋi** ' cook' indicates at least two different cas roles. This will be clear from the following sentences :

48. a. məhak lay phəjənə yek-y
he picture nicely paint -asp
'He nicely paints picture'

b. məhak T.V. yeŋ-ŋi
he T.V. see-asp.
'He sees T.V.'

c. tombi cak thoŋ-ŋi
Tombi rice cook-asp
'Tombi cooks rice'

Unlike the previous verbs in sentences (46) and (47) the verbs in sentences 48, **yek-y** 'paint' **yeŋ-ŋi** 'see' and **thoŋ-ŋi** 'cook', need to indicate at least two different case roles namely, an Agent (the person who paints, sees or cooks) and an object.

5.6.5.4 Three Assigned Case Roles

Similarly, if one uses in a sentence a verb like **pi** 'give' **yol-li** 'sell', **ləw-wi** 'take' there would be a need to denote at least two different case roles, namely an Agent, an Object, a Beneficiary or an ablative, as can be seen from the following examples :

49 a. jon-nə tombə-də həynəw əma pi
John Tomba-loc. Mango one give -asp.
'John gives a mango to tomba'

b. jon-nə tombə-də həynəw əma yol-li
John Tomba-loc. Mango one sell -asp.
'John sells a mango to tomba'

c. jon-nə həynəw əma phrij-dəgi ləw-wi
John Mango one fridge-abl.. take-asp.
'John takes a mango from the fridge'

It is seen that 'John' is the Agent 'Tomba 'is the Beneficiary or Goal', 'mango' is the Object while 'fridge' is the source. These are the case roles indicated by these verbs occurred in sentences 49. In this way the verbs of a language can be classified. More and above, another factor is also necessary for the classification of verb in a language. That factor is of nuclear and peripheral case roles.

5.6.6 Nuclear and Peripheral Case Roles

The case roles that represent the core meaning of a given sentence can be considered as its nuclear or obligatory case roles whereas the case roles that additional noun phrases represent in a sentence can be considered as its peripheral case roles. This will be more clear from the following examples :

50. a. əy-nə kar əma ləy
I- car one buy -asp.
'I buy a car'

b. əy-nə kar əma tombə-dəgi ləy
I- car one Tomba-abl.. buy-asp.
'I buy a car from Tomba'

c . əy numidaŋ-gi caklen puŋ nipan-də ca-re
I night -gen. meal hour 8-loc. eat-asp
'I have taken my dinner at 8 o'clock'

əy 'I' and **kar** 'car' in sentence 50 is treated as nuclear case role while **tombə-dəgi** 'from Tomba' the source is regarded as peripheral. In the same way 'I' and 'dinner' in 50 (c) an nuclear case role whereas 'at 8 o'clock' is peripheral case role. Because 'from Tomba' and 'at 8o'clock' are additional noun phrase .

One can provide certain additional information, peripheral case roles, for denoting the place of occurrence of the events or state. The case roles such as place, time, purpose, cause, source etc., in a language, can be treated as peripheral case roles.

8. Specified and Unspecified case roles :

51. a. ca-re (I/he) 'have eaten'
eat -asp

b. pu-khro 'Take it and go'
bring -dir.-comd.

c. əy pa-ri 'I am reading'
I read-asp.

Notice that in sentence 51 (a) and (b), beneficiary and object case roles are left unspecified while in (c) Agent is specified Case roles can be found out if the following relevant questions are put respectively :

a. kəna kəri ca-re 'What has eaten'?
who what eat -asp

b. kəna-nə kəri pu-ni ' Who will take what'?

c. nəŋ kəri pa-ri
you what read -asp. 'What are you reading'?

5.6.7 Covert and Overt Case Roles

Another aspect of the case roles is not represented by any specific noun phrases in the sentence. For example, in English the verb 'to bribe' which incorporates the object case role and the verb 'to harmmer' which incorporates the instrumental case role. In Manipuri also there are similar situations also. Consider the following examples :

52. a. məhak wa yal-li
he bamboo cut -asp
'He is cutting the bamboo'

b. məhak thaŋ-nə wa yal-li [thaŋ-nə 'dagger']
'He is cutting the bamboo with a dagger'

53. a. tomba-nə kobi thanəbə ləypak təw-ri
Tomba-nom. cabbage to plant ground dig-asp
'Tomba is digging the ground to plant cabbage'

b. tomba-nə kobi thanəbə yotpak-nə ləypak təw-ri [yotpak 'spade']
Tomba-nom. cabbage to plant ground dig-asp
'Tomba is digging the ground with a spade to plant cabbage'

54. a. məhak-nə ləy-du tha-khre
he-ŋom. flower-det. plant-def. -asp
'He has planted the flower'

b. məhak-nə ləy-du gəmla-də tha-re[gəmla-də 'flower pot'
'He has planted the flower in the flower pot'

It can be considered that (a) and (b) sentences as paraphrases. In 52 (a) and 53 (a) sentences instrument **thaŋ** 'dagger' and **yotpak** 'spade' are occurring as covert case roles. In the same way, in 54 (a) locative (gəmlə-də) is occurring as covert case role. But in (b) sentnces the respective case roles occur as overt case roles.

5.6.8 Post -Position

It is fairly marked the syntactic group of invariables, semantically serving the same purposes as is served by a case suffix. They are designated so, because they invariably take their place after the substantives, some of these follow adverbial stems as well as. In such a construction they form a part an adverbial phrase. Semantically, in a syntactic relationship, involving, special and temperal dimensions of it, the use of a post-position is of a special segnificance. There it helps in expressing the semantic nuance with a greater precision, in this language, dirctional like locative, genitive , and ablative are suffixed. There are non-directional also. So it is categorized into two -

(i) Non-directional and
(ii) Directional

5.6.8.1 Non -Directional :

1. **-dəmək** 'for'

It is used in all animate and inanimate; genitive marker precedes it.

55. a. əy-nə phurit əsi ica nupi-gi-dəmək ləy
I-nom. shirt this daughter-gen. for buy -asp.
'I buy this shirt for my daughter'

b. məhak ləw-iŋkhol-gi-dəmək yamnə khəl-li
he property-gen. for very think-asp.
'He ponders on much about estate'

c. ma-nə məhak-ki huy-gi-dəmək yamnə ceksil-li
he-nom. he -gen- dog-gen. for very care-asp.
'He takes much care for his dog'

2. **nəttənə** 'except'

56. tomba nəttənə kəna əmətə lak-te
Tomba except who one-only come -neg.
'No one has turned up except Tomba'

3. **loynənə** 'accompany with'

57. məhak tombə-gə loynənə ciŋ kay
he Tomba -asso. accompany hill climb-asp.
'He climbs the hill along with Tomba'

5.6.8.2 Directional

Non-directionals are very limited in number while directional are more. Directional post-positions go with case markers which are suffixed to them.

1. **mənuŋ** 'in, inside'

58. a . məhak ka mənuŋ-də cəŋ-ŋi
he room inside-loc. enter-asp
'He enter the room'

2. **məpan** 'outside'

59. məhak ka ədu-gi məpan-də ləy
he room that -gen outside-loc. stay-asp
'He is at the outside of the room'

60. məhak məpan-dəgi cəŋŋək-y
he outside -from enter -asp
'He comes in (from the outside)'

3. **məthək** 'on'

61. məhak-nə layrik ədu tebəl məthək-tə thəm-mi
he-nom. book that table on-loc. keep-asp
'He keeps the book on the table'

4. **məkha** 'under below'

62. layrik ədu tebəl məkha-də ləy
book that table under -loc. is -
The book is under the table'

5. **məmaŋ** 'front, before'

63. məhak-ki yum-gi məmaŋ-də pukhri əma ləy
he-gen house-gen. front-loc. pond one is
'There is a pond in the front of the house'

6. **məniŋ [mətuŋ]** 'behind'

64. məhak əy-gi məniŋ-də lep-pi
he I-gen beind-loc. stand-asp.
'He stands behind me'

7. **mənak** 'near'

-nak is a root and two other pronominals, i.e. **i-** first person and **nə-** second person can also be added accordingly.

65. tombə əy-gi i-nak-tə phəm-mi
Tomba I-gen. near -loc. sit-asp
'Tomba sits near me'

8. **nakən** 'beside'

66. yum ədu sorok-ki nakən-də ləy
house that road-gen beside-loc. is
'The house is beside the road'

9. **məyay** 'middle'

67. sorok-ki məyay-də əsibə lil əma ləy
road -gen. middle -loc. dead snake ome is
'There is a dead snake in the middle of the road'

5.7 PRONOUN

5.7.1 Pronoun

Pronoun forms a distinct class of substantive. It has been used in grammatical classifications of words to refer to a closed set of lexical items that, it is held, can substitute for noun or a noun phrase. Many linguists regarded it as a mechanical process used in producing more surface variants of underlying structures. It is for this reason that in the original verson of trasformational grammar pronouns were not located in the deep structure, but introduced trnsformationally.

Now-adays the term Anaphora has increasingly tended to replace pronoun. Anaphors are linguistic units that refer to objects that have already been introduced into discourse, that is, they express a partial or total identity between what is being denoted and what has already been identified. In another words, an item with little or no intrinsic meaning or reference which takes its interpretation from another item in the same sentence or discourse, its antecedent. For instance, in 'I asked Mona to open the door and she did it', the item 'she' and 'did it' are anaphors, laking their interpretations from their antecedents 'Mona' and 'open the door' respectively. Pronoun (more precisely, pro-NPs) are most familiar anaphors, but pro-N-bars, pro-VPs and pro-sentences also exist. Such is discussed in Transformational Grammar (TG Grammar).

In Manipuri, case suffixes can be added to pronouns ; though they function as subject or object of a verb, but unlike nouns they are small closed class of substantive.

5.7.2 Classifications

In this language, pronouns are divided into several distinct classes, including, personal pronouns, reflexive pronouns, demonstrative pronouns, indefinite pronouns and interrogative pronouns. All of these take case suffixes, but gender and number are not marked.

5.7.2.1 Personal Pronouns

The first person singular pronoun is **əy** 'I' and opposite to it is **əykhoy** 'we'. There is no question of inclusive and exclusive in the first person plural form. There is also dual form ibani (i-1st person pronominal, **-ni** 'two). It has also objective singular form **əyŋon-də** 'to me' **əyŋon-**

dəgi 'from me'. The second person pronouns are **nəŋ** 'you' (singular), **nəkhoy** 'you) (plural) and the dual form **nəbani** 'you two' (**nə** -2nd person pronominal and **ni** 'two'). The second person has two honorific singular form **ədom** and **əsom** which are used in formal relation or stranger. The third personal pronouns are **məhak** 'he' and **məkhoy** 'they' dual form is **məbani** (**mə-3rd** person pronominal, -ni 'two') ; the objective singular form **məŋondə** 'to him' or **məŋondəgi** ' form him'

Various Pronoun Forms

	Singular	Dual	Plural	Object	Honorific
Frist Person	əy I	ibani we two	əykhoy we	əy ŋon-də to me əy ŋon-dəgi from me	X
Second Person	nəŋ you	nəbani you two	Nəkhoy You	nəŋ ondə to you nəŋon-dəgi from you	əsom or (sig,) ədom 'you
Third Person	məhak she/he	məbani they two	Məkhoy They	məŋondə to him məŋ ondəgi from him	X

Possessive pronoun is formed by suffixation of genitive suffix **gi~ki**, as in the following illustrations :

əy-gi 'my'	ibani-gi 'ours (two)'	əykhoy-gi 'ours'
nəŋ-gi 'your'	nəbani-gi 'your (two)'	nəkhoy-gi 'yours'
məhak-ki 'his' or ma-gi	məbani-gi ' theirs (two)'	məkhoy-gi 'theirs'

Manipuri second person honorific pronouns, namely, **ədom** or **əsom** or **som** 'you (sing)' which is used in formal relation and to a stranger irrespective of age. It has no exact counter part plural form but a form **məyam** 'many' is used in formal relation.

1 a. som kəri ləmdəgi-no
you (hor) which place -abl.. -Q.mk.
'From which place are you?'

b. ədom kəna-gəloynə-bi-rək-y
you (hor) who -asso accompany - hon. do-asp.
'With whom did you come?'

5.7.2.2 Reflexive Pronoun

In this language, reflexive pronouns are derived by prefixation of respective pronominal markers i.e. **i**-for first person, **nə-** second person and **mə-** for third person, to a root **sa** 'body', thus literally meaning 'self''. (They do not have possessive meaning like English 'my', 'yours' singualr and that of objective 'him/her').

i+sa ➔ isa 'myself'
nə+-sa ➔ nəsa 'youself'
mə+-sa ➔ məsa 'himself'

2. a. **hswjik-ti əy isa-nə cak thoŋjə-bə ŋam-le**
now-def. I 1st P. self-nom. rice cook-refl-NZR can -asp.
'Now I myself can cook'

b. **nəŋ nəsa cət-lu-bra**
you 2nd.P. self go -dir-NZR-Qmk.
'Have you yourself been there ?'

c. **məhak məsa əsi-də lak-kədəbəni**
he 3rd.P.-self here-loc. come -asp.def.-NZR-cop.
'He himself must come here'

The respective antecedent pronouns **əy** 'I' in 2 (a), **nəŋ** 'you in 2 (b) and **məhak** in 2 (c) are optional as in 2 (d).

2. d. **həwjik-ti isa-nə cak thoŋ-jə-bə ŋəm-le**
'Now I can cook'.

In sentence 2 (d) **əy** 'I' is not occurred, only **isa-nə** 'myself' is occurred. Another point here is that case suffix also can be added, as in the following :

i-sa (I)		myself	}
nə-sa	'(you)'	yourself	+ Case Marker
mə-sa	(he)'	himself	

Consider the examples :

Genitive

isa			i-sa-gi
nəsa	+	genitive / gi/ →	nə-sa-gi
məsa			ms-sa-gi

isa-gi		'my	
nəsa-gi	layrik	'your	own
məsa-gi	book	his	book

locative **-də** (Dative meaning)

isa -də	'to I myself'
nəsa-də	'to you yourself'
məsa-də	'to he himself'

ablative : **dəgi**

isa-dəgi	'from I myself'
nəsa-dəgi	'from you yourself'
məsa-dəgi	'from he himself'

8

5.7.2.2.1 Anaphoric Reference

In the anaphoric reference, it 'self' refers its antecedent. Consider the following sentences :

3. a. tomba-nə məsa-gi phurit suy
   Tomba -nom. 3rd.P. self -gen shirt wash-asp.
   'Tomba washes his own shirt.'

   b. tomba-nə ma-gi phurit suy
   'Tomba washes his (some ones or Tomba's) shirt'

In sentence 3 (a), there is no ambiguity, that is, **məsa-gi co-refers to its antecedent noun** (Tomba), while sentence 3 (b) gives ambiguous meaning, i.e. **magi** may refers to 'some one's or 'Tomba himself'. There are some more sentences :

4. a . əy isa-gi layrik pay
   I 1st.p. -self-gen. book read-asp.
   'I read my own book'

   b. nəŋ nəsa-gi layrik pa-bra
   'Did you read your book?'

In pragmatic side, **məsa** has widely used in speech and their **məsa** can be treated as a anaphoric pronoun because it takes its interpretation or reference to its antecedent. In other words, it co-refers the arguments occurred in the sentence. In its extended function, any argument (following or preceding) that occurs in the sentence can be antecedent if there are two such arguments in a sentence either of them can ambiguously function as its antecedent. Consider the following sentences :

5. məsa-gi səyreŋ ədu meri-nə thoybi-bu təmbi
   3rdP. self -gen poem det Mary-nom.. Thoibi-acc teach-asp.
   'Mary teaches her (Mary's or Thoibi's) poem to Thoiobi'

Ambiguity does not depend on the positional occurrence of **məsa-gi,** as in the following sentences :

6. a. meri-nə məsa-gi səyreŋ thoybi-bu təmbi

   b. meri-nə thoybi -bu məsa-gi səyreŋ təmbi
   'Mary teaches her poen (Mary's or Thiobi's) to Thoibi'

However, there are constraints on its (məsa-gi) co-reference 1) if there is causative marker (to the verb), ii) if there is locative marker functioning as dative role and iii) by semantic boundary . In such cases, məsa-gi co-refers to the very argument with nominative markers (in the agentive function).

(i) Sentence with causative markers

7. məsa-gi cithi tomba-nə cawbə-bu i-həl-li
   3rd p.self -gen. letter Tomba -nom Chaoba asso. write -caus-asp.
   'Tomba makes chaoba write his (Tomba's) letter'

Even change of its position does not affect the meaning :

8. a. tomba-nə məsa-gi cithi cawbə-bu i-həl-li

b. tomba-nə cawba -bu məsa-gi cithi ihəl-li
'Tomba makes Chawba write his (Tomba's)letter'

(ii) Argument with locative marker is not co-referred.

9. məsa-gi phurit tomba-nə cawbə-də pi
3rd P. gen . shirt Tomba-nom. Chaoba-loc. give-asp.
'Tomba gives his (Tomba's) shirt to Chaoba

Even change of occurrence does not affect meaning :

10. a. tomba-nə məsa-gi phurit cawbə-də pi

b. tomba-nə cawwbə-də məsa-gi phurit pi
'Tomba gives his shirt to Chaoba'

(iii) Semantic boundary also constrains its co-reference

11. məsa-gi cara tomba-nə caknibə-də pi
3rd P. gen . meal Tomba-nom. beggar-loc. give-asp.
'Tomba gives his (Tomba's) meal to the beggar.'

Change of occurrence, here also, does not affect the meaning, as in sentences 12 (a) and (b).

12. a. tombə-nə məsa-gi cara caknibə-də pi
b. tomə-nə caknibə-də məsa-gi cara pi
'Tomba gives his meal to the beggar'.

The plural of **məsa** is **məsen** 'they themselves' (**mə**-pronominal marker and **sen** has no meaning), in the first person plural also **mə-sen** 'we ourselves' is used and the second person plural it is **nəsen** ' you yourselves'. However, it is acceptable to use **məsen** in the first person and in the second person plural. Consider the following :

13. a. əykhoy məsen khətnə-gumsi
we selves quarrel-let neg.
'Let us not quarrel among ourselves'

b. nəkhoy məsen/nəsen kərigi phunə-ri
you (pl) selves why fight -asp.
'Why are you fighting among yourselves'?

5.7.2.2.2 Intensive Reflexive

Reflexive can also give an emphatic meaning, it can be termed as intensive reflexive. In this language **i-sa** or **nəsa** can emphise, as in the following sentences :

14. a. əy isa məphəm ədu-də cət-lu-re
I 1st.P. self place that -loc. go-dir-prog.asp
'I myself have visited the place'

b. nəŋ nəsa məphəm ədu-də cətkə-də-bəni
'You yourself must visit that place'

c. məhak məsa əsi-də lak-kə-də-bəni hay-yu
'Tell him that he himself must come here.'

Futher degree of emphasis is more when a morpheme or suffix **mək** is added to i.e. **isa-mək, nəsa-mək** and **məsa-mək** .

15. nəŋ nəsamək məphəm -ədu-də cət-lu
'Go you yourself to that place'

5.7.2.3 Demonstrative Pronoun

In Manipuri there is no articles -definite or indefinite-. But it has two determiners, **-si** 'proximate' and **-du~tu** 'distal'. **-si** denotes the object or person being spoken of is near or currently seen or known to the speaker or topic of conversation, **-du~tu** indicates something or someone not present at the time of speech.

5.7.2.3.1 əsi and ədu Pronoun

There are two pronouns based on these determiners: **ədu** 'it (there)' and **əsi** 'it (here)' where **ə** is the attributive (in attributive adjective also **ə** is used). the difference is **əsi** and **ədu** are used only when there is a coreferential antecedent .

16. a. huy -du əy-gi-ni
dog-det. I-gen-cop.
'The dog is mine'

b. huy ədu əy-gi-ni
dog that I -gen-cop.
'That dog is mine (Dog that one, is mine)'

However, it is very possible to delete **ə** of **ədu** or **ə** of **əsi** in the running speech. But the difference will be clear from the following sentences :

17. a. əŋaŋ -gi-du pay-nu
baby -gen -dem.p touch -prohi.
Don't touch that thing, it is for the baby'

b. əŋaŋ -du-gi-ni
baby-det.-gen-cop.
'It is for the baby'

Notice that from the above sentences that **-du** in 17(a) is not a determiner ; it is a pronoun it refers to 'something' while **-du** in 17 (b) is a determiner to the noun **əŋaŋ** 'baby" (it does not refer to any other). The two sentences are occurring in the same situation i.e. there are continuation of a topic.

5.7.2.3.2 məsi and mədu Pronoun

There are two other pronouns which also based on the two determiners **-si** and **-du~ -tu** : they are **məsi** 'this' and **mədu** 'that'

18 a. mədu əy-gi huy-ni
that I -gen. dog-cop.
' That is my dog.'

b. məsi əy-gi huy-ni
' This is my dog.'

In this set of pronouns **məsi** and **mədu** , there is no meaning of 'proximate ' and 'distal', and **mə-** in this set is a third person pronominal marker. This set **mə(-si** and **-du)** differs from the set of ə-(**-si** and **-du**) in the following way

a. əŋaŋ { ədu / əsi } baby { it (there) / (here)
baby

*b. əŋaŋ { mədu / məsi } 'baby { that' / this
baby

From this it is noticed specially from (a) that **əsi** and **ədu** follows the NP. However, they (**əsi** and **ədu**) can precede the NP when genitive marker is suffixed to **əsi-** and **ədu-** (**əsi-gi** and **ədu-gi**) at the same time, this is known as split determiner. The respective determiner **-si** and **-du** are suffixed to the very NP, for examples :

19. a. əsi-gi əŋaŋ-si yamnə phəy
it-gen. baby -det. very good'
'This boy is very good'

b. ədu-gi ləysabi-du məsək phəjəy
it-gen. girl -det. face nice.
'She is very nice'

But in this way, **məsi** and **mədu** can occur, otherwise they are ungrammatical :

20 a. məsi-gi pakhəŋ-si məsa nal-li
this-gen. boy (adult)-det. handsome -asp
'This boy is handsome'

b. mədu-gi mi-du phəy
that-gen. man-det. good-asp.
'That man is good'

*c. mədu mi-du phə-y

These pronouns can have case markers and other suffixes also.

əsi-də] + (locative-də) 'here'
məsi-də

ədu-də] + locative-də 'there'
mədu-də

əsi-gi
məsi-gi] + genitive -gi 'of this'

ədu-gi
mədu-gi] + (genitive - gi) 'of that'

əsi-nə
məsi-nə
mədu-nə
ədu-nə] + (adverbial -nə) 'because of this/that'

əsi-dəgi
məsi-dəgi
ədu-dəgi
mədu-dəgi] (ablative -dəgi) 'because of this/that /then'

ədu-bu] 'but' (here -bu is not accusative marker)
mədu-bu 'that one also' [accusative]

əsi-bu
məsi-bu (Accusative pu~bu) 'such a thing'

5.7.2.4 Indefinite Pronoun

In this language indefinite pronouns are also formed by combination of (i) a question word (QW) plus the enclitic -su 'also' and (ii) another is QW plus the enclitic **kum** 'like' plus nominal - **pə~bə**.

(i) kəna+su ➔ kənasu 'none'
kəri+su ➔ kərisu 'nothing'

These above two can be treaed as 'Negative Polarity Pronouns ' because they occur only in negative environment as in sentences 20.

20 a. kəna-su yum-si-də ləy-te
none house -det-loc. stay-neg.mk.
'None stays in the house'
(There is no-body in the house)

b. ka-si-də kəri-su ləy-te
room-det-loc. nothing have-neg.mk.
'Nothing is in the room '
(There is nothing in the room)

* c. [kəna-su
kəri-su] ka-si-də ləy

kəna-su generally refers to person only while kəri-su indicates object and 20 (c) is ungrammatical because **kəna-su** and **kəri-su** cannot occur in positive environment. But when the enclitic **-su** 'also' is suffixed to other nouns, it gives the meaning of 'also', say, **'məhak-su'** he also **'bil-su'** Bill 'also' etc.

(ii) QW + [gum / kum] +bə

kəna-gum-bə 'some one'
kəri-gum-bə 'something' or 'sometimes'

Opposite to the above one, **kəna-su** and **kəri-su, kəna-gum-bə** 'some one' **and kəri-gum-bə** 'something' can occur in both the environments positive as well as negative ; **kəna-gumbə** refers to pronoun and **kəri-gumbə** to object. Consider the following sentences :

(a) Positive environment :

21. a. kəna-gumbə əma imuŋ-də cəŋ-khre
someone one inside house -loc. enter -asp
'Some one has entered the house'

b. kəri-gumbə khəra ka-si-də ləy-re
something some room-det. -loc. is-asp.
'There is something in this room'

(b) Negative Environment

22. a. kəna-gum-bə əmə-tə ka-si-də ləy-te
'There is none in this room'

b. kəri-gum-bə əma-tə ka-si-də ləy-te
'There is nothing in this room'

What it is noticed is that in the negative environment there is a lexical item **əma** 'one' with a specifier suffix **-tə**, i.e. **əmə -tə** 'only one'

5.7.2.5 Interrogative Pronoun

Manipuri has interrogative pronouns also. They are **kəna** 'who' **kəri** or **kərəmbə** 'which'.

23. a. məkhoy məyam-si-dəgi nəŋ kəna pam-mi
they many -det.-abl.. you (sg.) who like -asp.
'Who do you want among them ?'

b. nəŋ məyam -si-dəgi kərəmbə layrik pam-mi
you many-det-abl.. which book like -asp.
'Which book do you want among these ?'

5.7.3 Case Markers on Pronouns

Case markers can be suffixed to all the kinds of pronouns. Some examples are given below :

Demonstrative Pronouns :

		genitive	locative	ablation
məsi 'this' / mədu 'that'	+	gi/	-də/	-dəgi/

Interrogative Pronoun :

kəna 'who' / kəri 'What' + gi /-də/-dəgi

Reflexive Pronoun

məsa + gi /-də/-dəgi
he (self)

In this language suffixation of case markers do not affect the forms of personal pronouns except in locative and ablative in singular. They are given below :

	LOCATIVE		ABLATIVE	
first person	əy+də	➔ əyŋondə;	əy+dəgi	➔ əyŋondəgi
Second person	nəŋ+də	➔ nəŋondə;	nəŋ+dəgi	➔ nəŋondəgi
Third Person	məhak+də	➔ məŋondə;	məhak+dəgi	➔ məŋon-dəgi

Personal pronoun + case markers

əy + 'I'	nə	əy+nə I+nom.
	bu	əy-bu I+acc. (me)
	gi	əy+gi I+ gen.
	də	əyŋondə I+ dat.
	dəgi etc.	əyŋondəgi etc. I+ gen.
nəŋ + 'you'	nə	nəŋ-nə
	bu	nəŋ-bu
	gi	nəŋ-gi
	də	nəŋondə
	dəgi	nəŋondəgi
	etc.	
məhak + 'he'	nə	məhak +nə
	bu	məhak -pu
	ki	məhak -ki or magi
	də	məŋondə
	dəgi etc.	məŋondəgi etc.

Notice that addition of case marker **-də** and **dəgi** to the personal pronouns make the change of form as seen above **-əyondə** , **əyŋondəgi** etc. whereas the addition of **-nə, bu~pu** and **gi~ki** does not make the pronoun change, **əy-nə, əy-bu** and **əy-gi.** This is same to the second person and third person.

5.7.4 Pronominals

The linguistic phenomenon termed as Pronominalization 'is a widely used morphological feature of Tibeto-Burman (TB) languages. It takes place in two ways : (i) Nominal pronominalization and (ii) verbal pronominalization. Most of the Kuki-Chin languages of TB have verbal or nominal prominalization or both. But Manipuri has only nominal pronomilization which is regarded as a remnant of the pronominal linguistic feature of TB.

This feature of linguistic expressions, in a way, reflects the word view of its speaker about the various object of the universe. The underlying concept of the speakers of the language in the use of a personal pronoun, in its full, abridged or symbolic forms, or affix (prefix or suffix), with a noun is that in this world everything is possessed by someone or the other (in other words it indicates to whom it belongd). Manipuri has nominal pronominalization and according by all possessed things, viz., kinship terms, parts of body and inanimate. The pronominal markers, in this language, are all prefixes : the first person pronominal marker is i-, the second person pronominal marker is **nə-** and the third person pronominal marker is **mə-**.

The pronomonal prefixes i and **nə** are not so productive as **mə**. These pronominal prefixes can be prefixed to the following categories :

(i) Kinship terms : (some not to all)

i-ce	'my sister'	nə-ce	'your sister'
mə-ce	'her/his sister'	'i-ma	'my mother'
nə-ma	'your mother'	'mə-ma	'his/her mother'
i-pa	'my father'	nə-pa	'your father'
mə-pa	'his/her father'		

(ii) Body Parts : (some not to all)

kok	'head'	nəkok	'your head'
məkok	'his/her head'	səm	'hair'
nə-səm	'your hair'	mə-səm	'his/her hair'
khoŋ	'leg'	nə-khoŋ	'your leg'
mə-khoŋ	'his leg'	puk	'belly'
nə-puk	'your belly'	mə-puk	'his belly'
khut	'hand'	nə-khut	'your father'
mə-khut	'his hand'		

(iii) Some inalienable objects :

mə-məy	'its tail' [məy 'fire']	mə-ci	'its horn'
mə-ri	'its lace'/, (relative)	mə-ku	'its cover'
mə-hum	'its next'		

Of these roots **ci, ri, ku** and **hum** are bound.

In this language, use of pronoun is slightly delicate ; it needs the knowledge of 'social grammar or language in use' . The use of second person **nəŋ** 'you (sg)' is very limited, say, by the parents to their son or daughter, the old to young, among the very close friends etc. Even **nəŋ** cannot be used by the kids to their parents or to any seniors. When they are found use of **naŋ** to the seniors the parents will correct it. Futher the use of second person pronominal prefix to the nouns like **nəce** 'your sister' **nəpa** 'your father and **nəma** 'your mother' are not regarded as refine one.

5.8 VERB

In Manipuri, all verbal roots are bound roots; the exact verb forms are derived by affixation of modality, aspect markers etc. Of the two strategies (affixation and compounding) for constructing verb, affixation is more productive than compounding.

Root + aspect/modality marker ➔ verb
ca + ri ➔ ca-ri 'eating (continuous)
eat-asp
thək+te ➔ thək-te 'not drink'
drink-neg.mk.
cət+si ➔ cət-si 'Let's go'
go-propo.
sək+nu ➔ sək-nu 'Don't sing'
sing-prohi.

5.8.1 Various Categories of Suffixes

There are many suffixes which will be added to the verbal roots : they are in many kinds.

A. Aspect Markers :

Simple aspect (expressing the meaning of the habitual) : **- y~li~mi~ŋi~pi**
Progressive aspect : **-ri~li**
Perfect aspect : **-re~le**
Unrealized aspect : **-gəni~kəni**

B. ' be' verb : -ni

C. Modality :

Negative markers (suffixes)

Expressing habitual and action completed : **-te~de**
Expressing action in futurity (unrealized) : **-roy~loy**
Negative 'let' **-gumsi/kumsi**
Prohibitive marker **-nu**
Imperative markers (suffixes): **-o, -u, -ro~lo, -ru~lı , -kho**

D. Other Suffixes (named as 'D.suffix')

Definitizer - **-khi**
Definite +action completed - **-khre**
Causative marker - **hən~həl**
Remote action completed marker - **-ləm**
(1) Directional marker - **lək~rək**
(2) Directional (out to in) **-thok**

Expressing the meaning of start - **khət~kət**

Continution - **həω,**
Reciprocal - **minnə-**

Excess - **mən-**

(3) Directional (from out to inside) - **sin~sən**

Spread - **khay**
Falling downward, continuation - **thə**

5.8.2 Compounding

Some verbs in Manipuri, are formed by combination of two or more b Roots and they must be ended by aspect marker or modality. These compound verbs are very limited in number. They are given below :

pi+thək+le ➔ pi-thək-le 'has fed'
give-drink-asp
pi+niŋ+ŋi ➔ pi-niŋ-ŋi 'wish to give'
give-wish-asp
pi+thok+le ➔ pi-thok-le 'has handed over'
give-out-asp.
ca+niŋ+li ➔ ca-niŋ-li 'still wish to eat'
eat-wish-asp
a+niŋ+li ➔ a-niŋ-li 'still wish to read'
ead-wish-asp
pa+thok-le ➔ pa-thok-le 'has read out'
read-come out+asp

Noted that the second order bRoot **niŋ** 'wish' or 'want' and **thok~tok** 'come out' (from inside to outside) are very productive, in the sense that they can be added to any verb, as in the followings :

a. cət+niŋ+li ➔ cət-niŋ-li 'still wish to go'
go-wish-asp
cət-thok-le ➔ cətthok-le 'has gone out'

b. tum+niŋ+le ➔ tum-niŋ-le 'has felt sleepy'
sleep-wish-asp
tum+thok+le ➔ tumthok-le 'has started sleeping'

c. thək+niŋ+ŋi ➔ thək-niŋ-ŋi 'wish to drink'
drink-wish-asp
thək-tok-y ➔ thək-tok-y 'drink out'

d. phəjə+niŋ+ŋi ➔ phəjə-niŋ-ŋi 'wish to be beautiful'
nice-wish-asp
phəjə+thok-y ➔ phəjə-thok-y 'became beautiful'

e. pak+niŋ-li ➔ pak-niŋ-li 'still wish to widening'
pak+thok-li ➔ pak-thok-li 'still became widening'

5.8.3 Sequence of Suffixes

These above verbal suffixes cannot be added to the verbal root at random or at any order, in other words, they have specific order of suffixation to the verbal root. On the basis of their sequential suffixation, they can be divided into two types (a) medially occurred and (b) finally occurred suffixes. Both of them can immediately suffixed to the verbal roots. Medially occurred suffixes are given in (D) above named as D. Suffix while finally occurred suffixes are aspects markers or modality markers. Their order of occurrence are given here :

i. Only aspect markers or modality markers can occur with verbal roots
VR+asp.

ii. D.suffixes are followed by aspect markers or modality
VR+d. suffixes+asp.

iii. Regarding the occurrence of causative marker **hən~həl**, there are two specific rules.

a. In the simulteneous occurrence of **hən~həl** with aspect markers or modal markers, **hən~həl** precedes the latter (aspect or modal markers)
VR+hən~həl +aspect/Modal /rəm~ ləm /rək~lək

b. In the occurrence of **hən ~həl** with other suffixes, other suffixes (O.S.) like, **- sin, -thok~tok, -thə, minnə, -mən** etc. precedes the causative marker **hən~həl** VR+O.S. +**hən**

5.8.4 Classification of Manipuri Verbs

Manipuri verbs can be classified into two : Intranitive and Transitive. Intrasitive verbs can be made transitive by causativization (by suffixation of **hən~həl** to the intransitive verbs). Besides this classification. Manipuri verbs can be classified into three on the basis of semantics. They are : (a) Action verb (b) Process verb and (c) Stative verb. They are discussed one by one :

a. Action Verb

List of action verbs are given here :

phu-bə	'to beat or beating'	ca-bə	'to eat'
pay-bə	'to fly'	kaw-bə	'to kick'
yek-pə	'to draw'	khay-bə	'to divide'
cik-pə	'to bite'	i-bə	'to write'
cət-pə	'to go'		

Their occurrence in the sentences are given here :

1. məhak skul cət-li 'He goes to School'
he school go-asp

2. tombə-nə layrik əma tebəl-də thəm-mi
Tomba-nom. book table-loc. keep-asp.
'Tomba keeps a book on the table.'

b. Process Verb :

Process verbs are given in the following :

sat-pə	'to bloom'	pokhay-bə	'to break out'
niŋ-khay-bə	'to break down'	niŋkhay-bə	'to break down'
cakhaybə	'to speard out'	taw-bə	'to float'

Their occurrence in the sentences :

3. bəsənta-gi mətəm-da məkhəl məthel-gi ləy sat-li
spring-gen. time -loc. variety -gen flower bloom-asp.
'In spring time varieties of flowers are blooming'

4. cinar ədu mun-dənə cekhay-re
watermelon -det. ripe because of burst out-asp.
'The melon has burst out because of ripeness.'

C. Stative Verb

They are given below :

phəjəbə	'nice'	thibə	'ugly'
thumbə	'sweet'	khabə	'bitter'
cawbə	'big'	pik-pə	'small'

Their occurrence in the following sentences.

5. ləy-si phəjəy 'This flower is nice'
flower-det. nice

6. wa ədu yam-nə saŋ-ŋi
bamboo det. very long-asp.
'The bamboo is very long'

5.9 Tense or Aspects

5.9.1 Tense

Tense in the Tibeto-Burman languages, in general, is not so distinct as it is in the languages like English, Hindi, Sanskrit etc. Tense in this languages also is not so clear : it is felt necessary to analyse in different way. In the precise words of Comrie, 'Tense is grammaticalized expression of location in time', One can look at a particular form in a language, determine whether or not it is a grmmatical category, and then pronounce it is to be tense or something different. The difference between **Jack goes today** and **Jack went yesterday** in English is one of tense, whereas that between **Jack goes** and **Jack is going** and **Jack has gone** is rather one of aspects.

It is an empirical claim that tense is one of the grammatical categories and also claimed that tense is not found in all languages. The traditional Manipuri grammarians have held firmly that Manipuri has three tense - present, past and future ; each tense is again analysed into fou·· - indefinite, continuous, perfect and perfect continuous. There are some sentences :

1. a. jek ŋəraŋ kəythel cət-li (-y)
Jack yesterday bazar go

b. jek ŋəsi kəythel cət-li (-ri)
Jack today bazar go-

c. jek həyeŋ kəythel cət-kəni (-gəni)
Jack tomorrow bazar go-

What is noticed from the above three sentences is that the verbs ending in sentence 1 (a) and (b) are same though they occur with different adverbial time **ŋəraŋ** 'yesterday' and **ŋəsi** 'today' respectively. But in sentence 1(c) since there is adverbial time reference **həyeŋ** 'tomorrow' the verb ending is also changed into **-kəni** (or **-gəni**). In other word, there is the grammatical agreement between **həyeŋ** 'tomorrow' and the verb ending in 1(c) while in 1(a) and 1(b) no specific agreement is shown between the adverbial time and the verb endings (time reference is not grammaticalized).

It is certain that the question of absolute tense - past, persent, and future - does not arise. In this language one might say that the only tense distinction grammatically is future and non-future. Consider some other sentences in the followings :

2. a. jek kophi thək-khi
   Jack coffee drink-def.
   Jack has taken coffee (very definite)

   b. jek kophi thək-ləm-mi (-y)
   'jack has taken coffee' [Completed already]

   c. jek kophi thək-ləm-gəni
   'Jack may have taken coffee' [but not sure]

   d. jek kophi thək-khi-gəni
   'Jack will take coffee' [will continue]

Here it will be interesting to analyse the different verbal suffixes occurring in the above sentences (2). The suffix **khi** in sentence 2 (a) indicates 'definite-action-completion '(just like the action was witnessed by the speaker)'. Another suffix **-ləm~rəm** in 2 (b) denotes 'action already completed' (remote completion of the action) but it (i.e. **ləm~rəm**) cannot be the final in a sentence. The co-occurrence of **-ləm** and **-gəni** (**-kəni**) indicate 'doubt of an action'). The last point is when **-khi** co-occurred with **-gəni** it expresses 'continuation of the action'. So the treatment of **khi** and **ləm** as past tense marker by the traditional grammerians will be unlogical.

5.9.2 Aspect

Thus it would be more feasible to discuss 'Aspects' instead of 'Tense' in Manipuri. Aspects are different way of viewing the internal temporal constituency of a situation or an event. In other words, aspect indicates the internal structure of an event or situation. Aspect is not concerned with relating the time of the situation to any other time point, but rather with the internal temporal constituency of the one situation. An event or a situation in Manipuri can be divided into four units : the first is the simple habitual expression of the event; the second discusses about the event is going on ; the third expresses the event is completed and the fourth talks about the event will be performed in the next moment . So it will be more convincing to say that there are four aspects in the language. They are discussed below :

(i) Simple Aspect :

It expresses simple statement, habitual meaning and universal truth. The markers are **-y, -mi, -ni, -pi, -ŋI, -li** which occur under phonological conditions. Consider the following sentences :

3. a. numit-nə noŋpok-tə thok-y
   sun -nom. east-loc. rise-asp.
   'The sun rises in the east.'

   b. məhak cak thoŋ-ŋi
   he rice cook-
   'He cooks rice.'

   c. meri skul cət-li
   Mary school go-
   'Mary goes to school.'

d. tomba-gi məca nupi ədu yam-nə kəp-pi
Tomba-gen. his daughter det much cry-
'Tomba's daughter cries much'

(ii) Progressive Aspect :

This is indicated by **-ri~-li (-ri** occurs after vowels while **-li** after consonants). In other words, it expresses the action is continuing.

4. a. jek həwjik layrik pa-ri
Jack now book read-
'Jack is now reading'

b. məhak lay yek-li
he picture draw-
'He is painting'

c. əykhoy isəy ta-ri
we song hear-
'We are hearing the song'

(iii) Perfect Aspect

This is denoted by the suffix **re~le**, as in the following sentences

4. a. məkhoy philəm ədu yeŋ-le
they film that see-
'They have seen the film'

b. məhak hidak ədu ca-re
he medicine that eat
'He has taken the medicine'

There is a suffix **-khre** which indicates certainty of the completion of an action, as in the sentence 5.

5. məhak hidak ca-khre
'He has taken the medicine'

The speaker is very much sure about the completion of the action of taking 'medicine'. See the semantic difference between the following two sentences 6 (a) and (b).

6. a. məhak skul(də) cət-le
'He has started going to school'

b. məhak skul-(də) cət-khre
'He has gone to school'

6 (a) expresses that 'he' or the child has started going to school after absence from school for a few days, it does not mean that the action of going is completed, today he may not go to school. But 6 (b) indicates that he has gone to school, (right at this moment he is not at home).

This aspect marker can also be used in a very specific situation, say, reporting an action and informing of departure. Consider the following sentences :

7. a. məhak əsi-də cət-le
he this-loc. go-asp
'He has gone there'

b. əy cət-le
I go-asp.
'I am leaving '(I have gone)

7 (a) happens in such a situation that in the midst of the conversation of 'a person' (say Mr. X) and Mr. X is seen going by one of the member, then informed 'Mr.X is going there; (b) is used in the very context of taking leave, saying at the time of departure, informing 'I am leaving'.

(iv) Irrealis or Unrealized Aspect :

This is used for action which will take place in the near future. The relevent aspect marker is **-gəni~kəni**, as in the sentences 8.

8. a. məhak kəythel cət-kəni
he market go-
'He will go to market'

b. əkhoy həyeŋ ciŋ ka-gəni
we tomorrow hill climb-
'We will climb the hill tomorrow'

c. əykhoy ŋəsi myujiəm yeŋ-gəni
we today museum see-
'Today we will go to museum'

Now notice that there are four aspects. More and above, it is not possible to forget aspects in this language, and the suffix **gəni~kəni** is treated as irrealis or unrealized aspects, then the question of tense does not arise at all.

ADJECTIVES

5.10 Adjectives

Manipuri has no adjective form of word as 'good', 'tall' in English. An adjective is derived through the affixation of the attribute prefix or formative particle(FP) ə- to a verbal noun, e.g. **ə-phə-bə** 'good' (1).However, there are some adjectives which are without the attributive prefix **ə-**, e.g. **phəjəbə** 'nice' (2).

In this language, adjectives can be classified typologically into two groups : a) Adjective formed with the attributive ə-, as in example (1) and b) adjective formed without ə-, as in the example (2). Here is a point that in both the types, the nominalizer **bə~pə** ends the adjective form.

1. Adjective with ə-

1. Prefix + Root + NZR
ə+phə +bə ➔ əphəbə əŋaŋ 'the good child'
ə+sa+bə ➔ əsabə ləybak 'the hot country'
ə+pak+pə ➔ əpakpə ləm 'the wide land'
ə+pay+bə ➔ əpaybə ləycin 'the flying cloud'
ə+sin+bə ➔ əsinbə həy 'the sour fruit'

2. Adjective without ə-

2. Root +NZR
phəjə +bə ➔ phəjəbə ləy 'a nice flower'

nuŋŋay+bə ➔ nuŋŋaybə paw 'a happy news'
həraw+bə ➔ hərawbə numit 'a joyful day'
cokthə+bə ➔ cokthəbə nəha 'an exhausted youth'

It is here noted that formation of adjective by adding the attributive prefix **ə-** is possible only to monosyllabic root not to polysyllabic root. This **ə-** can not be prefixed when there is a suffix **lə~ rə** or **ri~li** or **khrə** or **ləm** between the root and the nominalizer **bə~pə**, as in the following example :

*3. əsatləbə ləyraŋ 'flower'[-sat-bloom]
* əwarəbə maythoŋ 'face' [-wa- sorrow]
* əpətləbə həy 'fruit'[-pət- rotten']

But without this very prefix **ə-**, all the above examples are possible, as in the following example and they will function as adjective.

4. Root +Suf.+NZR Noun

sat bloom	+	li lə ləm khrə	+	bə ləyraŋ flower 'a blooming flower'
sa hot	+	ri rə rəm khrə	+	bə yotcəy 'A hot iron'
pət rotten	+	li lə ləm khrə	+	bə həy fruit 'A rotten fruit'

There is another way of formation of adjective, that is, by adding the nominalizer **pə~bə** to the verb in progressive and perfect, as in the following examples.

5. Derived from Progressive

ca+ri+bə ➔ caribə ənaŋ 'the eating child'
thək+li+bə ➔ thəklibə nipa 'the drinking man'
yeŋ+li+bə ➔ yeŋlibə nupi 'the looking woman'

6. Derived from Perfect

thoŋ+lə+bə ➔ thoŋləbə cinjak 'the cooked food'
pət+lə+bə ➔ pətləbə yeŋsaŋ 'the rotten curry'
pok+lə+bə ➔ pokləbə əŋaŋ 'the born child'

There are other suffixes to which the nominalizer can be added and the very word can
9 functioned as adjective ; they are **-khi-**, **-ləm-** and **-khrə** consider the following examples.

ca+khi+bə ➔ cakhibə mi 'person who had taken meal'
ut+ləm+bə ➔ ut ləmbə philəm 'The film which was shown'
ləw+khrə+bə ➔ ləwkhrəbə layrik 'The book which was taken by'

(See in relalivilization also)

In short it can be said that adjective can be derived from any verbal root.

ADVERB

5.11 ADVERB

Adverbial expressions normally modify the verb with respect to place, time and manner of the action referred to by the verb. In Manipuri adverb is formed by suffixation of **-nə** to the verbal root. Three types of verb forms are stative, action and process. They can also reduplicate, as in (bs).

I. Stative Verb Root + nə ➔ kən-nə 'strongly'
təp +nə ➔ təp-nə 'slowly'
caw+nə ➔ caw-nə 'in large'
saŋ +nə ➔ saŋ-nə 'long'

1 a. məhak kən-nə cət-li
'he stongly go-asp'

b. məhak kən-nə kən-nə cət-li
'He goes very energetically'

2 a. məhak təp-nə cel-li
'he slowly run -asp.'

b. məhak təp-nə təp-nə cel-li
'He runs slowly and slowly'

3 a. məhak-nə saŋ-nə pawkhum pi
he -nom. long answer give
'He gives a long answer'

b. məhak-nə saŋ-nə saŋ-nə pawkhum pi
'He gives long answers'
(He has habit of giving long answers)

II Action Verb+ nə

ta+nə ➔ tanə 'by hearing'
kəp+nə ➔ kəp-nə 'cryingly'
yeŋ+nə ➔ yeŋ-nə 'by looking'
thoŋ+nə ➔ thoŋ-nə 'by cooking'

As they occur in the following sentences :

4. a. məhak isəy ta-nə thəbək təw-wi
he song hear -asp. work do-asp.
'He does the work by listening'

b. məhak isəy ta-nə ta-nə thəbək təw-wi
'He does the work by listening'

5. a. məhak kəp-nə cət-li
he cry- go-asp.
'He goes cryingly.'

b. məhak kəp-nə kəp-nə cət-li
'He goes cryingly'

III. Process Verb+ nə

sat+nə ➔ sat-nə 'in blooming'
pom+nə ➔ pom-nə 'in bud' (not blooming)
səw+nə ➔ səw-nə 'in boiling'

6. a. məhak-nə ləy sat-nə pambi ədu kəkthət-le
he-nom. flower blooming plant the cut -asp.
'He has cut down the plant while the flowers are blooming'

b. məhak-nə ləy sat-nə sat-nə pambi ədu kəkthət-le
'He has cut down the plant while the plant is blooming very much'

7. a. isiŋ səwnə phlaks-ta həy-gə-nu
water in boiling flask-loc. pour-asp.-proh.
'Don't pour the water into the flask in boiling state'

b. isiŋ səwnə səwnə phlaks-ta həy-gə-nu
water in boiling flask-loc. pour-asp.-proh.
'Don't pour the water into the flask in boiling state'

5.11.1 Kinds of Adverb

The followings are the kinds of adverb found in Manipuri. They are :

a. Adverb of manner
b. Durative adverb
c. Adverb of time
d. Adverb of quantity, and
e. Reduplicative adverb

They are discussed one by one in the followings.

a. Adverb of Manner

It is formed by addition of **-nə** to the stative verb, as given here a list : **təp-nə**, 'slowly', **kən-nə** 'stongly'; **thu-nə** 'quickly'; **poŋ-nə** 'proudly'; **lem-nə** 'gently'; **pak-nə** 'widely' ; **khu-nə** 'narrowly'; **ten-nə** 'shortly', etc. Consider the following sentences as they occurred.

8. a. tomba təp-nə cət-li
Tomba slowly go-asp.
'Tomba goes slowly'

b. təppak ədu pak-nə səndok-y
valley det. widely spread-asp.
'The valley spreads widely'

b. Durative Adverb

This is specifically formed by adding **-dunə~tunə** to the action and process verbal roots, as in the following sentences.

9. məhak isəy sək-tunə cət-li
he song sing-dur.adv. go-asp.
'He goes by singing'

10. əy-gi ləy-du sat-tunə ləy-ri
I-gen. flower det. bloom -dur.adv. stay-asp.
'My very flower is still blooming'

11. səŋgom səw-dunə ləy-re
milk boil-dur.adv. stay-asp.
'The milk has been boiling'

c. Adverb of Time

There are some lexical adverbs of time in Manipuri. They can be categorized into two according to the time reference : I) lexical items indicating past time, II) lexical items indicating future time. These are discussed below :

I. Lexical items of past time, in Manipuri, are **ŋəraŋ** 'yesterday' **nəhal** 'day before yesterday' **hakum** 'last year' **ŋəsay** 'last moment' (that time). Their occurrences in the sentences are given here :

12. John [**nəraŋ / nəhal / hakum / ŋəsay**] **kəythel-da lak-y**
John **market-loc. come-asp.**

'John came yesterday/day before yesterday / last year/ that time to the market.'

II. Lexical items of future time are horen 'hext moment', həyeŋ 'tomorrow', həŋcit 'day after tomorrow' məsem 'two days after tomorrow' mərəw 'three days after tomorrow' noŋməy 'next year'. Their occurrence in the sentences are given below :-

13. John [**həyeŋ / həŋcit / məsem / etc.**] **Imphal-da lak-kəni**
Imphal-loc. come -asp. unr. asp.

'John will come to Imphal tomorrow/day after tomorrow / two days after tomorrow/to Imphal'.

In this language, there are two lexical adverb of time. They are i) ŋəsi 'today' and ii) həwjik 'now' used along with past and future time,

(i) ŋəsi 'today' is used along with the meaning of past and future time, as in sentences (14) and (15) respectively.

14. məhak ŋəsi cət-khre
he today go-perf. asp (def.)
'He has gone today' (Past time meaning)

15. məhak ŋəsi cət-kəni
'Today he will go'

(ii) **həwjik** 'now' is used along with the meaning of future time, as in (16) and (17) sentences respectively :

16. məhak həwjik layrik pa-ri
he now book read-prog. asp.
'Now he is reading (continuing)

17. məhak həwjik lak-kəni
'He will come now '(future)'

d. Adverb of Quantity

In this language, there are three words, namely, **hen-nə** 'excessively', **wat-nə** 'in less' and **yam-nə** 'very' (formed by addition of adverb marker -**nə** to the roots **-hen, -wat, and yam-**) used as adverb of quantity. Their occurrence in the sentences are given below :

18. məhak-nə məca-də pəysa hen-nə thay
he-nom. his-son-dat. rupees excessively send -asp.
'He sends money to his son excessively'

19. məhak wat-nə cak ca-y
he less rice eat-asp.
'He eats his meal in less quantity'

20. məhak cak yam-nə cay
'He eats a lot'

e. Reduplicative Adverb

This type of adverb is formed by suffixing **-ləp~rəp, -li, -mi, -tək, -pet, -phet-, -bu** etc. to the verbal root and at the same time it is repeated. Consider the following illustrations :

-ləp :- saŋ-ləp saŋ-ləp [saŋbə . 'long']
waŋ-ləp waŋ-ləp [waŋbə 'tall']
te-ləp teləp[tenbə ' short']

-rəp :- parəp parəp [pabə 'thin']
cawrəp cawrəp [cawbə 'big']
sa-rəp sa-rəp [sabə 'hot']

-li :- təp-li təp-li [təppə 'slow']
mol-li mol-li [monbə 'slow']
pət-li pət-li [pət-pə 'rotten']

-mi :- nok-mi nok-mi [nok-pə 'to smile']

-tək :- - kən-tək kən -tək [kənbə 'hard']
ten-tək tentək [tenbə 'short']
patək patək [pabə 'thin']

e. . Reduplicative Adverb

This type of adverb is formed by suffixing **-lšp~ršp, -li, -mi, -tšk, -pet, -phet-, -bu** etc. to the verbal root and at the same time it is repeated. Consider the following illustrations :

-lšp :- sa ›-lšp sa ›-lšp [sa ›bš . 'long']
wa ›-lšp wa ›-lšp [wa ›bš 'tall']
te-lšp telšp[tenbš ' short']

-ršp :- paršp paršp [pabš 'thin']
cawršp cawršp [cawbš 'big']
sa-ršp sa-ršp [sabš 'hot']

-li :- tšp-li tšp-li [tšppš 'slow']
mol-li mol-li [monbš 'slow']
pšt-li pšt-li [pšt-pš 'rotten']

-mi :- nok-mi nok-mi [nok-pš 'to smile']

-tšk :- - kšn-tšk kšn -tšk [kšnbš 'hard']
ten-tšk tentšk [tenbš 'short']
patšk patšk [pabš 'thin']

-pet :- thum-pet thumpet [thumbš 'sweet']

-phet :- nok-phet nok-phet [nokpš 'to simle']
cšm-phet cšm-phet [cšmbš 'tasteless']
kuphet kuphet [kupš 'twinkle']

-bu :- lumbu lumbu [lumbš 'to make warm']
bu › :- sabu › sabvu › [sabš hot] 'warm'

These suffixes gave the meaning of 'slightly'. This can be examplified in the following sentences :

21. isi › šdu lumbu lumbu sa-hšl-lu
water det. warm heat-cau-comd.
'Make the water warm'

22. š ›a › šsi mšma ubšdš nokphet nokphet tšw-wi
child det. his mother see -NZR-when smole do-asp
'The child keeps smiling when he sees his mother'

23. thoybi tšp-li tšp-li cšt-li
Thoibi slowly go-asp
'Thoibi goes slowly'

24. Yu šsi thumpet thumpet tšw-wi
liquor det. slightly sweet do-asp.
'The liquor tastes slightly sweet .'

Among the above suffixes,**-lšp~ršp**, **-tšk** and **-phet** can be without reduplication, as in the following sentences :

25. cak šsi kšntšk tšw-wi
rice det. hard do-asp.
'The rice is felt slightly hard.'

But without **-nə, təw-wi** can occur, as in the following examples :

kup-tək təw-wi 'felt slightly small'
pet-tək təw-wi 'felt slightly soft'
saŋ-ləp təw-wi 'felt slightly long'

CONJUNCTION

5.12 Conjunction

In Manipuri, there are more than twenty conjunctions which can connect phrases and clauses. Regarding their forms, Manipuri conjunctions can be categorised into two : (a) Conjunctive suffixes (CS) (suffix to the noun) and (b) Conjunctive particles (CP) (made of words). They are discussed below :

A. Conjunctive Suffixes

They are : **-gə~kə, -gə........ gə, -ba, -su, -su.....su, -ne ......ne;**

Their occurrence in the sentences are given below :

7. əy məhak-kə wari sa-nəy
   I he story talk-asp.
   'I talk with him'
8. məhak tomba-ga cawba-gə loynənə isəy sək-y
   he Tomba-con. Chaoba-con. with song sing
   'He sings with Tomba and Chaoba'.
9. tomba-su philəm ədu yeŋ-gəni
   Tomba-also film det. see-asp
   'Tomba also will see the film'.
10. əy-su tomba-su mitiŋ yaw-gəni
    I-also Tomba -also meeting attend -asp.
    'I also and Tomba also will attend the meeting'
    (I will attend the meeting and Tomba also)
11. əy-ne tomba-ne mani-ne cət-kəni
    I-con Tomba-con. Mani-con. go -asp.
    'I,Tomba and Mani will go there'.
12. məkhoy-di ca-bə {su/gə/ne}, thək-pa{su/gə/ne} tumba {su/gə/ne}
    ədum təwdənə ləy-re
    'They are spending time by eating, by drinking and by sleeping'.

It is interesting that conjunctive suffixes such as **-su ... su, gə.....gə, ne....ne**, will occur with every noun or pronoun or verbal noun, as in the sentence (11) and (12).

B. Conjunctive Particles :

They are more in number than conjuctive suffixes and they cannot occur repeatedly with every nouns or pronouns or phrase or clause like as **su........su, gə......gə, and ne.....ne**, as in sentence (11).

The list of conjuctive particles are given below :

əmasuŋ or əmadi 'and'

ədudəgi	'then'
ədugə	'and'
ədubu	'but'
ədunə	'so'
nətrəgə	'either or'
nətrəbədi	'if not'
nəttrədəbu	'if it is not so?'
təωigumbəsuŋ	'but'
mərəmdi	'because'
mərəm ədunə	'therefore'

Their occurrence in the sentences are given below :

14. tomba əmasuŋ /əmadi thoybi həy hek-li
Tomba and Thoibi fruit pluck-asp.
'Tomba and Thobi are plucking fruit'

15. hannə munnə taω əduga khəl-lu
first carefully listen and /then think-comd.
'First listen carefully then think over'

16. məhak layrik parəm-mi ədudəgi sanəba thok-khre
he book read -asp. then play-nom. go out-def.+ asp.
'He read (for sometime) then went to play'

17. məhak layrəy təωigumbəsuŋ/ədubu məpukcel seŋ-ŋi
he poor but honest-asp.
'He is poor but honest'

18. məhak lak-te mərəm ədunə / ədunə əy-su cət-lə-roy
he come -neg. so I -also go-dur-neg.
'He did not come so I also would not go'

19. tomba nətrəgə thoybi tha-rək-u
Tomba or Thoibi send-dir-comd.
'Send Tomba or Thoibi'

20. ca-bə tumbə mətəm nay-yu nəttrəbədi nəsa phə-roy
eat-NZR sleep NZR time keep -comd. otherwise health good-neg.
'Be regular in eating and sleeping otherwise health will be bad'

Notice that the two types of conjuctions — conjuctive suffixes and conjuctive particles — are different in their functions. First, the conjuctive suffixes can occur repeatedly with the nouns or verbal nouns in a construction as in (12) and (13). Secondly, the conjuctive suffixes are often used for connecting between the words while conjuctive particles are for connecting between the clauses. However, the conjuctive particles **nəttrəgə** or **nəttrəbəsu** 'either or' can function between the words.

5.12.1 Types of Conjuction

On the basis of the nature of the function, conjuction in Manipuri can be classified into five. They are discussed

1. Co-ordinating Conjuction

They are **əmasuŋ** 'and', **ədubu/təωigumbəsuŋ** 'but', **ədum oynəmək** 'however'

21 a. caωba əmasuŋ tomba skul cət-li
'Chaoba and Tomba go to school'

b. caωba lak-le ədubu tomba-di cət-khre
'Chaoba has come but Tomba had gone'

c. caωba-nə kənnə ŋaŋ-ŋi ədum oynəmək tomba -nə tabi-de
'Chaoba talks seriously, however, Tomba did not listen it'

II. Correlative Conjuctions

They like coordinating conjuction connect the grammatically equal clauses but they occur in pair. They are **su... su , gə...gə and ne....ne**. (see sentences 11-13).

III. Comparative Conjuctions

Conjuctions of this type is used in cpmparision. They are suffix **-muk and -gum ~ kum**. They are shown in the following sentences.

22 a. məhak caωba-muk kəl-li
he Chaoba-as strong-asp.
'He is as strong as Chaoba'

b. məhak thoybi-gum cət-li
'He goes like Thoibi'

IV. Consequencial Conjuctions

They connect two or more clauses, one is the result of another. The conjuctions of this type are, **mətuŋda** 'after', **ədunə** 'or', **mərəm ədunə** 'so', **mərəm-di** 'because' etc.

mətuŋ-də :

23. məpa ləykhi-drəbə mətuŋ-də tomba-nə karbar ədu yeŋ-sil-le
his father exist-neg.-NZR after-loc. Tomba-Agent business det. look-into-asp.
'After the death of his father Tomba has taken up his father's business'

mərəm ədunə/ədunə :

24. məhak na-re mərəm ədunə/ədunə məhak
he ill-asp so he comė-dir-neg.mk.
'He is ill so he will not come'

mərəm-di :

25. pulis ədu pha-re mərəmdi məhak-nə heroin puthok-pusin təω-ωi
ploice det. arrest-asp. because he-agent heroin smuggling do-asp.
'The very police has been arrested because he does the smuggling of heroin'.

5.12.2. Double Occurrence of Conjuctions

In Manipuri two conjuctions — Conjuctive particles and conjuctive suffixes can occur simulteneously in a construction, as in sentence.

24. əy əmasuŋ tomba caωbəgə kəythel cət-li
I and Tomba Chaoba-with market go -asp.
'I and Tomba went to market with Chaoba'

CHAPTER–VI

MORPHOPHONEMICS

6.1 Morphophonemics

The morphological processes employed for various morphological words are : juxtaposition, prefixation, suffixation, reduplication, compounding, internal change and replacement. Of these, suffixation is the most commonly employed process. This will be illustrated in respect of noun stem formation, nominal / pronominal inflections and verbal formations.

When, in the process of stem formations or nominal/verbal suffixations. various morphological elements or morphs come together usually various types of morphophonemic adjustments or changes take place. It is an important aspect of the descriptional analysis of a language. It ireflects the relationship of the phonemic structure of the language to its grammatical structure.

6.2 Kinds of Morphophonemic Alternations

All the morphophonemic patterns of a language can be grouped as — (a) automatic alternations (b) non-automatic alternations, and (c) free variants. From among these the automatic alternations may be said as phonologically conditioned alternations and the non-automatic alternations as morphological conditioned and lexically conditioned alternations.

Roots in Manipuri are nouns and verbs. Noun affixation (only suffixation) is for gender, number and case (agentive, accusative, dative, locative, ablative, genitive and associative). Verb affixation (only suffixation) is for aspects (simple, progressive, perfect and unrelized or irrealis) and mood (interrogative, imperative, indicative). A sequence of morpheme can be added to these roots.

6.3 Morphophonemic Changes

The derivational processes found in Manipuri are compounding and affixation (prefixation and suffixation). In these, morphophonemic changes are usually occurred. They are discussed one by one in the followings :

6.3.1 Voicing Assimilation Rule (VA Rule)

Syllable - initial voiceless unaspirated stops are voiced between voiced segments, as formalized in Rule 1.

$$\text{VARule:}\quad \begin{bmatrix} \text{- Continuant} \\ \text{-sonorant} \\ \text{-spread glottis} \end{bmatrix} \rightarrow [\text{+voiced}]/[\text{+sonorant}] — [\text{+sonorant}]$$

The VA Rule applies in a limited number of morphological environment. First, the VA Rule applies when the nominalizer **-pə** is suffixed to a verbal root that ends in a voiced segment, as in example 1.

1. root root +nominalizer suffix -pə
pa 'read' pa +bə ➔ pabə 'to read'
phu 'beat' phu+bə ➔ phubə 'to beat'
pi 'give' pi+bə ➔ pibə 'to give'
thoŋ 'cook' thoŋ+bə ➔ 'to cook'
pen 'satisfy' pen+bə ➔ penbə 'to satisfy'

But the root does not end with a voiced segment, the initial stop of the nominalizer suffixed -**pə** does not become voiced, as in the following example 1

2. root root +nominalizer
lak 'come' lak +pə ➔ lakpə 'to come'
lot 'hide' lot +pə ➔ lotpə 'to hide'
kəp 'cry' kəp +pə ➔ kəppə 'to cry'

Second , the VA Rule applies to the case suffixes, namely, **-ki** genitive, - **kə** associative, and **-tə** 'locative', as in the following examples :

3. root root + case suffixes -ki, kə, and -tə
mi 'man' mi+gi ➔ mi-gi 'of the man' [genitive]
tha 'moon' tha +gi ➔ tha-gi 'of the moon'
məhak 'he' məhak+ki ➔ məhak-ki 'his'
dili 'Delhi' deli +də ➔ dili-də to Delhi [locative]
ciŋ 'hill' ciŋ+də ➔ ciŋdə 'to the hill'
[khut-tə 'to the hand']
əŋaŋ 'baby' əŋaŋ+gi ➔ əŋaŋ-gi 'of baby'

The VAR cannot apply in the followings :

First, the VA Rule cannot apply when the derivational suffixes, namely, **-thok** 'out' or **khət** 'up' are suffixed to roots. Consider the following example :

a. **-thok [thok** has two other allomorphs - **tok** and **-dok]**

4. root root+thok
hi 'trim' hi-dok-pə 'to make it clean'/ 'trim'
si si-dok-pə 'to put down an egine'
pi 'give' pi-thok-pə 'to give out'
su 'wash' su-dok-pə 'to wash away'
pu 'bring' pu-thok-pə 'to bring out'
lu 'to wash or cleanse' lu-thok-pə 'to wash out/cleanse'
pa 'read' pa-thok-pə 'to read out'
khoy 'plough' khoy-dokpə 'to plough out'
lay 'simplify' lay-thok-hən-pə 'to simplify out'
loŋ 'turnover' loŋ-thok-pə 'to turn over'
khik 'sprinkle' khik-tok-pə 'to sprinkle on'
kəp 'cry' kəp-thok-pə 'to cry out'

b. **khət** has two other allomorphs **-kət~gət~khət**

5.	root		root+khət	
	hi	'trim'	hi-gətpə	'to make it rough'
	ca	'eat'	ca-khət-pə	'to start eating'
	ma	'search'	ma-khət-pə	'to thrust hand upward'
	pay	'fly'	paykhət-pə	'to fly upward'
	loŋ	'spread'	loŋ-khət-pə	'to turn face upward'
	poŋ	'blown'	poŋ-khət-pə	'blown up'
	khik	'sprinkle'	khik-kət-pə	'to sprinkle upward'

Secondly, the VA Rule does not apply with prefixation or with compounds where the initial stem acts like a prefix. That is the VA Rule does not apply with the affixation of the pronominal prefix **i-** 'first person possessive', **nə-** second person possessive, and **mə-** 'third person possessive' where the voiceless initial root does not voice even though it occurs between the voiced segments. Consider, the following illustration :

6.	root		Pronominal Prefix - + root	
	pa	'father'	i-pa	'my father'
			nə-pa	'your father'
			mə-pa	'his father'
	ma	'mother'	i- ma	'my mother'
			nə- ma	'your mother'
			mə- ma	'his mother'
	ca	'issue'	i-ca	'my issue'
			nə- ca	'your issue'
			mə- ca	'his issue'
	ce	'sister'	i- ce	'my sister'
			nə- ce	'your sister'
			mə- ce	'his sister'
	kok	'head'	i- kok	'my head'
			nə- kok	'your head'
			mə- kok	'his head'
	səm	'hair'	i- səm	'my hair'
			nə- səm	'your hair'
			mə- səm	'his hair'

Thirdly, the VA Rule also does not apply with the affixation of the attributive prefix **ə-**, where the root initial voiceless consonants do not voice even though they occur between voiced segments, as in the following illustration.

7.	əten-bə	ə-tha-bə
	att-short-NZR	att-thick-NZR
	that which is short	'that which is thick'

Again the VA Rule does not apply with the prefixation of **mə-** which indicates manner of or method of or mode of V+ ing, another **mə-** indicating 'third person' when it is prefixed to the Noun) as shown in the following illustrations :

(i) **mə-** 'mode of'

8. a. mə-pa
mode-read
'mode of reading'

b. mə-tum
'mode of sleep'
'mode of sleeping'

c. mə-ca
mode-eat
'mode of eating '

d. mə-thək
mode -drink
mode of drinking'

(ii) **mə-** 'third person'

mə-səm ; mə-kok , mə- khoŋ 'his hair/head/leg'

Also VA Rule does not apply in the [N+N], [N+V], [V+V] or [V+N] compounds, as given in the following examples.

9. a. [Noun+Noun]$_N$

ləy-kon flower place 'garden'	məy-phəm fire-place 'fire place'
məy-ri fire- string 'flame'	u-na tree- leaf 'leaf of tree'

b. [Noun + Verb]$_N$

məy-sa fire-hot 'heat'	ləy-toŋ earth-mount 'earth mount'
wa-koy speech -move around 'talking round about'	wa-həŋ speech -ask 'question'
	ləy-haw earth-tasty 'manure'

6.3.2 Deaspiration Rule

Not only Manipuri has Voicing Assimilation rules, but also does occur 'deaspiration' in this language, and it is called 'Deaspiration Rule (D-Rule)'.

D-Rule : [-sonorant] ➔[-spread Glottis] / [+ spread Glottis] -.

The D-Rule applies when the derivational suffixes - **thok** 'out' or **khət** 'up' are suffixed to roots which begin with an aspirate. The application of this rule is illustrated in the following examples.

10.

root	root+ thok /-khat +pə
phiŋ 'short temper or anguish'	phiŋ-gət-pə 'to become anguish'
thon 'resurface'	thon-gət-pə ' to resurface upwared'
pheŋ 'clean'	pheŋ-gət-pə ' to wash out' (started)
pheŋ ' clean/wash'	pheŋ-dok-pə ' to wash out'

thin ' pierce' thin-dok-pə 'to pierce through 'or' pierce out'

6.3.3 Trilling Rule

The alveolar lateral **l** becomes a voiced alveolar trill **r** in the intervocalic position. This rule is substantialed by the following illustration and it is termed as T-Rule.

T-rule : [+ lateral] ➔ [-lateral]/[+syllabic] - [+ syllalic]

First it can be seen in the prefixattion of pronominal markers (**i-** first person, **nə** second person and **mə** third person') as in the following examples :

11.	ləy kay	'locality'	i-rəykay	'my locality'
	raŋ yay	'house'	i-raŋ yay	'my house'
	lən	'property'	nə-rən	'your property'
	ləy	'tomgue'	nə-rəy	'your tongue'
	ləybak	'land'	mə-rəybak	'his mother land'
	lembə	'remaining'	ə-rembə	'remainder'
	ləybə	'buying'	ə-rəybə	'the buying (thing)'

The T- Rule also applies when the progressive aspect marker **-li** and the perfect aspect marker **-le** are suffixed to a stem with a final vocalic segment (and in other environment the repective aspect markers are - **ri** and **-re**)

12.	i-ri	i-re
	write-prog. asp	write -perfect
	'is -writing'	'has written'
	phu-ri	phu-re
	beat -prog. asp.	beat -perf. asp.
	'is beating'	'has beaten'.
	cət -li	cət-le
	go-prog. asp.	go-perf. asp.
	'is going'	'has gone'

The T- Rule can also apply when some morphemes, like **-lə** ' action takes place towards the speaker' or 'action' occurs in speakers 'place', **-lu** and **-lək** action taken place somewhere (away from the speaker) then come towards the speaker and **-ləm** 'sequential' are suffixed to a root ending with a vocalic segment.

12 a. Suffixation of -lə ~rə

13.	ca-rəy	phu-rəy
	eat-V.suf.	beat-V.suf.
	'Come and eat here'	'Come and beat here'
	pha -rəy	ke-rəy
	arrest-V. suf.	make up-V.suf.
	'Come and arrest here'	'Come and make up here'

b. Suffixation of -lək

14.	ca -rək-y	pha-rək-y
	eat-V.suf. -asp.	arrest-V.suf. -Asp

	'Ate then came here'	'arrested then came here'
	thi-rək-y	li-rək-y
	search-V.suf. -Asp	narrate-V.suf. -asp.
	' Searched then came here'	'Narrated from there and came'

c. Suffixation of -lu

15.	ca-ruy	thi-ruy
	eat -V.suf	search-V.suf
	'went there and ate'	'went there and search'
	phu -ruy	phoy -ruy
	go-V.suf.	pluckout -V.suf.
	'Went there and beat'	'Went there and plucked out (the grass)'

d. Suffixation of -ləm

16.	ca-rəm-mi	phu-rəm-mi
	eat-seq-asp.	beat -V. suf.-asp
	'ate and went away'	'beat and went away'
	ki-rəm-mi	pi-rəm-mi
	fear-seq-asp	give-seq.asp
	'feared'	'give and went away'

The T-Rule also applies to some compounds : [N+N] and [N+N], illustration is given in 16.

16 a. [N+N] N

mi-raŋ mi-laŋ	} miraŋ	phi-ruk phi-luk	} phi- ruk
spider - mare 'cobweb'		cloth-basket 'a kind of basket'	
ce-rəy ce-ləy paper flower	} ce-rəy	lay-ruk lay-luk	} lay-ruk
'flower made of paper' (or a kind of flower)		god's meal 'God's meal'	

b. [N+V]

ləw-rok ləw-lok	} ləw-rok	ci-roŋ ci-loŋ	} ci-roŋ
paddy-harvest 'harvest season'		' horn-branches out' 'branch of horn'	

It is also mentioned already in the chapter of phonology that **l** and **n** are free variation in the final position of a syllable, e.g. **turel** or **turen** 'river'.

Besides this, there is also regressive assimilation, that is, when a syllable ended with **n** is followed by a suffix like **-li, -le, -lu, -lo, n** changes into **l** in the regressive mannner, as in the following.

19.	sen ' rear' or 'look after' (the cattle)	sel-li 'rears' or 'look after the cattle'
	cen 'run'	cen-le - 'has run'
	then 'arrange'	then - lo 'Arrange' (Command)
	yen 'distribute'	yen-lu 'Distribute' (Command)

6.3.4 Velar StopDeletion Rule

VS-D Rule + [- anteriorcoronal, -spread glottis, -voice] ➔ ϕ ---- [+ lateral]

There is also a rule for voiceless velar stops deletion before laterals. It is termed as VS-D Rule. This rule says that **k** of **thok** is deleted with the suffixation of the directional suffix **-lək** .

After the application of the V-Rule, the T-Rule applies, as in the following examples :

20.	tho-rək-pə	pha-do-rək-pə
	thok-rək-pə	pha-dok-rək-pə
	out-dirct -NZR	spread-out-dirct -NZR
	'come out'	'spread out'
	pay-tho-rək-pə	thaŋ-do-rək-pə
	fly out dirct-NZR	take out dirct -NZR
	'fly out'	'take out'

However, the VS-D Rule does not apply when the perfect marker **-le** and **-lə** are suffixed to the derivational suffix - **thok**.

This is shown in the following examples

21.	ca-thok-le	ca-thok-lə-gə
	eat -out-pref.	eat-out-pref. -con.
	'has eaten out'	'after having eaten out'
	pu-thok-le	pu-thok-lə-gə
	carry-out-pref.	carry-out-pref. con.
	'has carried out perfect'	'after having carried out'

6.3.5 Gemination Rule

There is also a rule for gemination in this language that is syllable consonants viz. **n~l~m~ω~p~ŋ** when they are followed by a vowel, takes place gemination. This is termed as Gemination Rule (G-Rule).

$$\text{G Rule } \phi \rightarrow \begin{bmatrix} \text{consonantal} \\ \text{-spread glottis} \\ \beta \text{ coronal} \\ \gamma \text{ anterior} \\ \beta \text{ feature} \\ \gamma \text{ anterior} \end{bmatrix} // \begin{bmatrix} \text{+ consonant} \\ \text{- spread glottis} \\ \beta \text{ coronal} \\ \gamma \text{ anterior} \\ \beta \text{ feature} \\ \gamma \text{ anterior} \end{bmatrix} \phi \text{ V}$$

This rule is applied when the simple aspect marker -y, the imperative marker -o and -u or the experiential evidence enclitic -e is suffixed to a verbal root ending with a consonant. Consider the following.

I -i Simple Aspect

19.					
	a.	cen	'run'	cel-li	'runs'
	b.	kəp	'cry'	kəp-pi	'cries'
	c.	coŋ	'jump'	coŋ-ŋi	'jumps'
	d.	təm	'learn'	təm-mi	'learns'
	e.	ləω	'take'	ləω-ωi	'takes'

II -o or -u 'imperative Marker'

yen	'distribute'	yel-lo/lu	'distribute (comd)
keep	'cover'	kup-po/pu	'cover (comd)
thoŋ	'cook'	thoŋ-ŋo/ŋu	'cook (comd)
thəm	'keep'	thəm-mo/mu	' keep (comd)

It should be noted that the Gemination Rule applies in the same environment as the rule of Voicing Assimilation. Thus if the Gemination rule applies first, the Voicing Assimilation rule cannot apply, and if the Voicing Assimilation rule applies first, the Gemination rule cannot apply. In order not to bleed each other, the two rules can be differentiated that the Gemination rule applies to syllable final consonants whereas the Voicing Assimilation rule applies to syllable unit consonants.

6.3.6 k to Glottal Stop Rule (G S-Rule)

k changes into a glottal stop in the environment that when the simple aspect marker -y or the imperative marker -**u** or the experimental enclitic is added to -**rək** 'directional suffix' (did something and came towards the speaker), this is termed as G-S-Rule. Examples are given
10 below:

20 .	ca-lək + i	
	ca-rək -y	thək-lə?-y
	ca-rək-y	thək-lək-y
	eat-dirct.-asp.	drink-dirct-asp.
	'ate and come here'	'drank and came here'

(ii) rək+Imperative Marker /u/

pu-rə?-u	thoŋ-lə?-u
pu-rək-u	thoŋ-lək-u
bring-drict-comd.	cook-dirct-comd.
	'cook it from there'

(iii) rək + Experimental Marker /e/

sa-rə?-e	yek-lə?-e
sa-rək-e	yek-lək -e
make-direct-exp.	paint -dirct-exp.
'made from there'	'painted it from there'

This rule can be entered also to the suffixation of **y**, **u**, **e** to **-thok**, 'out' as in the following examples :

21.	pa - tho?-y	su-do?-u
	pa-thok-asp	su-dok-u
	spill-out-asp.	wash-out-comd
	'spill out'	'wash off'
	cam-tho? -e	pu-tho? -e
		pu-thok-e
	cam-thok -e	'bring -out-exp.
	clean -out-exp	'bring out'
	clean off '	

6.3.7 Lateral Deletion Rule

There is lateral deletion rule also what this rule said is that the lateral l deletes after the voiceless veler stop k.

LD Rule :- l → ϕ /k-

The lateral Deletion rule applies with the affixation of the perfect aspect marker **-lə**, the progressive aspect marker **-li** or the sequential suffix **-ləm** as in the given example. A rule subsequently applies to inter vocalic **k** to change it to glottal stop (see the rule of **k** to Glottal Stop).

22. a. Affixation of perfect aspect lə [< le]

yo?əbə	lo?əbə	ko?əbə
yok-lə-bə	lok-lə-bə	kok-lə-bə
rear-asp.-NZR	harvest-asp.NZR	smear-asp.-NZR
'rear up'	'harvested'	'smearded out'

b. Affixation of sequential suffix

yoʔəmmi	laʔəmmi	soʔəmmi
yok-ləm-mi	lak-ləm-mi	sok-ləm-mi
rear-seql.-asp.	come-seql. -asp.	hurt-seql.-asp.
'reared up'	'came'	hurted'

However, it is worth to note that Lateral Deletion rule cannot apply when the directional **-lək** is suffixed to a verbal stem ending with the suffix **-thok**, as in the following example :

23.	ləŋthoʔləkle	paythoʔləky
	ləŋ-thok-lək-le	pay-thok-lək-y
	throw-out-dirct.-asp.	fly-out-dirct.-asp.
	'thrown out'	'Flown out'

6.3.8 Diphthongnization Rule

A rule of diphthongnization can be created from a vowel sequence

$V_j \rightarrow$ [-syllabic]/V_i-V_j

The diphthongnization rule applies when the simple aspect suffix **-y** or when the imperative marker **-u** or **-ro** is added to a root ending in a vowel.

24.	-y	'simple aspect'		
	u	'see'	uy	'see/s'
	pha	'arrest'	phay	'arrest/s'
	pa	'read'	pay	'read/s'
	ca	'eat'	cay	'eat/s'

-o or -u 'Imperative Marker'

pa	'read'	paω '-o'	'read'(Command)
ca	'eat'	caω 'u'	'eat' (Command)
ka	'climb'	kaω 'climb'	(Command)

The diphthongnization rule too applies when the simple aspect marker **-y** (i) is suffixed to a derivational suffix ending with a vowel as : **lə ~-rə** 'action taken place towards the speaker'. Consider the following examples :

25.	phu-rəy	pha-rəy
	phu-rə-i	pha-rə-i
	beat-dirct.-asp.	arrest-dirct.-asp.
	'Came and beat'	'came and arrested'
	pul-ləy	si-rəy
	pul-ləy-i	si-rə-i
	bind-dirct.-asp.	die-dirct.-asp.
	'came and bound it there'	'came and died here'

However, the Diphthongnization rule does not apply in the morphological environments where the Glottal Stop insertion rule applies.

In Manipuri, there are phonological rules which apply in certain morphological environments but fail to apply in others. More and above, it has been seen that certain rules need to be ordered with respect to each other : the Deaspiration rule must apply before the Voicing Assimilation rule, and the **k** to Glottal Stop rule must apply before the gemination rule. It has also been shown that there are certain cases, as in the interaction of the Lateral Deletion rule and the Velar Deletion rule, where both rule and the morphological environment must be specified for a correct characterization of the interaction of the rules.

CHAPTER–VII

CLAUSE STRUCTURE

7.1 Clause

It is convenient to begin with the study of Manipuri syntax at the level of the clause, a structure that is relatively independent and therefore, easily isolated. The core of this chapter is an inventory of clause types available in Manipuri. It is first discussed here about Manipuri word order, because this chapter is the introduction to Manipuri syntax.

7.2 Word Order

The vast majority of Tebeto-Burman languages have the basic word order of subject-Object-Verb (SOV) and all the Indian languages except Kashmiri and Khasi have also the same order of SOV. Manipuri has the very same order, SOV, as in the sentence 1.

1. məhak həynəw ca-y
   he mango eat-asp
   'He eats a mango'

The position of the qualifying adjective in relation to noun is that it (adjective) preceedes the noun , as in 2.

2. məhak əcəwbə həynəw ca-y
   he big mango eat-asp.
   'He eats a big mango'

But the numeral follows the noun, as in sentence 3.

3. məhak həynəω məŋa ca-y
   'He eats five mangoes'

Like numerals, qualifiers e.g. **khərə** 'some' **məyam** 'many' **pumnəmək** 'all' etc. follows the noun, as in the sentence 4.

4. əŋaŋ məyam lampak-ta sanə-ri
   child many grond-loc.. play-asp.
   'Many children are playing in the ground'

Demonstrative also follows the noun, as in sentence 5.

5. əy phurit əsi pam-mi
   I shirt this like -asp.
   'I like this shirt'

But adverb proceedes the verb.

Example

6. məhak yamnə yaŋnə cət-li
   he very fast go-asp.
   'He goes very fast'

Typologically, this is an agglutinative language; many suffixes can be added to verbal base. Different types of sentence formation, namely, negation, imperative and yes/no question can be constructed by suffixation of the respective markers to the verb. (see respective chapter for detail discussion). No doubt, this is a postpositional language opposed to prepositioned; all the case markers are suffixed to the noun and to the adverb of place, as in the following sentences

7. əy-gi huy əma ləy
I-gen. dog one have
'I have a dog'

8. layrik ədu tebəl məthək-ta thəm-mú
book that table on -loc keep-com.
'Keep the book on the table'

Notice that these order like demonstratives, numerals, qualifiers and adverbs are rigid while adjective can precede and follow, the normal order is to precede the noun.

7.3 Elements of Clause Structure

It is needed to recognize at least the following functional elements of clause structure in Manipuri; Subject, Direct and Indirect Object, Subject and Object complement, Locative, Temporal, Goal, Source, Benefactive, Verbal, and probably others such as cause, likeness, and comparative. In this language without a VP, all nominal arguments have the same status. The fact is that there is no positive evidence for verb+object constitnent in Manipuri; it may be an interesting typological fact, but it is more likely to be a consequence of sentence constituents rather than a pecularity of their function; evidence for a VP is typically lacking in verb-final languages. There is no morphological markings to indicate that it can be the only argument of an intransitive clause or the agent of a transitive. It is also useful to refer to the constituent that contains a verb head and subordinate elements as a verb phrase, even though it means abandoning the traditional binary constituency of the clause.

7.4 Case Marking

Except for the verb phrase, most of the clause elements have 'case marking' postposition associated with them ; these will be briefly illustrated here, and discussed more fully in case Chapter 5-6. Generally it is found overdifferentiation — different forms associated with a single role or underdifferentiation — a single form associated with several roles. In Manipuri, It is found mainly with the postposition.

Locative -də~tə :

9. phəmuŋ-gi nakən-də ləy-bə tebəl ədu-gi məthək-tə layrik əsi thəm-mu
bed-gen beside-loc.. stay-NZR that-gen. on -loc.. book this keep-comd.
'Keep this book on the table which is beside the bed'

Temporal -də~tə

10. məhak lak-li-bə 2nd Saturday-də London-dəgi thuŋ-lə-gəni
he coming-NZR -loc arrive-dur-asp.
'He is arriving on the coming second Saturday from London'

Goal - də~tə

11. məhak-nə tombə-nə pirək-pə bol ədu gol post-tə phəjə-nə kawsil-li
ne-nom. Tomba-nom. give-dic-NZR that goal post-loc.nice-adj. kick-deic-asp.
'He kicks the ball which is passed by Tomba into the goal post'.

Benefactive -də~tə

12. əy-nə ŋəraŋ ləyrək-pə phurit ədu tomba-də pi-thok-khre

I-nom. Yesterday buy-dic. NZR shirt that Tomba -loc. give-dic-asp.
'I have given to Tomba the shirt which was bought yesterday'

Source -dəgi~təgi :

13. təbəl ədu-gi məthək-tə layrik ədu əy-nə oja-dəgi ləω-rək-pə-ni
table that-gen. on-loc. exist-NZR book that I-nom teacher-abl. take-dir-NZR-cop.
'The book which is on the table is taken from my teacher'

7.5 Order of Clause Elements :

Manipuri consistently 'verb final' in both embedded and unembeded environments. The order of elements before the Verb is free, but certain orderings are much more common. Temporals and locatives tend to be early in the clause, before or immediately after the subject (if present); Adverbial manner (including instrumentals) are generally found directly before the verb.

7.6 Clause Types :

7.6.1 Core Verses Peripheral Elements

It is usual to make a distinction between elements centrally involved in Clause structure — core elements — and those peripherally involved — peripheral elements. Core elements are necessary for the completion of verbal meaning. Subject, objects (DO and IO), complements (SC and OC) and verbs are always core; other elements may be core elements but are usually peripheral. It is the core elements that are diagnostic of the type of clause.

7.6.2 Anaphoric Clauses

In English, and in many languages, the distinction between core and peripheral elements is supported by the grammatical distinction between oligatory and optional. Peripheral elements can be omitted without changing the meaning of the rest of the clause, while omission of a core element either changes the meaning of the remaining clause, or leaves it incomplete (elliptical).

In Manipuri, on the other hand, core elements particularly subject and Object, can be — and certain genres usually are — omitted, leaving the verbal as the only element of clause structure, as in sentence 14.

14. a. (S) həl-lək-ləm-ləgə əmuk cət-khre (....)
return-dic-compt.-du-con again go -def-asp.
'After coming back he again went to somewhere'

b. tum-khre - '(He) has slept'

c. ca-khre
'He has taken'

It is not very enlightening to lump all such clauses together in a clause type composed simply of a verb phrase. Such clauses will be considered tokens of other, filled out, clause types.

7.6.3 Anaphora versus Ellipses

A sentence such as /**niŋsiŋ-li**/ 'remember -asp.= I remeber (it)' is simply a transitive clause with subject and object omitted. It is, in other words, a complete sentence, albeit an anaphoric one. And this is the point : it is not elliptical. For 'elliptical applies to sentences or clauses, in which obligatory elements are omitted (Halliday and Hasan 1976), and elliptical sentences are therefore incomplete sentences. They can occur in situations :

a. Occur as one word answers to questions. These elliptical sentences are very commonly used in conversation.

15. Ques : nəŋ kəydəωŋəy Imphal-də thok-kə-ni
you when - loc.. return-asp.
'When will you go back to Imphal ?'
Ans : həyeŋ 'Tomorrow'
tomorrow

b. Through ellipsis of the main verb in conversation, it is possible to use a subordinate clause without any following finite verb. The elided parts are provided in the translation.

16. phi su- həω-dənə
clothes wash -start +_com. pleo.
'First , wash the clothes (when the sun shines then cook)'

17. cak ca-həω-dənə
rice eat -start + pleo.
'First have your meal (then do that work).

7.6.4 A Note on 'Ambient' Clauses

Subjectless clauses are classified in terms of semantically parallel non-anaphoric clauses that contain explicit central elements. Ambient verbs that predicate 'time of day', or 'state of weather' are usually said to require no arguments in semantic structure. They are verbs that "involve an all - encompassing event which is without reference to some particular 'thing' within the environmrnt" (Chafe 1970, 102). Manipuri has a propensity for subject verbs, those which can be predicated only of the weather, appear in surface structure, with a superficial argument'.

18. a. noŋ ta-ri 'It is raining'
rain fall -asp.

b. noŋ məŋ-ŋi 'It is promising to rain'
rain cloudy-asp.

---

1. Many other languages of Sino-Tibetan family also encode the ambient event as an instransitive clause : Thai / fon tok/'rain falls', / fáa lɛɛp/ 'sky sheet -lightens' ; Chinese / xia yu/ fall rain '(though /yu/ is an object' in Chao's analysis, by virtue of the fact that it follows the verb; no other argument is possible, however). Like Manipuri, Burmese has also prototypically ambient verbs, those which can be predicated only of the weather, appear in surface structure, with a superficial (though usually 'bound') argument, as in sentences 120.

120 a. moú yωa te 'It is raining'
sky rain VM [VM = Verbal marker] (end of the sentence)

b. moú oún te 'It is cloudy'
sky overcast VM.

c. moú hcoún te 'It is thundering'
sky thundery VM.
(Wheatley, 1982, p. 59)

d. noŋ khak-li 'It is thundering'
rain thundering (asp)

19. a. nuŋsa thok-le 'It is sunny'
sunlight come out-asp.

b. nuŋsa say 'It is hot'
sunlight hot-asp.

7.6.5 Intransitive Clauses

Clauses without object or (SBJ- or OBJ-) complement are Intransitive. By this definition, it encompasses containing intransitive verbs with obligatory 'adverbial components such as inner locative or goal, ablative or manner adverbial, as well as a special subtype, the 'possessive/existential' clause.

7.6.5.1. Ordinary Intransitive : (S) V

Ordinary intransitives are of two main types stative containing a verb with stative meaning and Dynamic, containing an action or process verb.

a. Stative

20. a. yum əsi caw-wi
house this big-asp. 'This house is big'

b. ləyrək ədu khuy-y 'That lane is narrow'
lane that narrow-asp.

c. məhak phəjəy ' She is nice'
she nice -asp.

b. Dynamic

21. a. ənaŋ ədu tum-li 'The baby is sleeping'
kid that sleep-asp.

b. ucek məyam pay-ri 'Many birds are flying'
bird many fly-asp.

c. thoybi cət-khre 'Thoibi has gone'
Thoibi go-def+ asp.

7. 6.5.2 Intransitive with Obligatory Adverbial Arguments

Verbs involving existence or physical orientation of animates (lives, die, stand, sit, lie etc.) and temporary adverbial take inner locatives as arguments :

22. a. əy imphal-də ləy 'I live in Imphal'
I Imphal-loc.. live

b. məhak ləymay-də phəm-mi
he floor-loc.. sit - asp.
'He sits on the floor'

c. məhak iray-də pok-y
he Friday - loc.. born -asp.
'He is born on Friday'

7.6.6 Transitive Clauses

Clauses containing an object are transitive. Transitive clauses can be furher subdivided into Mono- transitive: containing a single object and no complement; Ditransitive : containing two objects, one direct and one indirect, and Complete transitive, containing an object and an object complement.

6.1 Monotransitive Clauses : (S) (O) V

Various combinations of semantic roles are possible :

1. Agent and affected entity (i.e. patient or experiencer) :

23. a. məkhoy-nə səmbəl thuthek-y
they - nom. fench break-asp.
'They break the fench'

b. məhak-nə upu-du thəmbədə məteŋ paŋ-ŋi
he-nom. bos-det. keep-loc.. help help -asp.
'He helps to put the almirah'

c. thoybi-nə khəmbə sok-y
Thoibi-nom. Khamba touch-asp
'Thoibi touches Khamba'

2. Agent and effected entity (result) :

24. a. məkhoy-nə ənəωbə laybreri say
they-nom. new library build-asp.
'They build new library.'

b. məhak-nə ənəωbə layrik əma i-re
he- nom. new book one write-asp.
'He has written a new book'

c. məkhoy-nə khəmbə -thoybi-gi jəgoy say
they-nom. Khamba - Thoibi - gen. dance make-asp.
'They dance Khamba-Thoibi dance'

3. Affected entity (=experiencer) and goal

25.. a. məhak-nə tomba pam-mi
she-nom. Tomba like-asp
'She likes Tomba'

b. caksəŋ hek cəŋlək-pə-də ŋa thoŋbə-gi mənəm nəm-mi
kichen just enter-dir - NZR-loc.. fish cook-NZR-gen smell smell-asp.
'Just when (I) enter I got the smell of fish cooking'

7.6.6.2 Ditransitive : S (IO) (DO) V

Ditransitive clauses contain two objects — an indirect and a direct — in that order usually. However, direct object can precede also. Indirect Object can have accusative marker and locative marker.

26. məhak-nə tombə-də layrik əma pi
he -nom. Tomba-loc.. book one give-asp.
'He gives a book to Tomba'

The verb like **pi** 'give' (e.g. sentence 26), **thəm** 'keep' **ut** 'show', **təmbi** 'teach' etc. generally occur in ditransitive clause. (See 'case role' also in Case).

7.7 Complex Sentence

A sentence containing at least a matrix clause and other subordinate clauses is termed as complex clause or complex sentence.

7.7.1 Subordinate Clause

Subordinate clause is an dependent clause; it occurs with matrix clause (independent clause). How they do occur in a sentence is done by means of relativization (see Relativization):

7.7.1.1 Types of Subordinate Clause :

On the basis of their grammatical function in a structure, they can be broadly classified into three : (a) Noun clause (b) Adjective clause and (c) Adverb clause.

7.7.1.1.1 Noun Clause

In a noun clause formation, generally there is a factive element **haybə**, as in the following examples ;

As a Subject :

27. a. məhak sanəri haybə cum-mi
he play-asp fact true-asp.
'That he is playing is true'

b. məhak -nə ŋəsi ənabə-siŋ yeŋ-lə-roy haybə -du phə-te
he -nom. today patient-pl. see-dur-neg. fact -det. good -neg.
'That he will not see the patients today is not good'

Here **cum-mi** 'true+ asp' and **phət-te** 'good+ neg. + asp' are the verbs of the subjects **məhak sannə-ri haybə** 'that he is playing and **məhak-nə ŋəsi ənabə-siŋ yeŋ-lə-roy hay-bə-du** 'that he will not see the patients respectively'.

As an object :

Here, as an object, the factive element **haybə** is optional, as in sentence 28.

28. məhak lak-ye hay-bə əy khəŋ-ŋi
he come-asp. fact. I know-asp.
'I know that he has come'

Here **məhak lak-y hay-bə** is functioning as an object of the verb **khəŋ-ŋi** know-asp'.

7.7.1.1.2 Adjective Clause :

More detail can be seen in Relativization. Some examples are given below :

29. a. məhak lak-le hay-bə paω ədu yamnə nuŋŋay
he come-asp fact. news that very enjoy-asp.
'The news that he has come is very enjoyable'

b. əy-nə ibə layrik ədu miyam-nə pam-nəy
I-nom. write -NZR that people-nom. like-asp.
'The book that I wrote is liked by the people'

In the sentence 29(a), **məhak lak-le hay-bə** qualities the noun **paω** 'news' and in the same way **əy-nə i-bə** qualifies the noun **layrik** 'book'.

7.7.1.1.3 Adverb Clause

In adverb clause formation a non-factive element **haynə** is used, as in the following sentences :

30 a. məhak yamnə kənnə cət-li haynə əyŋon-də təm-mi
he very strong go -asp. non-fact. me -loc. inform-asp.
'I am told in this way he went very strongly (very actively)

b. məhak yamnə phəjə-nə ca-ri haybə əy tay
he very nicely eat-asp. non-fact. I hear
'I hear in this way that he eats well'

Adverb clause can have three types under semantic classification. They are (a) causal clause (b) conditional clause and (c) permissive clause. One interesting point is that in these types of clauses the non -factive element **haynə** is not used.

(a) Causal Clause :

31 a. məhak məsa ŋəm-dəbə mərəm-nə ŋəsi skul ka-rə-roy
he health able-neg. -NZR since -adv. today school go-dur-neg.
'since he is ill , he will not go to school today'

b. cabə phəbə-nə əŋaŋ ədu yamnə caω-re
eat-NZR good-Adv. baby that very grow-asp.
'As the baby eats well so the growth is fast.'

Notice that the adverb marker **-nə** is suffixed to **mərəm** 'cause' (since) in sentence 31 (a) and **phəbə** 'good' in 31 (b). It is also possible that without the lexical item **mərəm** (i.e. a connector) by addition of adverb marker-**nə** to the verbal noun causal clause can be constructed, as in sentence 32.

32. məhak məsa ŋəm-dəbə-nə ŋəsi skul ka-rə-roy
'since he is ill, he will not go to school today'

(b) Conditional Clause :

33 a. tombə lak-lə-bə-di nəŋ cət-pə ya-ni
Tomba come-Det-NZR-cond. you go-NZR allow-asp.
'If Tomba comes you can go'

b. nəŋ parikha-də məkok oyrə-bə-di ghəri ləy-bi-ni
you exam-loc.. first be -NZR -cond. watch buy - cop.
'If you top the exam I will buy a watch for you'

Here, in these two conditional clauses, it is seen a conditional marker **-di** (homophonous to morpheme particularization) is suffixed to the verbal nominals **lak-lə-bə-** (lak-lə-bə-di) in 33 (a) and **oyrə-bə-(oyrəbə-di)** in 33 (b).

(c) Permissive clause :

34. a. nəŋ-nə pam-bə məkhəy ləy-yu
you-nom. want -NZR thing -pl. that buy-comd.mk.
'Buy whatever you want'

b. nəŋ-nə ca-niŋ-bə məkhəy ca-ro
you-nom. eat-want-NZR all eat -comd.mk.
'Eat whatever you want'

In these clauses , only the verb (of the subordinate clause) i.e. **pam**- 'want' in 34 (a) and **ca-niŋ**- 'want to eat' in 34 (b) are nominalized by suffixing a nominalizing marker **-bə/-pə**. Thus formed the permissive clause in this language.

7.8 Coordinate Clause

It is a syntactic structure in which two or more members which are equivalent as to grammatical function are joined ('conjoined') in such a way that each of them has an equal claim to be considered a head of that structure. In Manipuri, they are joined, for example, by **əmasuŋ** 'and', **nətrəgə** 'or', **təωwigumbəsuŋ** 'but' **ədubu** 'but' **ədum** oynəmək 'however' etc. The examples are given below :

əmasuŋ 'and' :

35. tombə yum-gi thəbək-su təωωi əmasuŋ layrik-su yamnə pay
Tomba house-gen. work-gen. work-also do-asp. and book -also very read-asp.
'Tomba does domestic works and reads his lessons very well'

nətrəgə ' or' :

36. nəŋ kasi-də ləygə-dra nətrəgə məpan-də cen-gə-dra
you room-dem.-loc.. stay -pot-Q or outsude-loc.. run -pot-Q.
'Will you saty in this room or will you run outside ?'

təωwigumbəsuŋ or ədubu 'but':

37. məhak məsək-ti phəjəy ədubu drama-di həy-te
she face-part nice but drama-part. good-neg.
'She is nice but not good in drama'

ədum oynəmək 'however' :

38. məsi məphəm pumnəmək-tə sijin-nəbə yay ədum oynəmək mətaŋ əsi-də sijin-nəbə-nə yan-nə ca-nəy
this place all -loc.. use-NZR allow however. situation here-loc.. use-NZR-adv very appropriate-asp.

'This can be used in all situations, however, this is more appropriate to use in this particular context.'

CHAPTER–VIII
SENTENCE PROCESSES

8.1 Negation

There are two types of negative formation that appears in many languages. One of these is formed by verbal modifiers such as **not, never, hardly** etc., in English and **nai** in Japanese. Such negative formation is called sentential negation. The other type of negative makes use of negative prefixes such as **in-, dis-, un-, im-** in English and **hi-, hu-, mu-,** etc. in Japanese. This is called affixial negation. In Burmese sentences are negated by attaching the negative morpheme **ma-** to the head verb. In Manipuri, negative is formed by suffixation of negative markers, viz, **-te˜-de, -loy˜-roy** to the verb, as in sentence (1) and (2) {a^S are affirmative sentences while b^S are negative sentences}

1 a. məhak yu thək-y
he liquor drink-asp
'He drinks liquor'

b. məhak yu thək-te
'He does not drink liquor'

2 a. əy ŋəsi sinema yeŋ-gəni
I today film see-asp
'I will see film today'

b. əy ŋəsi sinema yeŋ-loy
'I will not see film today'

8.1.2 Negative Markers

In Manipuri ,there are five negative markers. They are given in the followings :

1. **-te~-de** used in realised aspect/non-future.
2. **-loy~roy** used in unrealised aspect/future.
3. **-kum~gum** used in let' negative
4. **- nu** used in prohibitive sentence
5. **nətte** is a lexicalized negator

They are discussed one by one in the followings

1. -te~-de

This marker is the combination of negative as well as aspect (of realised) and it is also used in expressing habitual sense (**-te** occurs after voiceless consonants while **-de** after vowels and voiced consonants) as in (3) and (4).

3. məhak ŋəraŋ skul cət-te
he yesterday school go-neg.
'Yesterday he did not go to school'

4. əy səyreŋ pa-de
I poem read-neg.
'I did not read poem.'

2. -roy~loy ~moy~poy~›oy[1]

This negative marker carries the meaning of futurity and used generally in unrealised aspect, as in (5) and (6).

5. tombš hšye› skul cšt-loy
Tomba tomorrow school go-neg.
'Tomorrow tomba will not go to school'

6. šy sa ca-roy
I meat eat-neg.
'I will not eat meat'

3. -kum ~ -gum

It is used in 'let' negative (or is a 'let' negative marker) and occurs phonologically, i.e. **-kum** occurs after voiceless consonants while **-gum-** after vowels and voiced consonants. This marker has to occur with a proposal (suggestive) suffix **-si**, otherwise the particular sentence is incomplete. Consider the following examples [aS are affirmatives, bS negatives]

7. a. šykhoy šwa›bš ci›-si ka-si
we high mountain -det climb-sug.
'Let us climb this high mountain'

b. šykhoy šw›abš ci›-si ka-gum-si
'let us no climb this high mountain'

8. a. šykhoy yu - thšk-si
we liquor drink-sug.
'Let us drink liquor'

b. šykhoy yu thšk-kum-si
'Let us not drink liquor'

9* šykhoy yu thšk-kum- (Incomplete)

4. -nu

This suffix is used in prohibitive sentence as in sentence 9.

9. nš› layrik-tu pa-nu
you book-det. read-proh.mk.
'Don't read that book'

This marker **-nu** can occur with the suggestive suffix **-si** then expresses the meaning of **-kumsi ~ gumsi** (i.e. the meaning of 'let' negative), as in the sentence 10 and 11.

---

1. They are allomorphs and occur in the following phonological conditions :
-roy after vowel : **ca** 'eat' **ca-roy** 'will not eat'
-loy after consonants : **cšt** 'go' **cšt-loy** 'will not go'
-moy after **m** : tum 'sleep' **tum-moy** 'will not sleep'
-poy after **p** : **kšp** 'cry' **kšp-poy** 'will not cry'
- ›oy after **›** : **tho›** 'cook' **tho›-›oy** 'will not cook'
-oy after **k** : **thšk** 'drink' **thšk-oy /loy** 'will not drink'

10. məphm-du-də cət-nu-si
place -det.-loc. go-proh-sug.
'Let us not go to that place'

11. məphəm-du-də cət-kum-si
'Let us not go to that place'

5. The Lexicalized Negator nətte

Various languages of the world, namely Tongan, Fijian, Maori (of Laninesian), Dieguens, Majave (of Yunan languages), Evenki (of Siberian group of Tungus family), Nenets, Nganasan (of Samoyrdic languages), Erzja (of Mordvin languages), Udmurt, Komi-Zyrain and Komi-Permjak (of Permic languages) and dialects of Lappish, Estonian, Livonian, Veps, have negative verb or auxiliary verb or as both.

Like these languages, Manipuri has negative verb functioning as **a** higher verb. This lexicalized negator nətte[1] is a negative form of copula verb **-ni** which strictly occurs in the sentence final position functioning as a linking verb in equative sentences of identification (12) class membership (13) and class inclusion (14).

12 a. məhak tomba-ni
he Tomba-be
'He is Tomba'

b. məhak tomba nətte
'He is not Tomba'

13 a. memi oja-ni
Memi teacher-be
'Memi is a teacher'

b. memi oja nətte
'Memi is not a teacher'

14 a. məhak məpa əma-ni
he father one -be
'He is a father'
(He has the quality of being a father)

b. məhak məpa əma nətte
'He is not a father'
(He has no quality of being a father)

---

1. **nətte** can be analysed as in the following :
By addition of the negative marker **-te** to copula verb **-ni** some phonological changes have occurred
1st. Step : i of **-ni**➔ə[under the phonological rule i.e. high front vowel followed by mid high becomes a central vowel i.e. i➔ə]
2nd Step Consonant t geminates
nət-
3rd step : ➔ **nətte**
nətte differs grammatically from **-ni** , **nətte** becomes a lexical item while **-ni** is a suffix.

On one hand, the negator **nətte** can be treated as a negative verb on the basis of Pyne's definition. i.e. "a negative verb always has at least some of the properties of regular verbs, such as occurrence with a verbal complementizer, or inflection for mood, tense aspect, person or number" (Pyne 1985, 207). This negator has two more aspects — progressive and perfect — as in (15) and (16) respectively.

15. əy ophis cət-pə nəttri (nət-tə-ri)
    I office go-NZR neg-be + prog. asp.
    'I am not going to office right at the moment'
    (Now I am not going office, I am going to meet a friend)

Other than this, like 'No' in English, **nətte** can function as a free negative, reply to a question, as in the following sentence.

16. a. nəŋ-nə pambə phurit-tu əsi-ra
       you-nom like-nom shirt-det. this-qmk
       'Is this the shirt that you like?'
    b. nətte 'No'

8.1.3 Negative Strengthening and Negative Polarity

Jespersen (1917:4) mentioned that generally negative is strengthened through some additional words. But in Manipuri, negation is strengthened by the addition of a prefix **suk-** which is prefixed to the verb. This prefix has two grammatical properties : (1) it is restricted to occur in a negative environment only that is why it is treated as a negative polarity item (NPI)[1], (2) by this prefixation the root (of the verb) is forced to reduplicate (i.e. the root thək 'drink' is reduplicated as in sentence (19) otherwise the sentence is ungrammatical.

18. əy yu thək-loy
    I liquor drink -neg.
    'I will not drink liquor'

19. əy yu suk-thək thək-loy
    'I will not drink liquor at all'

20. *a. əy yu suk-thək-loy
    *b *əy yu suk-thək thək-kəni

Sentence 20 (a) and (b) are ungrammatical because (a) the verb root is not reduplicated and (b) **suk-** cannot occur in positive environment.

Other NPI are words, e.g. **kərimətə** 'nothing', **kənasu~kənamətə** 'none' (no one), **kəydəwŋəydəsu** 'never' and **kədaydəsu** 'no where'. Here reduplication is not the question. Consider the following sentences.

21. tomba kərimətə ca-de
    Tomba nothing eat-neg.
    'Tomba eats nothing' '(Tomba does not eat anything)'

---

1. The term 'Negative Polarity Item (NPI) is used by Buyssens (1959), Klima (1964) and Baker (1970).

22. kənasu / kənaməta lan pam-de
no one war like-neg.
'No one likes war'

23. kədaydəsu məhak-kumba mi phəŋ-loy
nowhere he like person get-neg.
'In no where you cannot get such a person like him'

24. məhak kəydəωŋəydəsu kani ca-de
he never opium eat-neg.
'He never takes opium'

8.1.4 Non-overtly Negative Environments

There are three non-overtly negative environments found in this language. They are : (i) Conditional clauses (if you see any one) and questions (does she like him at all?) specially rhetorical questions (who would lift a finger for you?) all of which are compatible with (if not only with) the turrth of the corresponding negative (see sentences 25), (ii) Comparatives and equatives (better than ever, as good as anyone) which contain an implicit negative (see sentence 26), and (iii) negative incorporated adverbs and adjectives with or without negative morphology (never, not many, none, few, seldom, rarely, impossible, hard etc.) (see sentence 27).

1. Conditional

25 a. nəŋ-nə -bu thibə phəŋŋəbə-di ləω
you-nom-acc. search get -if take -com
'If you get it in searching take it'

b. ma-nə-bu nəŋ nuŋsi-bro
he - nom. acc. you love-qmk.
'Does she love you?'

c. kəna-nə məhak-kidəmək leppi-gəni
who-nom he for stand -asp.
'Who will stand for him'

2. Comparative and Equatives

26. məhak-kum-nə pukcel seŋbə mi phəŋ-gə-dra
he -like-top. honest person find -asp-q.mk.
'Can you find an honest person like him?'

3. Negative Incorporated

27. sa-si yam-nə kən-khre
meat-det very hard-def-asp
'The meat is too hard' (it cannot be chewed)

Noted that there is no negative element in the respective sentences but they express negative sense. On the contrary, there are sentences with double occurrence of negative markers expressing weaker meaning.

8.1.5 Double Negation

In mathematics and algebra, there is a principle or formula that two negatives become a positive. But language is not mathematics. What can be applied to mathematics cannot be applied to language. Whenever two negatives really refers to the same idea or word the result is invariably positive. However, the negative donot exactly cancel each other : the longer expression is always weaker. In this language, double negation is used preferably in literary expression (the two sentences (28) and (29) are quoted from songs).

28. əy-di isəy sək-lə-roy khəl-luy ya-de
I -det song sing-dur.-neg think-asp can-neg
'I decided not to sing anymore but I cannot do so'

29. khəl-lə-roy ŋəm-de pubə wa-re
think-dur-neg can-neg. bear - NZR. sad-asp
'I am unable not to think on but felt very sad'

There is another type of construction of double negation in this language. That is the 'Aspect - less' negative morpheme (neg.M) **-tə-~də-** occurs along with other negative markers **-te- ~ -de** occurs only in the morphological negation. (This will be discussed in the morphological section). Consider the following sentences.

30. meri cak ca-də-nə skul cət-te
Mary meal eat -neg.-adv school go-neg.
'Mary does not go to school without having meal'

31. thəω-dəbə thaŋ-nə yanbə ya-roy
sharp neg. NZR dagger-inst. cut be-neg.
'The unsharp dagger cannot cut it'
(It is not possible to be cut by unsharp dagger)

Notice that the negative markers **-te** and **-roy** in sentence (30) and (31) is suffixed to the verbal root respectively while the negative morpheme **-də-** occurs in different word class, i.e. the word **ca-də-nə** in sentence (30) functions as adverb to the verb **cət-te** whereas the word **thəω-də-bə** functions as adjective qualifying the noun **thaŋ-**. Now it is learnt that there are two types of double negative constructions.

The third type of double negation is formed by the occurrence of the negative morpheme **-tə ~ -də** along with the lexicalized negator **nətte**, as in the following examples :

32. nuŋsi-də-bə nətte nəŋbu kərəmnə haysi-ge nəŋon-də
love-neg.-NZR neg. you-acc how say-sug-inst you-loc.
How I have to say you it is not that I did not love you?

33. niŋsiŋ-də-bə nətte əy nəŋ-nə haykhibə pumnəmək
remember neg. -NZR neg I you -neg say-def-NZR all
'It is not that I did not remember all what you said to me'

8.1.6 Morphological Negation

Morphological negation occurs whenever the negative morpheme must be considered to form part of the derivational morphology of the verb. In Manipuri, morphological negation occurs in noun, adjective and adverb which are categorized by their respective functions. The negative suffix **-te~-de** umlauts to **-tə~-də** in the morphological negatives.

Illustrations are given here :

I. [Root + tə/də + NZR-bə]

Root neg. morpheme Nominalizer

ca -də-bə 'Not to eat'
thək-tə-bə 'not to drink'
phu-də-bə 'not to beat'
lot-tə-bə 'not to hide'

II. [Rook + roy/loy+də + Nominalizer]

Root Neg. Mk specified mk. norminalizer

ca- roy - də -bə 'not to eat' (pointing out)
pa-roy-də-bə 'not to read' (pointing out)
cət-loy-də-bə ' not to go' (pointing out)
sil-loy-də-bə 'not to copy (pointing out)

III. [Root + tə/də + Adv.mk] Adverb

Root Neg. Marker Adv. mk

thək-tə-nə 'without drinking'
pa-də-nə 'without reading'
i-də-nə 'without writing'
khəŋ-də-nə 'without knowing'

b. Root + together + tə/də +nə

pa-minnə-də-nə 'without reading together'
ləy-minnə-də-nə 'without staying together'
sa-minnə-də-nə 'without playing together'

c. Root + Causative + tə/də+nə

tum-hən-də-nə 'without making (some one) sleep'
ca-hən-də-nə 'without feeding (some one)'
yeŋ-hən-də-nə 'without making (some one) see'

8.1.7 Formation of Opposite Words by tə/də

English has some prefixes for making opposite forms, for instances, un-, in-, in-, dis- etc. In Manipuri, opposite words can be formed by affixation i.e. by suffixation of the negative morpheme -tə/də. Consider the following set of example.

lu-bə lu-də-bə
'clean,' 'unclean'
poŋ-bə poŋ-də-bə
'proud' 'not proud'
ya-bə ya-də-bə

'accept'	'unaccept'
thoy-bə	thoy-də-bə
'win'	'not win'
waŋ-bə	waŋ-də-bə
'tall'	'not tall' (short)
ŋəω-bə	ŋəω-də-bə
'white'	'not white'
yaŋ-bə	yaŋ-də-bə
'fast'	'slow'

In case the opposite is formed from the adjective then the adjective marker prefix ə- is deleted, otherwise it is ungrammatical.

Consider the set of examples.

əphəbə	phət-tə-bə
'good'	'bad'
əωaŋbə	ωəŋ-də-bə
'tall'	'short'
əpak-pə	pak-tə-bə
'wide'	'not wide'
əŋəωbə	ŋəω-də-bə
'white'	'not white'

It is learnt that Manipuri has two strategies for negative formation - affixal and sentential negation. Double negation is frequently used in literary expression and also in day today expression.

INTERROGATIVE

8.2 Interrogative Sentences

8.2.1 Interrogative Features

Interrogative features of natural languages can be classified into three groups : Intonation, Order and Segmental elements. They are discussed one by one in the followings :

1. Intonation-which includes sentences and tag intonation as well as particle and interrogative word accent (rising pitch in declarative sentence).
2. Order - Which includes main constituent, inversion, positional relationship of affix to stem and of tag, Q -particle or Q-word to clause constituent.
3. Segmental elements - Which include interrogative particle (and affixes), words and tags.
4. Interrogative gesture (eyebrow lifted, head inclined forward etc).

In Manipuri, interrogative features can be classified in the following ways :

I. Intonation - Yes/No questin in Manipuri can be formed by raising the intonation;

II. Q-particle suffixation -Yes/No question is generally formed by suffixation of Q-marker;

III. Q-word- Wh-question is generally formed by using Wh-question words, and

IV Tag-question-Yes/No question can also be possible by sentence - final tag question.

8.2.2 Kinds of Interrogatives

There are basically two kinds of interrogatives: Yes/No question and inquiry question generally known as Wh-question.

8.2.2.1 Yes/No Question

It is said that in Yes/No question, the speaker seeks confirmation of the entire content of the questioned sentence. In Manipuri, inversion of word order is not a strategy for the formation of Yes/No question ; there are two strategies for the indication of Yes/No question a) by rising intonation and (b) by addition of Yes/No question suffix to the verb in the infinitive form. They are discussed below.

a. By rising intonation

Any assertive sentence can become an Yes/No question sentence and can become an Yes/No question by rising intonation, as in the following sentences :

1 a. nəŋ layrik-tu pa-re
you book-det. read-asp.
'You have read the book ?'
(Have you read the book?)

b. əŋaŋ-du para pha-re-ko
child-det. lesson know-asp-pleo.
'The child has understood his lesson?'
(Has the child understood his lesson?)'

8.2.2.1.1 Yes/No Question Suffixes

It has two separate suffixes **ra~la** and **-dra~tra** . They are used in different aspects. That is suffix **ra~la** is used in simple aspects, progressive aspect and perfect aspect while the other suffix **-dra** is used in unrealized aspect.

a. Yes/No Question Suffix -ra~ -la

The second strategy for the formation of Yes/No question is the addition of the question suffix **-ra~ -la** to the nominal (derived from the verb).

To form Yes/No question of simple aspect (of habitual meaning), the aspect marker **y** will be deleted, then the noninalizer suffix **-bə/-pə** will be added to the verbal root and the yes/No question suffix **-ra~ -la** wil be added, as in the following illustration.

2. məhak yu thak-y
he liquor drink -asp (simple)
'He drinks liquor'
First, By deletion rule, the aspect suffix **-y** is deleted

a. məhak yu thək-
Second, By addition rule , the nominalizer suffix **-bə~pə** is added;

b. məhak yu thək-pə
Third, By addition rule, the Yes/No question suffix -ra~-la is added

c. məhak yu thək-pa-ra [pə+ra> pra]
'Does he drink liquor?'

But in the case of progressive and perfect aspects the deletion rule of thee aspect respectively is not applicable. To form Yes/No question of progressive aspect (suffix **-li ~li** and the nominalizer suffix **bə~pə** are added then the Yes/No question suffix is added, as in the following example.

3 a. məhak ca thək-li-bə-ra[bə+ra> bra]
'Is he drinking tea?'

b. məkhoy layrik pa-ri--bə-ra[bra]
they book read-asp-NZR. -Q.
'Are they reading books?'

It is said already, deletion of perfect aspect marker (**re~le**) is not necessary, i.e. **e** of **re~le** should be change into ə, then addition of nominalizer suffix **bə~pə** and the Yes/No question suffix **ra~la** is added, as in te following illustrations.

4. a. məhak ca thək-lə-bə-ra/[bra]
'Has he taken tea"

b. məkhoy layrik pa-bə-ra/[bra]
'Have they read their books?'

The Yes/No question sufix **-ra~la** is also discussed in the Verb 'be' (9.1.1) also as interrogative verb 'be' form and has the grammatical property of direct addition to the noun, even to propernoun, pronoun etc. (functioning as a verb 'be') as in the following sentences. (For detail see Verb 'be')

5. a. məsi ŋa-ra
this fish-qmk.
'Is this a fish?'

b. məhak məri-ra
He/She mary-q.mk.
'Is she Mary?'

c. ŋəraŋ lak-pə-du nəŋ-la
yesterday come-NZR-det. you-Q.mk.
'Are you the person came yesterday?'

Now it is seen that the yes/no question suffix **ra~la** is functioning as verb 'be' i.e. its suffixation to noun **ŋa** 'fish' in 4 (a), to propernoun Mary in 4 (b) and to pronoun **nəŋ** 'you in 4 (c)'.

b. Yes/No Question Suffix -dra~tra

The last strategy for the formation of the Yes/No question of unrealized aspect (irrealis) is the addition of the Yes/No suffix **dra~tra**, as in the following sentences :

6. a. nəkhoy imphal-də cət-kə-dra
you (pl) Imphal-loc. go-asp-q.mk.
'Will you go to Imphal ?'

b. nəŋ manipuri təm-gə-dra
you (s) Manipuri learn-asp-q.mk
'Will you learn Manipuri?'

8.2.2.2 Inquiry Question or Wh-question

In inquiry or wh-question, yes/no question suffixes do not occur at all. The wh-question words, in this language, are **kəri** 'what', **kəri** or **kərəmbə** 'which', **kəna** 'who', **kərigi** 'why', **kədaydə** 'where', **kəydəwŋəy** 'when', and **kərəmnə** 'how' (**kəya** 'how many').

7. a. nəŋ kəri pam-mi
   you what want-asp.
   'What do you want?'

   b. nəŋ kərəmbə/kəri isəy taniŋ-ŋi
   you which song hear-want-asp.
   'Which song do you want to listen?'

   c. kəna manipuri təm-gəni
   who Manipuri learn-asp
   'Who will learn Manipuri ?'

   d. nəŋ kərigi manipuri grammar iri-no
   you why Manipuri grammar write-asp-wh q.mk.
   'Why are you writing Manipuri grammar ?'

   e. nəkhoy kəday-də əmuk cət-kəni
   you(pl) where again go-asp
   'Where will you go again ?'

   f. nəkhoi kəydəwŋəy əmuk cət-kəni
   'when will you go again ?'

   g. nəŋ kərəmnə grammar əsi i-khi
   you how grammar this write-def.
   'How did you write this grammar ?'

   h. nəŋ kəya yamnə layrik pakhi
   you how many book read-asp.
   'How many books did you read books ?'

8.2.2.2.1 Question Suffix -no (Ineterrogative Verb 'be')

In wh-question, there is a suffix **-no** which is also treated as Interrogative verb 'be'. It has three grammatical properties a) addition to wh-question words b) addition to noun and c) addition to verb.

a) Addition to the wh-question Words

8. mədu [kəri 'what' / kəna 'who' / kərəmnə 'how' / kərigi 'why' / kədəydə 'where' / kəya 'how much'] + no
   that

kəri 'what'	'what is that' ?
kəna ' who'	'who is that' ?
kərəmnə ' how'	'which one is that' ?
kərigi 'why'	'why is that' ?
kədəydə 'where'	'where is that' ?
kəya ' how much'	'how much is that' ? etc.

b) Addition to the Noun

One very interesting point here is that **-no** functions as an iterrogative verb 'be'. Like this when the suffix -no is added to any noun e.g. book, Tomba, dog etc, it functions as an interrogative verb 'be', as in the following sentences :

9. a. nəŋ-nə pa-ri-bə layrik ədu kəri layrik-no
you-nom. read-asp-NZR. book that which book -be
'Which is the book that you are reading ?'
'(The book which is reading by you is which book)?'

b. kərəmbə huy-nə-no tomba-də cik-pə-ədu
which dog-nom-be Tomba -det. bite-NZR-that
'Which is the dog that bites Tomba'

c. məhak kərəmbə tombə-no
he which Tomba-be
'Which Tomba is he ?'

c) Addition to the Verb (Optional)

But when the suffix **-no** is added to the verb, it does not function as an interrogative verb 'be'; it is very much optional, as the following sentences

10. a. nəŋ kəri layrik pa-ri
you which book read-
'Which book are you reading ?'

b. nəŋ kəri layrik pa-ri-no
'Which book are you reading ?'

8.2.2.2.2 Wh-question Words as a Sentence

Without any addition to the wh-question words, they can be a sentence in the running discourse.

Example

11. a. kəri 'what is ?'
b. kəna 'who is ?'
c. kərəmbə 'which one ?'
d. kəday 'where ?'
e. kəydəωŋəy 'when ?'
f. kərəmnə 'how ?'
g. kəya 'how much/many ?'

8.2.2.2.3 Reduplication of wh-question Words :

Reduplication is very common in Manipuri ; it is widely available in the realm of verb, adjective, adverb, noun and pronoun. (see detail in the chapter, Reduplication). Besides these, reduplication is also found in all the wh-question words except the two wh-question words viz. **kəydəωŋəω** 'when' and **kərəmnə** 'how' they indicate pulural meaning. They are given below :

12. a. nəŋ kəri kəri pam-mi
you what what want-asp
'What do you want?'
(What are the things you want ?)

b. nəŋ kərəm kərəmbə ləy pam-mi
you which which flower want -asp
'Which flowers do you want ?'

c. nəŋ kəna kəna pam-mi

'Who do you want ?'
(Who are the persons you want ?)

d. suti-də nəŋ kəday kəday-də cət-kəni
holiday-loc. you where where go-asp
'Where will you go in the holiday ?'
(What are the places you are going in the holiday?)

e. klas əmaməm-də əŋaŋ kəya kəya lak-y
class each-loc. child how how many come -asp.
'How many children are coming in each class?'

8.2.3 Different Types of Question

8.2.3.1 Echo Question

Echo questions are questions used to confirm part of the interlocutor's preceding conversational turn, either because that previous turn was not heard, or the person asking the echo question believes that he may have misheard part of it or because what he heard is incoherent or surprising. In this language, there are two kinds of echo questions.

The first is response to a statement, and takes the basic form of the statement and repeats more of the constituents of that statement or repetition of the whole statement plus a new word **haybə** 'to say' or addition of question suffix **ra**, i.e. haybə-ra (the extended meaning of 'to say') as in the following sentences 12b.

13. a. ŋa əsi lupa 100 pi
fish this rupee 100 cost
'This fish costs hundred rupees'

b. ŋa əsi lupa 100 pi haybə.[haybə-ra]
'Is this fish cost one hundred rupees ?'

The second type of echo question is in response to a preceding question (Yes/No and wh-question), and the person asking the echo question seeks confirmation that he has correctly heard the original question (in practice many individuals use this as a stalling device to gain time to work out their answer). Both the questions (Yes/No and Wh-question) can be formed echo question by repeating the same question plus a word **haybə** or **haybə-ra**, as in

14. ŋa ədu kilo kəya-no haybə[haybə-ra]
fish that kg. how much-be
'How much kg. is that fish'
'Are you asking me how much kg. is that fish)

15. əy iroybə həybə-ra hay-bə-ra
I swimming know-Q. mk. say NZR -Q. mk.
'Are you asking me that I know swimming ?'

8.2.3.2 Rhetorical Questions

A rhetorical question has the form of a question (Yes/No or Wh-question) but its intent is that of a statement with the opposition polarity. This can be illustrated clearly with general questions :

16. əy nəŋon-də wari-si hay-də-bə-ra
I you-loc. story-det. say-neg-NZR -Q.mk.
'Didn't I tell you the story'

In this sentence (15), the intent is to say that 'I did tell you the story already' i.e. roughly equivalent to English 'I told you so'.

With wh-questions, a positive question has the effect of a sentence where the interrogative word is replaced by 'no one' while a negative question has the effect of a sentence where the interrogative word is replaced by 'everyone', as in sentence (16).

17. kəna inakkhunbə pam-də-bə-ge
Who to be rich like-neg.-NZR-int.
'Who doesn't like to be rich'
(The sense is that everyone wants to be rich)

8.2.3.3 Alternative Question or 'Either or' Question

Alternative question or 'either or' question can be constructed with disjunction constituent **nətrəgə** 'either or' which does occur between the two verb phrases, as in sentence 17 (a) and (b). It seeks information in 'Yes' or 'No'.

18. nəŋ məhak-pu khəŋbə-ra nətrəgə khəŋ-də-bə-ra
you he-ass know -NZR-Q or know-neg-NZR-Q
'Do you know him or not ?'

The disjunction constituent **nətrəgə** duly occurs in between the two verb phrases, say, khəŋ-bə-ra (VP1) without negative suffix) and khəŋ-də-bə-ra (VP-N, with negative suffix). This order of VPs is rigid i.e. the VP-N cannot precede the VP1 otherwise the sentence is ungrammatical as in 19 (a). One point of the disjunction constituent **nətrəgə** is that its occurrence is optional, as in sentence 19 (b).

19 a*. nəŋ ədəgi ucek əsi ubə ŋəmdə-bə-ra ŋəmbə-ra
b. nəŋ ədəgi ucek əsi ubə ŋəm-bə-ra ŋəm-də-bə-ra
you far bird this see-NZR-Q can-neg-NZR-Q
'Can you see that bird or not ?'

8.2.3.4 Negative yes/no Question and wh-Questions

It is formed by addition of the negative suffix **-tə-~də-** to the verb before the question suffix **-ra~la**.

See the examples.

20. nəŋ manipuri ŋaŋ-də-ra
you Manipuri speak - neg. Q.
'Didn't or doesnot you speak Manipuri ?'

21. nəŋ thoybi-də nuŋsi hay-roy-dra
you Thoibi-loc. love say-neg-Q
'Will you not say to Thoibi that you love her ?'

22. nəkhoy kəna yu thək-te
You (pl.) who liquor drink-neg.
'Who among you did not take liquor ?' (do not)

8.2.3.5 Tag Question

A question which immediately follows a statement and which serves to seek confirmation, wither explicitly (as in He is Manipuri, isn't he ?) or rhetorically (as in He is Manipuri, is he?). Consider the examples :

23. a. yen thoŋbə -si haω-wi , haω-tə-bə-ra
Chicken -det. tasty taste-neg-NZR-Q
'This chicken is very tasty, isn't it?'

b. yen thoŋbə-si haω-te , haω-bə-ra
chicken det. tast-neg. taste-NZR-Q.
'This chicken is not tasty, is it?'

Tag question has two types : this type, sentence 23(a) and (b) is known as reversed tag question (because the prosition and tag part are in reversed). Opposite to the reversed tag question is the constant tag question (in which the proposition and the tag part is in constant).

See the examples :

24. a. yen thoŋbə-si haω-wi , haω-bə-ra
'This chicken is tasty, is it ?'

b. yen thoŋbə-si haω-te, how-tə-bə-ra
'This chicken is not tasty, isn't it ?'

Manipuri has no sentence 24(b) type of constant while there is 24(a) type of constant. It is seen from the above example, the construction of tag question, that only the verb phrase is retained in the tag part (the VP is in interrogative form whether it is in negative- interogative or not). Reversed tag question is generally taken as common in many of the languages.

The most commonly identified function of reversed polarity tag is 'to obtain confirmation, i.e. the speaker thinks the proposition is true, but wants the hearer to confirm it. But it is not necessary for the speaker to be uncertain about the turth of the proposition, as this definition implies (otherwise he wouldn't be asking for confirmation of it), the proposition can be analytically true, in which case the speaker must know for certain that it is true.

IMPERATIVE

8.3 Imperative

As a general feature Imperative sentence has three features (a) underlying of subject, (b) second person being underlying subject and (c) Futurity. In imperative there are two types, namely, command and request. Pragmatically, in this language, they are found significantly different. Command is generally used to the juniors while request is used to seniors and strangers.

8.3.1 Command

Command in Manipuri is constructed by the suffixation of Command markers, viz., **o, u, ro, ru, kho** etc. to the verbal -root. There are other two command suffixes **nu** and **gumsi** which are used in different syntactic structures . They are all discussed one by one.

2.1 The command suffix **o/u** has no difference in meaning and used in general command construction as in the following sentence.

1. nəŋ ca-du thək-o/u
   you tea -det. drink-comd.
   'Drink that tea'

There is a phonological rule that when the verbal root is ended by **m, n, p, l, ŋ**, they are lengthened and suffixed the marker, for instance, the verb cam-mo/mu 'as in sentence 2. (Phonological condition is shown in Morphophonemic Chapter).

2. ceŋ-du cam-mo/mu
   rice-det wash-comd.
   'Wash the rice'

8.3.2. Command Suffixes

a. Command Suffix ro~lo

This command suffix **ro~lo** has deictic meaning (directional) as towards the speaker 'or 'here' as in the following sentences (**-ro** occurs after vowels while **-lo** occurs else where).

3. phurit əsi yeŋ-lo
   shirt this see comd
   '(Come here and) see this shirt'

4. məhak ŋaωsən-nəy phu-ro
   he naughty-asp. beat-comd.
   'He is naughty, so (come and) beat him'

5. ca thək-lo
   tea drink-comd.
   '(Come here and) have tea'

b. Command suffix ru~lu

Opposite to the command suffix **ro~lo** is the suffix **ru~lu** in deictic sense : it indicates 'away from the speaker' or 'there', as in the following sentences.

6. ca thək-lu
   '(Go and) have tea'

7. məhak ŋəωsən-nəy phu-ru
   'He is naughty, so (go and) beat him'

The deictic difference of the two command suffixes **lo~ro** and **lu~ru** can be clearly seen in the following illustrations :

8 a. nəŋ imphal-də lak-lo
   you Imphal-loc. come -comd.
   'You come to Imphal'

   b.* nəŋ imphal-də lak-lu

Notice that sentence 8 (b) is ungrammatical because **lak** 'come' cannot occur with the command suffix **lu**, because **-lu** has the meaning of 'away from the speaker' in the sense that it has the meaning of 'go there' rather than the meaning of 'Command'. It will be more clearer now from the following sentences.

9 a. nəŋ dukan cət-lo

you store go-comd.
'You (come here and) go to store'

b. nəŋ dukan cət-lu
'you go to store'

Sentence 9 (a) says that the addressee should come first to the place of speaker then he should go while the meaning of 9 (b) is that addressee can go direct to the store instead of coming to the speaker's place : in 9 (a) the addressee cannot go direct to the store because he has no money in hand to buy and he did not know what are the things to buy.

c. Command Suffix -kho

This suffix **kho** has additional meaning of aspects: one meaning of futurity it does not give immediate future while others indicate it, it gives near future), another meaning of continuity, as in the following examples.

10. cak ca-kho
meal eat-comd.
'Have your meal' (the speaker does not serve right at the moment).

11. ma-gi phurit-tu yeŋ-kho
he-gen shirt-det. see-comd.
'See her/his shirt ' (not showing the right at the moment)
Its meaning of continuity will be clear from the following sentences :

12 a. laybreri cət-lu 'Go to Library'
library go-comd.

b. laybreri cət-kho
'Keep going to Library'

d. Prohibitive Suffix -nu

Prohibitive sentence is formed by addition of this suffix **-nu** to the verbal root. Examples are given below :

13. nəhak thəbək ədu təω-nu
you (pl.) work that do -proh.
'Don't do that work'

14. məcu ədu yan-nu
colour that mix proh.
'Don't mix that colour.'

8.3.3 Occurrance of Command Suffixes

Syntactically co-occurrence of the command suffixes are restricted in order ; it can be categorized in this way and in this order : a) **-lu + -kho**, b) **-lu + -nu** and c) **lu+ro** not in the order of **ro+lu** nor **ro+kho** nor **nu+lu** etc. Examples are given below :

a. -lu+kho

15. nəkhoy məyam əmuk sannə-ru-kho
you(pl) all again play-comd-comd
'You all again (go and) play'

b. -lu+nu

16. nəkhoy məyam isiŋ ədu thək-lu-nu
you (pl.) all water that drink-comd-proh.
'You all don't drink that water'

c. -lu+ro

17. nəkhoy məyam ka ədu-də sannə-ru-ro
you (pl.) all room that -loc. play -comd-comd
'You all (go and) play in that room'

One point is that this double occurrence of command marker does not give any emphatic meaning to the command.

8.3.4 Indirect Command

Indirect command, in this language, is formed in two ways : a) by interrogative form with intentional suffix **ge** which is followed by question suffix **ra/la** and b) by infinitive form with a clause **phəy** (good+asp) i.e. it is good'.

a. By Interrogative Form

18 a. layrik əsi tomba-də pi-ge-ra
book this Tomba-dat. give-int.-Q.
'Will you give this book to Tomba'

b. nəŋ məkhoy-gə cətmin-nə-ge-ra
you they -asso. go-toge. -int-Q.
'Will you go with them?'

b. By Infinitive Form

19 a. layrik əsi tomba-də pi-bə phəy
'It is good to give this book to Tomba'

b. nəŋ məkhoy-gə cət-pə phəy
'It is good for you to go with them'

Though these two sets of sentences belong to different construction, they have implied imperative meaning like 'you can give this book to Tomba' or 'why don't you go with them'. But they are more formal than 'Give this book to Tomba' or 'Go with them' to used to a stranger.

8.3.5 Kinds of Imperatives

In Manipuri there are four kinds of imperatives. They are given below :

I. 'Let' Imperative. It is formed by addition of the suffix **si/se** to the verbal root, as in the following examples.

20. əykhoy ciŋ əsi ka-si
we hill this climb-Prop
'Let us climb this hill'

Another kind of 'let' imperative can be formed by simultaneously addition of causative suffix **hən** and command suffix **lo/lu/kho**, as in the following sentences :

21 a. əykhoy ciŋ əsi ka-həl-lu/lo/kho

'Let us make climb this hill'

b. məkhoy ciŋ əsi ka-həl-lu/lo/kho
'Let them climb this hill'

c. məkhoy ciŋ əsi ka-hən-si
'Let them climb this hill'(proposing and seeking permission).

II. Permission Imperative :

22. nəŋ-nə əpambə məkhəy ləy-ro
you-nom. want whatever buy-comd.
'Buy whatever you want'

III. Conditional Imperative

23. para əsi pha-o , əy nəŋ-gi sannəpot ləybi-ge
lesson this learn I you-gen. toy buy-int.
'Learn this lesson, I will buy toys for you'

IV. Wish Imperative

24 a. nuŋay-nə pal-lu
happily - exist-comd.
'Live happily'

b. məkhoy nuŋaynə pan-sənu
'Wish they should live happily'

8.3.6 Command Sentences with Tag Question

Command sentences can be followed by tag question ; this is generally used by seniors to juniors, say, specially by the parents to their children. One constraint is that prohibitive can not be followed by negative tag-question (constant tag), as sentence 25 (b). But constant tag of 25 (a) can be used.

25 a. nəŋ məkhoy-gi-də khəra cət-lu , cət-ke-ra
you they-gen.-loc. go-comd. go-int.-Q
'Go to their place, will you ?'

b* nəŋ məkhoy-gə tinnə-nu , tinnə-roy-dra
you they -asso. mix-proh. mix-neg-Q

Reversed tag is generally used, as in sentence 26 (a) and (b)

26 a. nəŋ məkhoy-gi-də khəra cət-lu, cət-loy-dra
'Go to their place, won't go ?'

b. nəŋ məkhoy-gi-də khəra cət-nu , cət-ke-ra
'Don't go their place will you?'

It is also said about that command sentence with tag-question is generally used by the parents in threatening their children 'to do this' or 'not to do this' and tag-question is formed only with verb+respective suffixes (see detail in Interrogative)

8.3.7 Request

The use of honorific especially for making request is quite prevalent in this language. Similarly, rank, blood -relation and stranger are the main parameters for making request form. In one hand, use of honorific shows maturity of language in use. And it is also regarded as a formal speech. Along with honorific, gestures and body movement can also show that one is giving respect and honour to the others. In this language request can be formed in the following three ways

8.3.7.1 By Addition of Honorific Suffix -bi/pi

This is very simple and commonly used also that request can be formed by just addition of suffix **bi/pi** to the verb and simultaneously the command suffix is also suffixed after, as in the following example:

27 a. ca-bi-yu
eat -hon -comd.
'Please have it'

b. ca -thək-pi-yu
tea drink-hon.-comd.
'Please have tea.'

Notice that the order of addition of suffix **bi/pi** is that when there is causative and deictic suffix, the honorific suffix should be added later, for instance, **ca-hən-bi-yu** 'eat-caus-hon-comd. 'Please let me/him eat'

8.3.7.2 By Request Word and -bi/pi

Request can also be formed by using request word viz. **canbidunə, thəωjanbidunə** and **nuŋsibidunə** 'kindly or please' and simultaneously addition of the suffix **bi/pi** to the verb, as in the following sentences. (use of these request words are becoming now very formal)

28 a. canbidudunə məkhoy-gi-də khəra cət-pi-yu
kindly they -gen. -loc. go-hon.-comd.
'Kindly pay a visit to their place'

b. thoujanbidunə əy-gi mərəm khərə khənnə-bi-yu
please I-gen. case consider-hon.-comd.
'Please consider my case favourably'

8.3.7.3 By Using Polite Forms

To form a very formal request form rather than the above one (i.e. request construction by RQ_bi), it is necessary to use polite forms. A table is given below :

Noun

(+polite form)	Common form (-polite)	Gloss
luk	cak	'rice'
səŋgay	yum	'house'
layjə	isiŋ	'water'
khaŋcet-nəmkhaŋ	phi-rol	'dress'

cərəy	phi	'cloth'
poyrəy	maykəy	'direction'

Verb

(+ polite form)	Common form(-polite)	Gloss
leŋ-bə	cət-pə	'to go'
ha-bə	ca-bə	'to eat'
phan-bə	thək-pə	'to drink'
cep-pə	tum-bə	'to s;eep'

Pronoun

(+ Polite form)	Common form (- polite)	Gloss
ədom/əsom	nəŋ	'you'
məyam	nəkhoy	'you(pl)'

There is a constraint that the + polite form of noun or verb cannot co-occur with the -polite form of noun or verb ; as in the following sentences

29 a. luk ha-bi-ro ' Please have you meal'
eat eat-hon.-comd.

b. cak ca-bi-ro ' Please have your meal'

30 a. səŋgay-də leŋ-bi-ro ' Please go to the house'
house-loc. go hon.-comd.

b. yum-də cət-pi-ro ' Please go to your house'

31 *a. cak ha-bi-ro
rice eat

*b. luk ca-bi-ro

Sentence 31 (a) and (b) are not acceptable because they do not follow the constraint that + polite cannot co-occur with - polite forms.

8.3.7.4 By Interogative Form

Request can be constructed by the interrogative form also. This is more polite than the Request by polite form because there is no any command suffix in the construction, as in the following sentences.

32 a. yum-də cət-lə-dra
house -loc. go-dir-Q
'Would you go home ?'

b səŋgay-də leŋ-lə-dra
'Would you go home ?'

Sentence 32 (b) is more polite than 32 (a). It is no doubt that more polite can be formed with the proposal suffix -si as in the following sentences.

33. səŋgay-də leŋ-lə-si-ra
'Would you go back (home) ?'

In this, different aspects of imperative are discussed along with pragmatic significance. In addition, polite forms and request sentences are extended to the very close friends but where the meaning of polite or request is not found.

CHAPTER–IX

SYNTACTIVIZATION

9.1. Verb 'be'

In this language, there are three different forms of verb 'be', namely, **ləy, oy** and **-ni**. On the basis of their respective grammatical functions, verb 'be' in Meiteilon can be divided into three groups

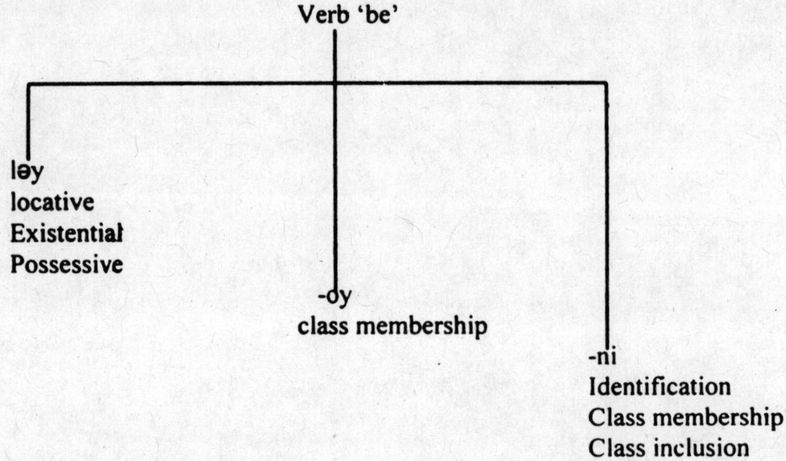

The concept of 'being' and 'existence' are conveyed by the verb **ləy** and it also conveys the meaning of possession; **ləy** and **oy** differ from **-ni** at morphological level in the sense that **ləy** and **oy** are independent lexical items while **-ni** a suffix.

In this language, there are other different forms of verb 'be' depending on the types of sentences, that is, in affirmative sentence **-ni** is used, in negative **nətte** is used while in interrogative - **ra~la** and **-no** are used. Grammatically there is a slight difference : **-ni, -ra/la** and **-no** are suffixes while **nətte** is a lexical negator. More and above, they function as copula in the constructions.

Keeping in view the status of verb 'be' in various constructions ranging from existential construction to copula constructions, it may be claimed that verb 'be' has basic functions :

i. In existential constructions (EC), and
ii. In non-existential constructions (Non-EC)

In EC it is present in the base because in it verb 'be' functions as a main verb with full semantic content. Taking this concept into consideration, it can be said that Manipuri has one verb 'be' form, **ləy** used in EC.

In Non -EC it is inserted at a later stage through transformations. Non -EC includes copulative, auxiliary, locative, possessive constructions. The function of verb 'be' as a copula is that of a linker. Bach (1967:447) also expresses similar views when he says that the contribution of copula to the meaning of a sentence is "determined completely by the items that link". Also, initially, it is absent in child language as well as in baby talk, its acquisition comes at a later stage.

9.1.1 Verb 'be' and its Polysemous Functions

Verb 'be' has multiple functions to perform in various types of constructions in the language of the world. These functions which range from copulative to existential are strikingly diverse in nature. They do not exhibit any apparent relation among themselves.

9.1.1.1 Existential Function

Verb 'be' **ləy** functions as existential in this language. Consider the following sentences

1. lay ləy
   God exist 'God exists'

2. əcumbə ləy
   truth exist 'Truth exists'

These sentences denote absolute existence of abstract entities and **ləy** functions as verb 'be' which does not take complements and functions as almost as a main verb.

9.1.1.2 Locative Function

Verb 'be' form **ləy** can also function as locative, as in the following sentences :

3. John yum-də ləy
   John house-loc. stay
   'John stay at home'

4. John Imphal-də ləy
   'John lives at Imphal'

By this, **ləy**, temporal existential construction can also be formed, as in the following sentence.

5. ŋəsi suti ləy
   today holiday is
   'There is holiday today
   (Today is holiday)

In locative construction, it serves as a linker only. In such constructions, there is a subject NP, say, John in sentence (3) and (4) and to specify the location of the subject NP (on temporal or spatial scale), there is a locative element, not verb 'be'. Verb 'be' merely links the nominal and the locative element at a purely grammatical level. That is why, if we delete verb 'be' in a locative construction (say, sentence 4 John Imphal-də) which we do in telegraphic speech and in the newspaper headline, the location is specified all the same by the locative element.

9.1.1.3 Possessive Function

Not only verb 'be' **ləy** can function as existential and locative it also can function as possessive. Consider the following sentence :

6. əy-gi huy əni ləy
   I-gen. dog two have
   'I have two dogs'

Possessive function performed by another verb 'be' form **-ni** is different, as in sentence 7.

7. huy əni əni-du əy-gi-ni
dog two-det. I gen -be
'The two dogs are mine'

Possessive construction can be formed by verb 'be' -**ni** in other two ways as in sentence 8 and 9. (**ni** will be discussed in detail latter).

8. əni-du əy-gi huy-ni
two-det. I -gen dog-be
'(The two mine dogs are)'. 'The two dogs are mine'

9. əy-gi huy əni-du-ni
I-gen. dog two-det-be
' These are my two dogs'

Similarly in locative construction. in possessive construction, verb 'be' is not crucial semantically for two reasons, first. possessive constructions are at the underlying level derived from locative 'be' which functions merely as a link. Secondly, it may be noted that in many langauges (which have case marker) it is the case ending which reflects the special kind of relation of possession that exists, between the two NPs — the possessor and the possessed. verb 'be' acts merely as a link between the two NPs

9.1.1.4 Copula Functions

When in a sentence consisting of a subject and a predicate, verb 'be' serves as a link, between the two ; it is called copula. Copula function is performed by verb 'be' -**ni** . Copulative functions are grouped into two :

1. Equative, and
2. Participle formation.

These are described hereunder :

Equatives include identification, class inclusion, and class membership.

A. Identification

10. a. məhak thoybi-ni
she Thoibi -be
'She is Thoibi'

b. əy John-ni
I -be
'I am John'

B. Class Inclusion

11. a. məhak nupa-ni
he man-be
'He is a man'

b. oja-du American-ni
teacher -det American -be
'That teacher is American'

C. Class Membership

12. a. John oja-ni
John teacher-be
'John is a teacher'

b. məhak pilot-ni
he pilot-be
'He is a Pilot'

There is a form oy which can replaced the very verb 'be' form **-ni**, very specifically only in class inclusion and class membership. Consider the following sentences.

13. məhak nupa oy (Class inclusion)
'He is a man'

14. John oja oy (Class membership)
'John is a teacher'

Sentence 13 carries the meaning of 'he' is really a man 'having the quality of being a man not a woman'. So there is a slight different meaning from sentence 11(a). But the meaning of sentence 14 and 12 (a) is same. Grammatically **oy** and **-ni** are different : **oy** is an independent lexical item while **-ni** is a suffix. More and above, participle formation cannot be constructed from any sentence **-ni** being the verb 'be' (11-12). But participle formation can be made from sentences 13 and 14 in which oy is functioning as verb 'be'. For participle formation, a nominalizer **-bə ~ -pə** will be added to **oy- (oy-bə)**. Consider the following sentences :

15. nupa oy-bə məhak
man be -NZR a man

16. oja oy-bə məhak
teacher be-NZR he
'He who is a teacher'

Participle can also be formed by addition of **-bə ~pə** to the verb 'be' **ləy- (ləy-bə)**. Consider the following sentences :

17. a. upu mənuŋ-də ləy-bə phurit-tu
almira inside-loc. be -nom. shirt-det
'The shirt (which is) in the almira...'

b. u-kha-də ləy-bə nupa-du
tree -under-loc. be NZR man-det
'The person (who is) under the tree...'

These sentences are derived from the following sentences respectively.

18. a. phurit-tu upu mənuŋ-də ləy
'the shirt is in the almira'

b. nupa-du u-kha-də ləy
'The man is under the tree'

It is already said that **-ni** is a suffix and it is used in equative sentence of identification, class inclusion and class membership. Other than this, **-ni** has some other grammatical properties. It can suffixed to, (proper) nouns, noun, pronouns, predicative noun, numeral, ordinal etc.

A. Peoper Noun+ni

19. məhak john-ni
he -be
'He is John'

B. Noun +ni

20. məsi əy-gi huy-ni
this I -gen. dog-be
'This is my dog'

C. Pronoun +ni

21. əy-ni 'It is me'
(Replying to the question 'Who are you')

D. Predicative Nominal+ni

22. yum-du phəjəbə-ni
house -det. nice-be
'The house is nice'

E. Numeral +ni

23. məkhoy mi məri-ni
they people four-be
'They are four'

F. Ordinal +ni

24. məhak -nə əhanbə-ni
he-nom. first-be
'He is the first'

It is already mentioned above Manipuri has other verb 'be' form, rather than these, depending on the types of sentences--- Interrogative and negative.

9.1.2 Interrogative Verb 'be' Forms

Manipuri has interrogative verb 'be' form. They are Yes/Nó question marker -ra~la and -no used in Wh-question. Why they are treated as Verb 'be' will be cleared from the following illustrations :

26. məsi lil-la
this snake be
'Is this a snake?'

27. məkhoy əphəbə mi-ra
they good people-be
'Are they good people?'

28. layrik ədu əsi-ra
book that this-be
'Is that the book?'

29. ŋəraŋ lak-pə-du nəŋ-la
yesterday come-NZR-det. you-be
'Are you the person who came yesterday ?'

It is very cleared from the above sentences (26-29) that Yes/No question marker **-la~ra** functions as verb 'be'. It (**-ra~-la**) functions as linking verb, say, the two **məsi** 'this and **lil** 'snake' are linked by **-la**. In all the sentences **-ra~-la** functions as verb 'be', and it can be added to the very Wh-question word as well as to the verb also. Consider the following sentences :

30. məhak kəna -no
    he who-be
    'Who is he?'

31. məsi kəri-no
    this what -be
    'What is this?'

Here **-no** functions as a linking verb.

9.1.3. Lexical Negator nətte

The texical negator **nətte** is just opposite to verb 'be' **-ni** ; that is, **-ni** is used in Affirmative sentence. **nətte** is taken as verb 'be' because it functions as copula in a sentence. Consider the following sentence :

32. məhak John nətte
    he John be
    'He is not John'

33. məhak huranbə nətte
    he thief be
    'He is not a thief'

Notice that **nətte** functions as copula and if **nətte** is replaced by **-ni** (suffixed to John and **huranbə** respectively) they became affirmative sentences, as in sentence 34 and 35 respectively.

34. məhak John-ni
    'He is John'

35. məhak huranbə-ni
    'He is a thief'

Thus, it is known that Manipuri has different verb 'be' forms depending on the function and depending on the types of sentence. That is for affirmative it is **-ni**, for interrogative it is **-ra~-la** and **-ni** ; and for negative it is **nətte**.

NOMINALIZATION

9.2 Nominalization

1. Nominalizations are regarded as nouns derived from verbs with the general meaning of an action or process having the capability of declining or taking prepositions or postpositions in the same way as non-derived nouns and showing 'reasonable' productivity. The Tibeto-Burman languages are highly nominalizing. Nominalized constructions in these languages not only occur in non-final position, but nominalized forms occur at the end of final clause.

In Manipuri even the stative verb can also be nominalized; the nominalizing suffix is highly productive and it occurs finally.

9.2.1 Nominalizing Strategies

a. bə~-pə

The nominalizer (NZR) in this language is a suffix, viz., **bə~pə (-bə occurs after vowels and voiced consonants while -pə occurs after voiceless consonants).** All the action, process and stative roots are bound and known as verbal roots. They can be nominalized by suffixation of the NZR **-bə~-pə**, as in the following two ways, (I) addition to the direct verbal roots and (ii) after other suffix.

Direct to the Roots :

a. Action Verbal Roots :

ca+bə ➔ ca-bə 'to eat'
eat-
pi+bə ➔ pi-bə 'to give'
give-
phu+bə ➔ phu-bə 'to beat'
beat
thoŋ+bə ➔ thoŋ-bə 'to cook'
cook-

thək+pə ➔ thək+pə 'to drink'
drink-
kəp+pə ➔ kəp-pə 'to cry'
cry
cət+pə ➔ cət-pə 'to go'
go

b. Process Verbal Roots

ta +bə ➔ ta-bə 'to fall'
fall
pathə +bə ➔ pathə-bə 'to spill down'
spill
pay+bə ➔ pay-bə 'to fly'
fly
taω +bə ➔ taω-bə 'to float'
float

c. Stative Verbal Roots

waŋ +bə ➔ waŋ-bə 'to be tall'
saŋ+bə ➔ saŋ-bə 'to be long'
ten+bə ➔ ten-bə 'to be short'
pa+bə ➔ pa-bə 'to be thin'

ŋəω+bə ➔ ŋəω-bə 'to be white'
ŋaŋ+bə ➔ ŋaŋ-bə 'to be red'
təp+pə ➔ təp-pə 'to be slow'
sa+bə ➔ 'to be hot'

9.2.2. Occurrence of other Suffixes

In this category, the NZR **-bə˜-pə** occurs after aspect markers (progressive, perfect and unrealized or irrealis), causative marker and after morphological negative marker **-də˜-tə.** They are discussed in detail in the followings.

9.2.2.1 After Aspects :

In the case of aspects, the different aspects — simple, propgressive, perfect and unrealized -have different norms or rules for nominalization.

Simple aspect. In this the very marker is deleted, then the NZR is added.

cət-y 'go'- [Asp.]

Deleted

thoŋ-ŋi - cook [Asp]
cət+ pə> cət-pə 'to go'
thoŋ+ bə > thoŋ-bə 'to cook'

1. a. əy cət-pə pam-mi[pam-y]
I go-NZR like -asp
'I like to go'

b. məhak cak thoŋ-bə cət-li [cət-y]
he rice cook -NZR go- asp.
'He goes to cook'

Progressive Aspect [-ri~li]

In this case, the NZR is just added, as in the following .

ca-ri 'is eating'
eat-prog.
pa-ri 'is reading'
read-prog.
kəp-li 'is crying'
cry-prog.

2. a. layrik pa-ri-bə əŋaŋ.....
book read -prog-NZR child
'The reading child (the child who is reading)'.

b. cel-li-bə nupa məca.....
run -prog. -NZR man - small ..
'The running boy...'

Perfect Aspect : [-re~le]

The e of the perfect aspect [re~le] is, at first, changed into ə, then added the nominalizer.

ca-r[e]
Umlaut to ə
thək-l (e) drink
Then added NZR ca-rə + bə ➔ ca-rə-bə '.... that is taken'
thək-lə+ bə ➔ thək-lə-bə '..... that is drunk'

3. a. ca-rə-bə mi məkhəy
eat-asp-NZR kid group
'All who have taken men.........'

Unrealized or Irrealis [-gə-ni~ kə-ni]

Here -ni of gəni~kəni is deleted and added an enclitic də, then added the NZR

ca-gə[ni]
thək-kə[ni]
(both: deleted)

Then added enclitic
ca-gə-də
thək-kədə

Then added the NZR

➔ ca-gə-də-bə
➔ thək-kə-də-bə

4. a. ca-gə-də-bə mi-siŋ...
eat. asp encl -NZR man-pl.mk.
'The person who have to eat...'

b. thək-kə-dəbə əŋaŋ -siŋ
drink-asp-encl. -NZR kid -pl. mk.
'The kids who have to drink'

9.2.2.2 After Causative Marker [-hən~-həl]

The nominalizer **-bə~-pə** can be added after causative marker also , as in the following examples :

5. ca-hən-bə 'to make (some one) eat'
yeŋ-hən-bə 'to make (someone) see'
thoŋ-hənbə 'to make (someone) cook'

9.2.2.3 After Morphological Negative Marker [-də~ tə],

The NZR can also be added after the morphological negative marker, as in the following examples

ca-də_bə ➔ ca-də-bə 'not to eat'
thək-tə+bə ➔ thək-tə-bə 'not to drink'

6. a. əy philəm əsi yeŋ-də-bə pam-mi
I film this see-neg. -NZR like -asp
'I like not to see this film'

b. mədu thək-tə-bə phəy
that drink-neg. NZR good
'It is good not to drink that (something)'

9.2.3 Addition of Noun Categories to the Nominals

9.2.3.1 Case Markers to the Nominals

Derived nominals by the suffix **bə~pə** can have case markers. Consider the following illustrations :

7. a. həωjik nəŋ əthumbə ca-bə-gi kanə-bə ləy-te[gen]
now you sweet eat-neg.-NZR-gen. useful has-neg.
'Now there is no need to eat sweet for you'

b. kati-nə cəp-pə-nə mədu phəgəni [inst]
scissor-inst cut-NZR-inst. that good-Un . asp.
'That will be good to cut with a scissor'

c. ca-bə-də məci oybə ca-u [loc.]
eat-NZR-dat/loc. proteine eat-comd mk.
'Eat protein when you are eating'

d. ca-bə-dəgi həkcaŋ-də kanə-də-bə haybəbu morok-ni [abl)

eat-NZR -abl body -dat/loc. useful-neg.NZR quot. is chilly-cop.
It is the chilly (red) that is not useful to health in eating
(From the eating of red chilli we cannot get any useful component to the health).

9.2.3.2 Addition of Number Marker

The plural suffix **-siŋ** can be added to the derived nominals, nominalized by **-bə~pə**, as in the following examples :

8. a. sannə-bə lak-li-bə siŋ ..
play -NZR come-asp. -NZR -pl.
'The persons coming to play..'

b. yu thək-kə-də-bə siŋ ...
liquor drink -Un. asp-NZR-pl.
'The person who will to drink...'

Notice that the above derived nominals, say, **lak-li-bə** .. (8 a) and **thək-kədə-bə** (8 b) express or refer to noun like 'person' or somebody'.

9.2.4 Different Functions of Nominalization

The NZR **-bə~pə** is employed in a diversity of functions to

1. To derive noun, the nominalizer **pə~bə** is suffixed to the verbal roots (see 2.1).
2. In relativization, the NZR **bə/pə** is suffixed to the predicate of the subordinate clause. (see for detail in Relativization)
3. In complementation, the nominalizer **bə~pə** is suffixed to the predicate of the complementation (see for detail in Complementation).

COMPLEMENTATION

9.3 COMPLEMENTATION

Complementation is taken as a grammatical process by which sentences are formed to function as the arguments of matrix sentences. Complement constructions are intricate and are varied in many natural languages. Complement constructions consist of a combination of two types of modality meanings, the Information and the Evaluation Modalities, both of which have consequences for the propositional content of the complement and its co-occurrence with different meanings and forms.

The Information Modalities, consisting of four modalities of Truth, Future Truth, Occurrence, and Action, which describe information about someone's knowledge or behaviour in the world. The other Evaluation Modalities, consisting of four modalities with a Pre-determined, Determined, Undetermined, and Indeterminate meaning, which describe evaluations of alternatives.

9.3.1. Matrix Sentences and the Complement Modalities

Although higher sentences have their own meaning and forms independent of their complements, they can affect the meanings and forms of their complements. The type of predicate in the matrix sentence can have an important effect, as does its time reference and the type of nominal roles it takes. The polarity and modality of the higher sentence also can affect the complement.

First, it depends on the basic type of higher predicates — wheth^r the matrix predicate is subject or object embedding. The object embedding makes predications about animate, usually human, subjects, and will be called reactions because they explain a persons reaction to a proposition. The subject embedding predicates make predicates about the subject proposition and will be called appraisals because they explain a persons appraisal of a proposition.

These reactions and appraisals can be divided into three classes. One class consists of emotive predicates. These are emotive reactions, which involve someone's emotional respond to a proposition (regret, be afraid, hope, desire, like, be willing), and emotive appraisals, which involve someone's emotional evaluation of a proposition (be amazing, the hopeful, be desirable). A second class consists of linguistic predicates. There are linguistic reactions, which involve someone uttering a proposition (say, predict, command, promise), and linguistic appraisals, which involve someone's linguistic appraisal of a proposition (be said, be rumoured, be predictable). Finally, there are cognitive - physical reactions, which involve someone's cognitive or physical response to a proposition (know, discover, believe, show, wonder, expect, watch, see, force, manage, try, be able, decide, intend), and cognitive physical appraisal of a proposition (be known , be true, be likely, be possible, be necessary, be important, be acceptable, behove, begin, take place).

9.3.2 Types of Complementation

There are three different types of complementation in Manipuri. They are I) Complementation by nominalization, 2) complementation by adding a complementizer (the factive **haybə** or the non-factive **haynə**), and 3) Complementation by adding the prefix **khu-** or **mə-** to the predicate.

9.3.2.1 Complementation by Nominalization

The NZR **-pə/bə** is suffixed to a verb to form nominal complements, as in sentence 3 in which there is equi-NP. (əy pam-mi 'I like'; əy cen-bə ' I run-NZR)

3. əy cen-bə pam-mi
   I run-NZR like -asp.
   'I like to run'

There is another type of nominal complements in which there is a different NP while the matrix has another NP, as in the following sentences :

4. a. tomba skul-də cət-khi-bə əy khəŋ-ŋi
      tomba school-loc. go-comp-NZR I know-asp
      'I know Tomba's going to school'
   b. məhak lak-pə əy thəjəy
      he come -NZR I believe
      'I believe his coming'

The predicates (of these two sentences 4 (a) and (b) convey primarily deontic mood). Regarding the linear order, in this type of complement there are two orders : one is the matrix follows the complement, as in sentence 4 (a) and (b). In another the complement is embedded into the matrix (that is between subject and predicate), as in sentence 5.

5. əy tomba skul-də cət-khi-bə khəŋ-ŋi
   I Tomba school-loc. go -compl. -NZR know-asp.
   'I know Tomba's going to school'

The matrix predicate can also take nominal complement containing purposive suffix **nə** in the predicate. Consider the following sentences :

6. a. məhak ŋa pha-nə-bə sem-li
   he fish catch -Purs-NZR make-asp
   'He is making to catch fish'

   b. əy yum sa-nəbə təω-ri
   I house build-ours-NZR do -asp.
   'I am trying to build a house'

There is another sentence which has two different NPs, as in sentence 7.

7. əŋaŋ-siŋ ca-nə-bə mama-nə cak toŋ-li
   child-pl. eat-purs-NZR-nom. rice cook asp
   The mother is cooking for her children.

9.3.2.2 Sentential Complement

The second type of complement, in this language, is formed by two types of complementizers, namely the factive complimentizer (F-Com) **haybə** and the non-factive complimentizer (Non-F-Com) **haynə**. These roots **hay** 'say' through the suffixation of the adverbial suffix **-nə** (In the Relalivisation, 9.4, **haybə** is called as Quotative, there is no difference). The compliments formed by using these two NZR are classed as sentential complements because they are made up of full-fledged sentences ending either in **haybə**, the F-Com or **haynə**, the Non-F-Com. The complements ending in **haybə** refer to a fact (a state, process or action) whereas **haynə** to a statement. Because of this difference, the use of these complementizers are responsible to some prepositional differences. This can be clear from the following pairs of sentences :

8. a. tomba-nə phurit ədu pam-mi haybə əy tay
   Tomba-nom. shirt that like F-com I hear-asp
   ' I hear that Tomba likes that shirt.'

   b. tombə-nə phurit ədu pam-mi haynə əy tay
   'I hear that Tomba likes that shirt'

Though the meaning of these two sentences are same, each of them shows slight differences, that is according to 8 (a) Tomba likes the very shirt, its colour, its design because he had an intention to have such a type from the early days. But in 8 (b) Tomba likes the shirt, its colour and its design but he had no longer intention of having it.

The complement-taking matrix predicates can be classed into three groups depending upon whether they take (i) the F-coms, (ii) the Non-Fcoms, or (iii) both. What to be noted here is that the predicates belonging to the first indicate the epistemic mood (atleast the expression of possibility and certainty), Commitment of the speaker), while group mostly denotes the deontic mood (concerned with permission, obligation and prohibition).

9.3.2..2.1 Predicates Belonging to F-coms.

The predicates belonging to the F-coms are **oythok** 'possible', **man** 'appear', **kaw** 'forget', **cum** 'true' **niŋsiŋ** 'remember' '**nuŋŋay** 'be happy' **ŋək-e** 'wonder' **khəŋ**-'know'
Examples :

9. a. tomba-nə manipuri təmbi haybə əy khəŋ-ŋi
   Tomba-nom Manipuri teach Fcom I know-asp

'I know that Tomba teaches Manipuri'

b. **manipuri-də tens məyek seŋ-de haybə cum-mi**
Manipuri-loc. tense clear -neg Fcom true-asp
'It is true that in Manipuri tense is not significant'

c. **məhak thəbək əsi təω-ωi haybə əy kaω-ωi**
' he-nom. work this do-asp Fcom I forget-asp
'I forget that he did this work'

9.3.2.2.2 Predicates Belonging to Non-Fcom

The predicates belonging to the Non-Fcom are **həŋ** 'ask', **hay** 'say', **ni** 'request', **pən** 'mention' **ŋaŋ** 'advice' or 'tell', **tək** 'persuade', **yet**' agrue', **cəy** 'abuse/scold' **niŋ** 'wish', **lep** 'decide', **khən** 'think', **ləω** 'take' (from an opinion)
Examples :

10. a. **manipuri-də voice ləy-te haynə əy ləω-ωi**
Manipuri-loc. voice have-neg. Non-Fcom I take-asp.
'I take in this way that there is no voice in Manipuri'

b. **məhak parikha ŋəm-gəni haybə əy khəl-li**
he exam. pass-asp. nom. Fcom I think-asp
'I think that he will pass the exam.'

c. **manipuri grammar əma i-ge haynə əy lep-le**
Manipuri grammar one write-int nom. Fcom I decide -asp
'I have decided that I should write a Manipuri grammar'

9.3.2.2.3 Predicates Belonging to the F-com and Non F-com

Predicates belonging to this group are **khəŋ** 'know', **thajə** 'believe', **ciŋnə** 'doubt', **ta** 'hear' **u** 'see', **ya** 'agree', **wa** 'worry', **təm** 'be the destiny', **laωthok** 'announce' etc.
Examples :

11. a. **tombə ləndon-də cət-khre haybə əy tay**
Tomba London-loc. go-asp Fcom I hear -asp
'I hear that Tomba has gone to London'

b. **tombə ləndon-də cət-khre haynə əy tay**
'I hear that Tomba has gone to London'

12. a. **məhak isəy sək-y haybə əy thajəy**
he sing sing-asp Fcom I believe-asp
'I believe that he sings'

b. **məhak isəy sək-y hay-nə əy thəjəy**
'I believe that he sings'

13. a. **manipuri-də Subject-kə verb-kə agreement ləy-te haybə əy yay**
Manipuri subject-ass. verb-ass have-neg. Fcom I agree
'I agree that in Manipuri there is no grammatical agreement between subject and verb.'

b. **manipuri-də Subject-kə verb-kə agreement ləy-te haynə əy yay**
'I agree that in Manipuri there is no grammatical agreement between subject and verb.'

Out of the above given predicates (Predicates belonging to both) there. are two predicates, namely, **ciŋnə** 'doubt' and **niŋsəŋ** 'remember'. They are rather semantically interesting. That is, while **ciŋnə** 'doubt' occurs with the F-com, it gives the meaning of 'negative' in the context (exact meaning of 'doubt') whereas while occurring with the Non-Fcom it has the meaning of epistemic (meaning of 'possibility'). Consider the following pair sentences :

14. a. məhak lak-kəni haybə əy ciŋnəy
he come-Un. asp Fcom I doubt-asp
'I doubt that he will come' (I don't think that he will come)
b. məhak lak-kəni haynə əy ciŋnəy
'It appears to me that he may come'
(There is the possibility of his coming)

The another is the case of **niŋsiŋ** 'remember'. When it occurs with the F-com it has the epistemic meaning 'remember' whereas when it goes with the Non-F-com it gives the denoting meaning 'remind'. See the following illustrations.'

15. məhak hidak əma cagədəbəni haybə əy niŋsiŋ-ŋi
he teblet one eat-un.asp.-NZR-cop F-com I remember -asp
'I remember that he should take a tablet'
b. məhak hidak əma ca-gədəbəni haynə əynə niŋsiŋ-ŋi
'I remind him that he should take a tablet'

9.3.2.3 Complementation by Prefix khu-/mə-

The third way of complementation in this language is the addition of the prefix **khu-** or **mə-** to the predicates of complement sentences in order to indicate (I) the way of performing the activity (in the case of action sentences), (ii) the manner in which an event occurs (in the case of process sentences), and (iii) the kind of feature that is specified (in the case of stative sentences).

Two grammatical features arise when the prefix is added to the verb, one is the addition of genitive marker to the arguments, another is the verb loses its all suffixes occurring after it. Consider the following sentences :

16. a. məhak yu thək-y
he liquor drink-asp.
'He drinks liquor'
b. məhak-ki yu khu-thək lu-de
he -gen liqour pre-drink nice-neg-cop
'The way of his drinking is not nice'

17. a. meri ŋa taω-ri
Mary fish fry-prog. asp
'Mary is frying fish'
b. mari-gi ŋa khu-taω phəjəy
'The way of Mary's frying fish is nice'

18. a. meri phəjəy
Mary beautiful-asp.
'Mary is beautiful'
13 b. meri-gi khu-phəjə əsi pukniŋ sumhətniŋ ŋay-ni
'The beauty of Mary is facinating'

It is also possible to add genitive suffix **gi/ki** to the second argument in the complement of the above sentence 16 (b) like **məhak-ki yu-gi khu-thək** ...... and of 17 (b) sentence like **meri-gi ŋa-gi khu-taω** ....

9.3.2.4 Complementation both by Nominalization and by Prefixation

In this language complementation can also be made by occurring nominalization and prefixation ; In this the verbal form is reduplicated : the first verbal form is nominalized, ending in the nominal suffix **bə/pə** while retaining other suffix (the possible suffixes are progressive **ri~li** or remote **rəm** or causative suffix **hən**) and the verbal has the prefix only **khu** or **mə**. Consider the following sentences.

19. a. məhak-ki curup thək-ləm-bə khu-thək .... [Rem. prog.]
he-gen. cigarette drink-R. prog.-NZR pref. -drink ...
'The way of his smoking (in those days)...'

b. məhak-ki curup thək-li-bə khu-thək .... [prog.]
'The way of his smoking (Continuing now)'...

c. məhak-ki cak thoŋ-hən-bə khu-thoŋ...[Caus.]
he-gen rice cook-NZR pref. -cook ...
' The way of causing (someone) to cook rice ....'

Notice that there is reduplication of verbal forms and two strategies of complementation are involving, as given in the above sentences 19 (a), (b) and (c).

9.3.3. Equi-NP Deletion

In this language subject can be deleted in many cases. There also arises equi-NP deletion in sentential complementation. When there is co-reference between an argument of the matrix sentence and an argument of the complement sentence, one of them is being deleted, as in the following illustrations :

20. a. thoibinə khəmbə nuŋsi
Thoibi-nom. Khamba love-asp
'Thoibi loves Khamba'

b. thoibi-nə ləypak miyam-də ut-li
Thoibi country people-loc. show-asp
'Thoibi shows it to the people'

c. thoibi-nə khəmbə nuŋsi haybə ləypak miyam-də ut-li
'Thoibi shows to the people that she loves Khamba'

Notice that Thoibi occurs only once in the sentence 20 (c). This is because of equi-NP deletion, so an argument is deleted.

Equi-NP deletion is also prevailed in the complementation by nominalization, as in the following sentences :

21. a. jəgoy say
I dance do-asp
'I dance'

b. əy isəy sək-y
I song sing
'I sing'

c. əy jəgoy sa-bə, isəy sək-pə pam-mi
'I like to dance and to sing'

9.3.4. Case Markers on Complementizer

It is known that case markers are added to the noun phrase; it is also known that suffix **nə** with any verbal root functions as adverb, e.g. **kəp** 'cry' **+nə** (**kəp+nə** 'cryingly'), **nok-** 'smile' **+nə** (**nok-nə** 'smilingly'); and sufix **-bə/-pə** with any verbal root functions as noun, e.g. **ca**'eat' **+bə** (**ca-bə** 'to eat'), kəp 'cry' **+pə** (**kəp-pə** 'to cry'). So the complimentizer **hay-bə** is basically nominal in nature while the other complementizer **haynə** is basically adverbial in nature. The grammatical result is that the complements ending in **haybə** can be further followed by different case markers depending on the relation that the complements have with the matrix verb. However, the case markers show somewhat different connotations.

The genitive suffix **-gi/ki** is added to the complementizer **haybə** in order to indicate the reason for the occurrence of the main events, as in the following examples :

22. məhak nay haybə-gi əy lak-pə-ni
he ill-asp Fcom -gen. I come-NZR-cop
'I come here since he is seek'

b. məhak drama əsi-də yaw-wi haybə-gi əy yeŋ-ŋi
he drama this-dat. take-asp Fcom-gen. I see-asp
'I saw this darma because she took a part'

Genitive

In complementation by nominalization also, the genitive suffix can be added after NZR bə/pə. Here nominalization functions exactly as complementaion, as in sentence 23.

23. məhak na-bə-gi əy lak-pə-ni
'I come here for his sickness'

(ii) The use of locative suffix **də** with the Fcom **haybə** is for indicating the fact that the event of the complement constitutes the time in which the event of the matrix sentence occurred as in the following sentences.

24. məhak-nə cət-lə-si haybə-də əy-nə ya-de
he-nom. go-dir-pro Fcom,loc. I-nom agree-neg
'I do not agree when he says that let's go'

25. a. məhak-nə məsi thək-u haybə-də əy-nə thək-pə-ni
he-nom. this drink-com Fcom-loc. I-nom drink-NZR -cop
'I drink it when he asks me (to drink it)'

b. khəmba-gə thoybi-gə cət-minnə-khi haybədə noŋbal saω-ωi
Khamba-assoc. Thoibi-assoc. go -together-compl. Fcom-loc. Nongbal angry-asp
'Nongbal is angry when he is told that Khamba and Thoibi went together.'

The locative suffix **-də** not only indicates the constituent time of the event, as in 18 (a), it (the suffix **də**) also denotes that the subordinate event is the cause of the main event, as in sentence 25 (a) and (b)

25. a. **məhak-nə məsi thək-u haybə-də əy-nə thək-pə-ni**
he-nom. this drink-com Fcom-loc. I-nom drink-NZR -cop
'I drink it when he asks me (to drink it)'

b. **khəmba-gə thoybi-gə cət-minnə-khi haybədə noŋbal saω-ωi**
Khamba-assoc. Thoibi-assoc. go -together-compl. Fcom-loc. Nongbal angry-asp
'Nongbal is angry when he is told that Khamba and Thoibi went together.'

The same meaning, (i.e. X is the cause of Y) is also similarly indicated by the use of the locative suffix də along with the genitive suffix -gi after the Fcom (haybə-dəgi), that is, the subordinate event is the cause of the main event, as in sentence 26 (a) and (b).

26. a. **məhak-nə caω haybədəgi əy ca-bə-ni**
he-nom. eat-com. Fcom -loc.-gen. I eat -NZR-cop
'I eat since he asks me to eat'

b. **məhak-nə philəm əsi yeŋ-si haybədəgi əy yeŋ-bə-ni**
he-nom. film this see-prop Fcom -loc. gen. I see -NZR -cop
'I see this film since she proposes (Let's see)'

Locative

Locative suffix -də can also be added to nominalization. Here is the illustration

27. **məhak (-nə) cət-pə-də əy(nə) ya-de**
'I disagree to his going'

(iv) The associative suffix gə/kə also provides a temporal meaning, that is, the main event takes place immediately after the subordinate event. Consider the following sentences.

28. a. **məhak-nə cət-lo haybəgə əykhoy cət-le**
he-nom. go-com Fcom-assoc. we go-pref. asp
'We have left immediately when he asks to go'

b. **pulis yəw-rək-le haybəgə miyam ədum kay-re**
police arrive -dir. come-NZR-Asso mass automatically disperse -pref. asp
'The crowd has dispersed just when the police arrived'

Notice that the addition of these case suffixes to the Fcom haybə some performs adverbial function. So they are regarded as adverbial rather than complements exactly.

Associative

This suffix also provides temporal meaning in the complementation by nominalization. Consider the following sentence.

29. **police yəwrək-pə-gə miyam ədum kay-re**
'The crowd has dispersed as soon as the police arrived'

This senteces does not perform the function of complementation.

RELATIVILIZATION

9.4. Relativilization

In a natural language, the essential semantic property of relative clause (RC) is the functional property of modification of noun. This is a property only some RC's those referred to adjectival relative clauses. TB languages, in general, have neither relative pronoun nor non-restrictive relative clause. In TB languages, grammatical subordinatation typically involves nominalization which forms relativization

9.4.1 RC Forming and its Type

Manipuri has only restrictive relative clause. It is formed by addition of nominalizer (NZR) **-pə ~-bə** to the embedded verb and a determiner (Det) **-du (ədu)~ -do (ədo) ~-si (əsi)~ -se (əse)** is used as a correlative marker.

Example :

1. [əy-nə ŋəraŋ ləybə] layrik ədu tomba-də pi
   I-nom. yesterday buy-NZR book det Tomba-loc. give -asp
   'The book which I bought yesterday is given to Tomba'

It is also noticed that Manipuri has only one strategy for forming RC, it is prerominal Rc because the embedded clause **əy-nə ŋəraŋ ləybə** precedes the head noun **layrik** 'book'. In other word, the **əy-nə ŋəraŋ ləy-bə** 'that I bought yesterday..' precedes the matrix (main) clause **layrik ədu tomba-də pi** 'the book is given to Tomba'. Consider two more examples :

2. thoybi-nə hek-pə ləy-du əy-nə lay-də kət-li
   Thoibi-nom. pluck-NZR flower-det I-nom. God-loc. worship-asp.
   'The flower that Thoibi plucks I worship it to the God.'
3. məhak-nə i-bə səyreŋ ədu miyam-nə pam-nəy
   he-nom. write-NZR poem det people-NZR like-asp
   'The poem that he writes is appreciated by the people'

There is another strategy for forming RC. This RC is formed by the use of quotative (Qut) **hay-bə** (Factive) which is the extended meaning of **hay-bə** 'to say', as in sentence (4).

4. tomba-nə yeŋ-ŋi hay-bə drama ədu....
   Tomba -nom. see-asp. qut. drama det. ....
   'The drama that Tomba sees ...'

What is the difference between the two RCs — RC with Qut (4) and RC with NZR (sentences 1-2) — is that the RC with Qut. (4) has a relative marker (subordinate marker) **haybə** and the verb of the embedded clause is a finite verb whereas the RC with NZR (1-3) there is no relative marker, the verb of the embedded clause is not a finite verb but in nominalized form. In other word the embedded clause is more 'participle like'. The RC is regarded as participle like which is based on factors like the absence of a relative pronoun, relative marker (subordinate marker) and the embedded verb is not a finite verb.

Manipuri has a peculiar type of RC in which the head NP is not present in the surface structure. It is agreed that in this type of RC the speaker and the addressee have shared knowledge. Consider the following example :

5. tomba-nə nuŋsi-bə-do əsi-də cət-le

(tomba-nə nuŋsi-bə ləysabi-do əsi-də cət-le)
Tomba-nom love-NZR girl-det here-loc. go-asp
'Here goes the girl that Tomba loves'

In this sentence the head NP **ləysabi** is not present in the surface structure. In this language, RC of different aspects can be constructed. Consider the following sentences :

6. tomba-nə yek-li-bə lay ....[Cont. asp -li-]
Tomba-nom draw-asp-NZR picture....
'The picture which is drawing by Tomba ....'

7. tomba-nə yek-lə-bə lay ..... [Pref.asp -lə<le]
'The picture which has been drawn by Tomba ...'

8. tomba-nə yek-kədə-bə lay .... [Unreal.asp -kə<kəni]
'The picture which will be drawn by Tomba....'

What is learnt from the above discussion is that there is no relative pronoun. Answer is that RC is formed by the addition of NZR -pə~bə to the embedded verb and a determiner (functioning as correlative marker) (subordinate marker). One peculiar is that there is relativization of headless NP. It is come to know that there is only prenominal RC strategy for forming RC in Manipuri.

CAUSATIVIZATION

9.5 Causativization

A causative construction indicates a situation in which two events are involved: a preceding causing event and a subsequent caused event. They occur in such a way that if there had been no causing event, the caused event could not have followed. This situation is called 'macrosituation" which is thus comprised of two micrositutions: a causing microsituation or antecedent and a caused microsituation or consequent.

your silence caused her to be worried

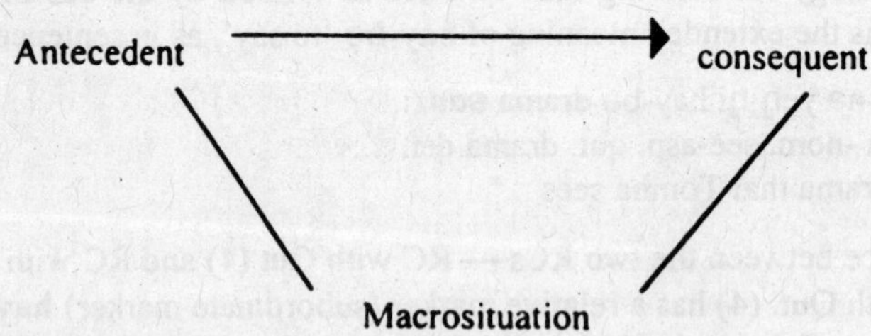

The causing microsituation is "your silence", as a consequence of which "she was worried". It can be asserted that had you not been silence she would not have been worried.

Causative forms are of two types morphologically regular and productive forms, and non-productive forms which are morphologically irregular. Productive causative constructions involved either the use of auxiliary causative verbs or the use of affixes. Languages of the isolating type have a tendency to use auxiliary causative verbs, while agglutinative languages tend to use affixes.

Manipuri is an agglutinative language, and has both productive and non-productive types of causatives.

9.5.1 Lexical Causatives

Manipuri has some suppletive pairs of simple causative verbs, e.g.

si-bə	'to die'	hat-pə	'to kill'
ca-bə	'to eat'	pijə-bə	'to feed' (solid food)
thək-pə	'to drink'	pi-thək-pə	'to feed' (liquid)
yeŋ-bə	'to see'	ut-pə	'to show'
tum-bə	'to sleep'	sum-bə	'to lull/' to put to sleep'
məy-cakpə	'to catch fire'	məy tha-bə	'to fire'
təω-bə	'to dig'	phumbə	'to bury'
ləω-bə	'to take'	mət-pə	'to make myself owner of something'
mun-bə	'to snatch'		
mut-pə	'off (light)	munthət-pə	'to put off'
kay-bə	'to break'	thugay-bə	'to make it broken'
tət-pə (in thread or wire)	'to break'	thəthət-pə	'to make the thread or wire break'

Notice that lexical causative are very irregular that is why they are classed as un-productive.

The causative marker **-hən~-həl** can be suffixed to these pairs, given above. One interesting, here, is that the meanings are not same : addition of **hən** to the non-causative verb gives one meaning while addition of to causative verb is another. This can be clear from the following examples

1 a. məhak-nə tomba si-həl-li
he-nom. Tomba die-caus.-asp.
'He has caused Tomba death'

b. məhak-nə tomba hat-həl-li
'He has caused (Tomba) killed by some one'

The above two sentences are obviously found different 'he' in (1a) is the Subject as well as the Agent of being died of 'Tomba' while 'he' is (1b) is the subject but not the Agent of killing. In other words, 'he' hired some one to kill Tomba, indirectly related with the action but not directly.

2 a. məma-nə əŋaŋ-du səŋgom thək-həl-le
his mother -non. baby-det milk drink -caus-asp.
'The mother has made the baby drink milk'

b. məmma-nə əŋaŋ-du səŋgom pithək-həl-le
'The mother has made the baby drink milk (by someone)'

This sentece (2) has the same difference with sentence 1 :in (2a) the mother feeds her baby but in 2b) the mother made someone to feed the baby (another agent is involved to feed the child). This difference in meaning i.e., involvement of another 'agent' in sentence (bs) is created by the suffixation of **-hən ~həl.**

A sentence can be analysed in the following way :

3. huy əma si-re
dog one die-asp
'A dog has died'

4. əy-nə huy əma hat-le
I-nom. dog one kill-pref.-asp
'I have killed a dog'

Although the two roots **si-** 'die' and **hat-** 'kill' have no phonological similarity, they can be easily related by means of the generative semantic approach; the causation is not overtly marked in the surface structure, but it is there at the abstract semantic level. The verb **hat** 'kill' contains in its underlying structure the verb **si-** 'die'. Hence the semantic interpretation for **hat-** can be stated as CAUSE DIE, even though the verb **si-** never actually appears in the surface structure of the sentence. Thus a sentence like **məhak-nə kəy əma hat-li** 'He kills a tiger', in which the element of CAUSE is not present in the surface structure, can still be viewed in terms of a causing event to say:

5. məhak-nə kəy əma hat-li ədubu kəy-du si-de
he-nom. tiger one kill-asp. but tiger -det. die-neg.
'He kills a tiger, but that tiger does not die'

In fact, both lexical and productive causatives share semantic properties.

9.5.2. Morphological Causatives.

There is much evidence that the Tibeto-Burman languages (Tibetan, Kachin, Burmese, Lissu etc.) once had a highly-developed morphological process of forming causatives from simplex verbs by addition of a prefix * s- which was a regular process of forming causative verbs.[1] Maintaining the process of regularity for forming causative verbs in Tibeto-Burman, Manipuri has still a uniform strategy for forming causatives from all kinds of non-causative verbs. All verbs (intransitive and transitive) form their corresponding morphological causatives by suffixing the causative marker **-hən~-həl** direct to the root, as in the following way :

I [Root + Caus. marker + Asp] $_{\text{Verb}}$
ca + hən + y = Simp Asp
eat li ~ri - Cont.
re~le - Pref.
gəni ~kəni- Unreal.

Example :

ca+hən +y ➔ ca +həl-li 'to cause (him) eat'
+li ➔ ca-həl-li 'action continuing'
+ le ➔ ca-həl-le 'action completed'
+gəni ➔ ca-hən-gəni 'action to perform in unrealized time'

II [Root + Caus.mk. + NZR] $_{\text{Nominal}}$

---

1. This process survives faintly but unmistakably in present-day Lahu as well. There remain more than a dozen pairs of verbs related to each other semantically as simplex/causative or intransitive / transitive, and differing phonologically from each other only by tone (and sometimes voicing of the initial consonant).

Example :

thək+hən+bə ➔ thək-hən-bə 'to cause (him) drink'
cət+hən+bə ➔ cət-hən-bə 'to cause (him) go
tum+hən+bə ➔ tum-hən-bə 'to cause him sleep'

III [Root + Caus.mk. + X ....]

Example :

cət+hən+niŋ +khi+de
go-caus - desire +def. +neg
'Having no intention to make (him) go'
pa+hən+ləm-dri-ŋəy-də
read-caus. - neg.-when-pleo.
(Before he was not made read)

IV. * ə + [Root + Caus. mk. + NZR]

Example :

*** ə+[ca+hən+asp/NZR /X]**
*** ə+[ca +hən +li]**
*** ə + [ca +hən +bə]**

The syntactic constraint here is that the adjective formative ə- cannot occur with causative marker - hən in any condition.

Here are some sentences :

6. əy-nə məhak-pu cak ca-həl-li
I-nom. he-accus. rice eat-caus-asp.
'I-make him eat his meal'

7. məhak-nə tombə -bu siloŋ-də cət-həl-li
He made Tomba go to Shillong'

Notice that the causative marker - hən~həl can be added to all categories of verbal base. From an intrasitive base :

8. a. cəysu tek-le
stick break-asp
'The stick has broken'

b. məhak-nə cəysu tek-həl-le
he- nom. stick break caus-asp
'He has broken the stick'

From a transitive base :

9. a. məhak-nə ωa yal-li
he -nom. bamboo cut-asp
'He cuts the bamboo'

b. tomba-nə məhak-pu ωa yal-həl-li
Tomba-nom. he -accus bamboo cut-caus-asp
'Tomba makes him cut the bamboo'

9.5.3 DOUBLE CAUSATIVE

Here is a sentence having two objects :

10 məhak-nə dactər-bu ənabə layeŋ-həl-li
he-nom. doctor-Accus patient treat-caus-asp.
'He makes the doctor treat the patient'

An interesting point here is that when the case marker **-bu** (accusative) that is added to **daktər** 'doctor' in sentence (10) is replaced by dative case marker **-də** [daktər-də] and simultaneously the case marker **-bu** is added to **ənabə- [ənabə-bu]**, a new causative phenomenon comes up, as in sentence (11) :

11. məhak-nə daktər-də ənabə-bu layeŋ-həl-li
he-nom. doctor -dat patient-Accus. treat -caus-asp
'He makes the doctor have the patient treated'

What must be looked into carefully is that this sentence (11) is different from (10), even though they have the same constituents except for the case marker **-də** present in sentence (11). In sentence (10) daktər **-bu** is the agent (i.e. this doctor and not any other doctor has to give treatment to the very patient), but sentence (11) has no agent. **daktər** is not the agent in this structure ; instead the sentence has the sense of "double causative", i.e. 'He' and Doctor 'cause somebody else, say Mr. X, to give treatment to the very patient.

9.5.4 Ballastic Causation

Another type of causative construction is illustrated in sentence 12.

12 məhak-nə john-bu Memi-nə layrik təmbi -həl-li
he-nom. -accus -inst book teach -caus.- asp
'He makes Memi teach John'
(i.e., He causes John to be taught by Memi)

In this sentence, the **-nə** suffix on Memi is the instrumental marker. It appears that the embedded subject has been demoted down to an oblique position . Sentence 13 is another such sentence :

13. miyam-nə ma-bu john-nə phu-həl-li
people-nom. he-accus. -nom beat -caus.-asp
'People cause John to beat him'
(i.e., People make him to be beaten by John)

Sentences 12 and 13 are different from sentences 10 and 11 if the nature of the caused event is considered. The kind of causation in 12 and 13 appears to concide what Shibatani (1973) refers to as 'ballastic causation" which involves an action, as against "Continuous causation" where a state or process is depicted (as in sentences 10 and 11). Here the current of the action is running against the normal continuous causation.

9.5.5 Factitives and Permissive

Generally, morphological causatives are accompanied by two meanings: one is facititive (to make some one do something) and the other is permissive (to let someone do something). Manipuri makes no distinction between the factitive and the permissive.
For example :

14. məhak-nə ma-bu ka-də cəŋ-həl-li
he-nom. he-accus. room-loc. enter-caus.-asp
'He makes /lets him enter the room'

15. əy-nə məhak-pu hospital-də cət-həl-li
I-nom. he-acuus hospital-loc. go-caus.-asp
I make /let him go to the hospital.'

Sentences 14 and 15 show that Manipuri does not make semantic distinction between factitive and permissive.

9.5.6 Volition

Another important semantic factor is that of volition. The causative verbs that signify volitional events cannot occur with inanimate causers. In other words, inanimate causers can occur only with non-volitional verbs in Manipuri, as sentence 16 and 17 show :

16. miyam -nə ma-bu huranbə-du phu-həl-li
people-nom. he-accus thief -det beat-caus-asp
'People make him beat the thief'

17. saωniŋməndunə ma-nə huranbə-du phu-y
anger -much-being he-nom. thief -det beat-asp.
'He beats the thief out of angry'

Sentence 17 cannot be changed into sentence 18 which is ungrammatical.

18. * əsaωbənə-nə ma-bu huranbə-du phu-y
'Anger makes him beat the thief'

The difference between 16 and 18 is that the former has an animate causer while the latter sentence has an inanimate causer. Sentence 17 does not have a causer at all, and no causative marker on the verb.

However, a non -volitional event can take an inanimate causer, as in 19.

19. P.C. Sarkar-gi mejik-nə miyam-bu ŋək -həl-li
-gen. magic-inst. people-accus. surprise -caus. asp.
'P.C. Sarkar's magic surprises the people'

9.5.7. Quotative Causative.

In this construction Manipuri uses a bound morph **hay- (hay-bə)** 'to say' along with the morphological causative **-həl**,as in sentence 20.

20. Mr. X-nə Mr. Y-də John-bu isəy ta-hən-nəbə hay
-nom. -dat -accus. song hear-caus. suf say
'Mr. X tells Mr. Y to make John hear the song'

Notice that this construction includes another derivational suffix following the causative marker **-hən** which is not found in the construction of morphological causatives, that is **-nəbə**. Without this suffix (-nəbə), the quotative causative construction is ungrammatical, as in sentence 21.

*21. Mr. X-nə Mr. Y-də John-bu isəy ta-hən hay

Lexical causatives can also occur in this quotative construction, as in sentence 22 :

22. əy-nə John-də ucek-tu hat-nəbə hay
I -nom. -dat. bird -det. kill - say
'I tell John to kill the bird'.

The same meaning of sentence 20 is conveyed by the suffixation of **-həl** to **hay [hay-həl-li]** as in sentence 23.

23. Mr. X-nə Mr. Y-də John-bu isəy ta- nəbə hay-həl-li
'Mr . X tells Mr. Y to make John hear the song'

It is clear now that morphological causative is very regular and can be suffixed all categories of verb. More and above, it is also learnt that it has many semantic roles.

REDUPLICATION

9.6 Reduplication

9.6.1 Introduction

Reduplication is that repetition, the result of which constituted the unit word. Reduplication can be classified into four, namely complete, partial, echo and mimic. Complete reduplication, according to Apte (1968) is of three main types : (1) repetition of a one-word utterance, (ii) repetition of a clause or phrase and (iii) repetition of single morpheme and / or words. Reduplication is a linguistic feature analysed in 'India as a linguistic area 'by Masica (1976). T-B languages (i.e. Burmese, Lahu etc.) are rich in reduplication.

Manipuri is also rich in reduplication and is used very commonly in speech. The four types mentioned above are found in the language.

9.6.2 Types of Reduplication

9.6.2.1 Complete Reduplication

Complete reduplication refers to the phenomenon when a single word or clause is repeated once in the same sentence without any phonological or morphological variations. Complete reduplication can occur in :

Noun

yum	yum ;	ka	ka
house	house	room	room
məphəm	məphəm	ləybak	ləybak
place	place	country	country
əŋaŋ	əŋaŋ	pukhri	pukhri
child	child	pond	pond
məcet	məcet	mərik	mərik
piece	piece	drop	drop

As they occur in sentences :

1. nupa məca -siŋ yum yum-də hən-khre
boy -plu house house -loc. return-asp
'The boys have returned to their respective houses'

2. ləybak ləybak-ki məsa-gi phiral ləy
country country own -gen flag has
'Every country has its own flag'

It is, here, a point that addition of case marker to the second repeated word is syntactically preferred (-də and -ki) respectively.

wh- Question Words

In Manipuri, very often a repetition of wh-question words is used. Reduplicable wh-question words are given below :

kəri kəri ; kəna kəna
which which who who
(what what)
kərəm kərəm ; kəday kəday
how how where where

They can be seen occurring in the following sentences

3. nəŋ kəri kəri sannəpot ləy-gəni
You which which toy buy-asp
'Which toys do you buy ?'

4. kəna kəna peristə cət-kəni
Who who - loc. go-asp
'Who will go to Paris ?'
(How many of you will go to Paris ?)

Adjectives

There is also reduplication in adjectives. The paired construction in which the first is a base while the second repeated form is a complete adjective (attributive) from (i.e. -bə is added to the second while it is not in the case of first), as given here :

I	II
əŋaŋ	əŋaŋ +bə
red	red

— ↑ is added to the second not to the first

* əŋaŋ +bə əŋaŋ+bə (ungrammatical)

Other examples are

əŋəω	əŋəω-bə	;	əpik	əpik-pə
white	white		small	small
əsa	əsa-bə	;	ətek	ətek-pə
hot	hot		fresh	fresh

As they occur in the sentences;

5. əy [əŋaŋ əŋaŋ-bə / əŋaω əŋaω-bə / ətek ətek-pə] ləy pam-mi
I flower like-asp
'I like red/white/fresh flowers'.

Adverbs :

Here are some examples :

yam-nə	yam-nə	;	kəp-nə	kəp-nə
very	very		cryingly	cryingly
ŋaŋ-nə	ŋaŋ-nə	;	ta-nə	ta-nə
talking	talking		listening	listening
təp-nə	təp-nə	;	yaŋ-nə	yaŋ-nə
slowly	slowly		fast	fast

Their occurrence in sentences :

6. məhak skul-də ŋaŋ-nə [kəp-nə kəp-nə / ŋaŋ-nə / təp-nə təp-nə] cət-li
he schol-loc. go-asp

'He goes to school cryingly / in talking / slowly'

7. John yu yam-nə yam-nə thək-y
liquor very very heavily'
'John drinks liquor very heavily'

Verbs

In the case of verbs, reduplication differs from other reduplication of nouns, adjectives, adverbs and wh-question words: repetetion of verb is generally constructed in subject-objectless structure; it is a sentence, no doubt, so named as sentential reduplication. This is grammatically possible in different types of sentence constructions such as informative statement, command and request,

1. Informative (reporting) statement : that informing the addresses by a speaker about an action or event, as in sentence 8.

8. cət-le cət-le
go-asp go-asp
'I am going'

The underlying structure of this sentence 8, **əy cət-le əy cət-le** 'I am going'. Informing that 'I am leaving' occurred just at the 'moment of departure', **-le~re** normally indicates, 'perfect', but in this context it does not indicate perfect aspect'. The sentence 8 is also ambiguous. It can give the meaning of : 'He is going' informing the very person is going. It further said that both the subjects first person or second person can be the subject. The context and the situation decide which person is ?

Command

Here the subject is definitely a second person though it is not overtly in the structure, and repetition of such type is very commonly used in speech. This is a subject-object-less structure. Command is formed by the suffixation of / **ru/~/lu** / and **-lo~ro** etc. (see in Imperative 8.3.) to the action oriented verb root . Here are two sentences :

9. a. cət-lo —cət-lo

go-comd. go-comd.
'Go'

b. ca-ro ca-ro
eat-comd. eat-comd.
'Have it'

Request

It can be also used in request sentence, for instance :

10. leŋ-bi-ro; leŋ-bi-ro
go-hon-comd go-hon. -comd
'Please go'
(Detail discussion can be seen in Imperative 8.3.)

9.6.2.2 Partial Reduplication

Partial reduplication refers to the paired construction in which the second word is not an exact repetition of the first but is similar or related to the first either on the sentence or phonetic level. Here are the examples.

cət-thok cətsin ; mərək sarək
go go between
(to go to and fro) ; (not coming to a complete shape)
(movement)
haydok hayjin ; puthok pusin
open close bring out bring in
(repetition of opening and closing) ; (repetition of bringing out and bringing in)

As they occur in sentences :

11. məhak cətthok cətsin ŋəm-də-re
he to go to and fro able-neg-asp.
'he is unable to move here and there'

12. thoŋ-du haydok hayjin təω-gə-nu
door-det open close do-asp-proh.
'Don't keep the door in opening and closing'

Here in sentence 11 and 12, they function as adverb; they also can function as nominal, as in sentence 13 and 12

13. cətthok cətsin toy-nə təω-nu , phət-te
to go to and fro often do-neg. good-neg-asp
'Don't move here and there, it is not good.'

cətthok cət-sin in sentence 11 function as adverb while in 13 it funcion as nominal. There is also noun in partial reduplication :

nə-səm nə-na ; sa-phi lan-phi
your-hair your ear (dress for battle) 'war dress'
sa-rəm ŋa-rəm ; həy-nəm ləy-nəm
aminal-way fish-way fruit-smell flower-smell
'the path where the animal

goes and back' 'the smell of fruits and flower'

sa-mi lan-mi
animal-man war-man ;
'army'

As they occur in sentences :

14. nəsəm nə-nə təru təru-nə thəm-mu
your hair neat and clean keep -comd
'Keep your hair in neat and clean'

15. ləykol əse həynəm ləynəm-nə thəl-le
garden this fruit-smell flower smell ful-asp
'The garden is full of smell of fruits and flowers'

What it is found in these partial reduplication is that they look like phrase or idiom and so they are not productive. Looking through their morphological structure, they are all compounding the first unit also and the second unit also. Very briefly, an underlying meaning can be established. (Detail will be discussed in Word-formation 4). For instance

sa-phi (sa-phabədə set-nəbə phi) 'the dress to be worn in hunting'

lan-phi 'the dress to be worn in war'

9.6.2.3 Echo Words

Refer to a situation where the second word in the paired construction does not have any meaning of its own, when it is attached to the first word, an idea of generality is obtained.

isiŋ maysiŋ ; mityeŋ nayyeŋ
'water' 'the way of looking'
phəyreŋ tureŋ ; phəmuŋ phanuŋ
not properly moving bed
seran turan ;
wrong doing

Their occurrence in sentences :

16. a. nəŋ isiŋ maysiŋ sok-cil-ləbra
you water collect-in-asp -Q.mk.
'Have you collected water'?

b. ləmbi-də yu ŋaorəgə phəyreŋ tureŋ cət-nu
road -loc. liquor drunkard imbalancing movement go -proh.
'Don't go on the road imbalancing manner after drinking alcohol'.
(Don't go improperly on the way after drinking)

Though the second has no meaning at all in the paired of the echo word, but in the sentence structure it gives a little wider spectrum which will be discussed in detail in section, Various Meaning of Reduplication.

9.6.2.4 Mimic Words

Like other reduplicative types, mimic words also pertain to situation where there is a complete reduplication, but the morphemes are onomatopoetic. In other words, mimic words are compounds and represent natural sounds or emotional feelings verbally, Examples are

ŋrəŋ ŋrəŋ 'roaring sound (of tiger or thunder)
It can also reffer to child's continuous cry.
cek cek 'chirping sound (of bird)
srit srit 'very slppery'
phən phən 'hopping (of bird)'

Note that without the words in bracket the mimic words do not indicate a complete sense. The mimic words generally modify the verb. Their occurrance in the sentences are given below.

17. a ta-o, ətiya-də noŋ-nə ŋrəŋ ŋrəŋ ŋəŋ-li
hear-comd. sky-loc. rain-nom. roar-asp
'Listen, in the sky there is the thundering sound'

b. ucek-nə phən phən coŋ-li
bird-nom hop-asp
'The bird is hopping'

9.6.3 Various Meaning of Reduplication

Reduplication, generally, has many different semantic shades in a language. Reduplication has the meanings of distributiveness, plurality and emphatics. Manipuri has these meanings and it employs reduplication for several interrelated sorts of semantic effect ; the precise shade of meaning conveyed by a reduplication depends on the context. Reduplication has other functions as well : e.g. to give frequentive or continuous meaning to verb (in Burmese also) yó- yó thωa 'become slacker and slacker' ; or familiarity when applied to knidship terms : e.g. dodo 'aunti from 'ado', in Burmese.

9.6.3.1 Plurality Meaning

Complete reduplication of wh-question words expresses the meaning of plurality, as in sentences 18.

18. a. nəŋ kəri kəri layrik pam-mi
you which which book want-asp
'Which books do you want ?'
(Which are the books you want ?)

b. nəŋ kəri layrik pam-mi
'Which book do you want?'

18.a. implies a plural meaning (more than 'one book') while (b) only 'one book'. Same is the case of **kəna** 'who', as in sentence 19.

19. a. kəna kəna moyraŋ cət-kəni
who who Moirang go-asp
'Who will go to Maoirang ?'
(Who are the persons to go to Moirang)?

b. kəna moyraŋ cət-kəni
14 who Moirang go-asp
'Who is going to Moirang ?'

19.a implies 'some' have to go to Moirang among many (but who are those) while (b) refers to 'one' ('one' has to go to among 'many'). Plurality is also expressed by a complete reduplication of adjective, as in sentence 20.

20. a. məhak-ki əŋəw əŋəwbə həwdoŋ ləy
he -gen. white white cat has
'He has many white cats'

b. məhak-ki əŋəwbə həwdoŋ əma ləy
'He has a white cat'

The statement that a complete reduplication of adjective indicates plurality, can be more clarified by the sentence 21.

* 21 məhak-ki əŋəω əŋəωbə həωdoŋ əma ləy

This is ungrammatical because əŋəω əŋəωbə (this reduplication) can not co-occur with the singular marker əma 'one'. This repetition carries meaning of pluratily not singularity.

9.6.3.2 Distributive Meaning

Reduplication (complete) of a noun indicates the meaning of distributiveness, as in sentences 21(a) and (b).

21. a. əŋaŋ-siŋ ka ka-də hən-khre
child -plu room room-loc. return-asp.
'The children have returned to their respective rooms'

b. yum yum-də ce-si yenthok-u
house house -loc. paper-det. distributive-comd.
'Distribute this paper to each house'

It is noted that sentences 21(a) and (b) without particular lexical item **khudiŋmək or khudiŋ-də** 'each' or 'every', expressed the meaning of distributiveness which is indicated by the repetition of nouns **ka ka-or əŋaŋ əŋaŋ-** in the sentences respectively.

9.6.3.3 Modifying or Emphatic Meaning.

Rather than distributiveness and plurality meaning reduplication (mimic word) denotes modifying or emphatic meaning, as in 22(a) and (b).

22. a. ləmbi-si srit srit nal-li
road -det slippery -asp.
'The road is very very slippery'

b. meri english breŋ breŋ ŋaŋ-ŋi
Mary English speak-asp.
'Mary speaks English very fluently'
(English is not her mother tongue but she speaks very well)

The mimic words exactly express the meaning of 'very' or 'degree' as in 22 (a) and (b). This statement can be examined again by comparing with the following sentence 23 (a) and (b), sentences without mimic words respectively.

23. a. ləmbi-si nal-li
'The road is slippery'

b. meri English ŋaŋ-ŋi
'Mary speaks English'
(English is not her mother tongue but she can speak)

Mimic words, in this language, are imaginary; they actually visualize our senses. Not only the mimic -words express a modifying meaning but a complete reduplication of adverb can also denote, as in sentences 24 (a) and (b)

24. a. məhak təp-nə təp-nə cət-li
he slowly slowly go-asp
'He goes slowly slowly'

b. məhak kəp kəp-nə cət-li
'He goes cryingly'

In Burmese also 'continuous meaning' is found and it gives certain verb : **yó- yó thωa** 'become slacker and slacker'. reduplication of adverb can exprcss durative meaning or span of time.

9.6.3.4 Durative Meaning

Here is a sentence

25. məhak kωa jon-nə jon-nə əhal oyrək-le
he betalnut sell sell adv. old become -asp.
'He has become old in selling betelnut'
(He lives on selling betelnut, now he is becoming old in age).

The reduplicated word **jon-nə jon-nə**, adverb, fully express the span of time.

9.6.3.5. Familiarity Meaning

Meaning of familiarity can also be expressed by reduplication. This is generally used to kinship terms, by the children in calling their elders.
For examples,

dəω dhəω	' grandy'	from	idhəω	'grand father'
bok bok	'grany	from	əbok	'grand mother'
nene	'Aunty'	from	ine	'Aunt' (father's sister)

These are very informal kinship terms used by the kins and this also indicates familiarity and attachment relationship.

In general, the echo words and partial reduplication are seemed readymade phrases or idioms; they are not productive. Regarding the meaning, any of them shows a little wider sense ; it can feel to our sense but what are included is physically undefinable for instance ; **sa-rəm ŋa-rəm**[1]

1. It is a phrase, however, only one (either sa-rəm or ŋa-rəm) can also be used in different context; and indicates the meaning of variety as in sentences

a. sa-rəm təret pha-rə-gə lay-də kət-kə-də-bə-ni
animal - variety seven catch -dur-assoc. God-det. Worship-Asp-NZR-COP.
'By catching seven varieties of animal you must worship God.'

b. ŋə-rəm təret -nə əŋaŋ-du caωum-le
fish-variety seven -inst. baby -det start eating -asp. solid food'
'The baby has started eating of solid food with seven varieties of fishes'.

sa-rəm ŋarəm 'the usual path of animal/fish going to and fro
animal path fish path (partial reduplication)
isiŋ maysiŋ 'water and ....'
water X
huy nuŋ ' dog and ....'
dog X

Let's see the following two sentences :

26. a. huy cəŋ -hən -gənu
dog enter-caus -asp. -proh.
'Don't let the dog enter'

b. huy-nuŋ cəŋ-hən-gənu
Don't let enter the dog and others'

26(b) covers some others also i.e. 'dog and others' but not particularizes the second animal.

9.6.4 Reduplicative Environment

In this language, there is a syntactic environment which needs reduplication of root or base by the prefixation of some prefixes. The prefixes are : i-, pəŋ-, khəŋ, tə-, pum-~puŋ-, suk-, etc. By the prefixation of these prefixes the root is reduplicated otherwise it is ungrammatical.

[i- / pəŋ- / khəŋ / tə- / pum- / suk-] + Root ➔ [i- / pəŋ- / khəŋ / tə- / puŋ- / suk-] +Root +Root

They indicate different meaning and even the same prefix changes its meaning according to the context. More and above, they can occur in both the environments — negative and affirmative. But the prefix **suk-** can occur only in negative environment.

9.6.4.1 Prefix

i- has different meaning according to the context.
Let'us see 27 (b) as a reply to a question 27(a)

27. a. nəŋ təl ca-bəra , cak ca-bə-ra ?
you bread eat -NZR. Qmk. rice eat-NZR. -Qmk.
'Do you take either bread or rice ?'

b. əy i-ca ca-y
i - eat eat-asp
'I eat anything'

'superlative meaning'

28. u əsi-nə i-ωaŋ waŋ-ŋi
tree this-nom. -tall-asp
'This tree is the tallest one'

i- 'normally'

29. **məhak məyaŋ i-kəŋ kəŋ-ŋi**
he body -thin thin-asp
'He is normally thin'

i- 'almost'

30. **kobi-si i-pət pət-le**
cabbage-det -rotten rotten -asp.
'The cabbage has almost rottened'
(not completely rotten)

khəŋ - 'at once' or 'suddenly'

31. **paω-du hek ta-bə-gə məhak khəŋ-saω saω-re**
neaws -det. just hear-NZR.- he -angry angry -asp
'Just when he heard the news he started angry suddenly'

pum - 'completely'

32. **məna-məsiŋ-si pum-pət pət-le**
vegetable-det. -rotten rotten -asp.
'This vegetable is completely rotten'

puŋ-˜pəŋ- 'anything'

33. **məhak-ti puŋ-/pəŋ- ca ca-y**
he -def. -eat eat -asp
'He eats anything'
(He eats anything whether it is tasty or not).

suk- 'never'

This occurs only in negative environment.

34. **məhak yu suk-thək thək-te**
he liquor -drink -neg-asp.
'He never drinks liquor'

There are two prefixes i-, and pəŋ - changing their meaning depending on the environments they occur; if they (i-, and pəŋ-) occur in affirmative environment, as in sentence (27-33), they have those meanings. In case they occurred in negative environment, they give the meaning of 'less degree', as in sentence 35.

35. **məhak yu pəŋ-thək thək-te**
he liquor drink drink -neg-asp
'He rarely drinks'
(He drinks but not often)

9.6.4.2 Suffixes

Rather then these prefixes, there are some suffixes which force the root to be reduplicated. The suffixes are -trik˜drik, - throk, -droŋ, -suk, -səŋ, - driŋ, sit, -sin, -dreŋ, sroke etc. By

their suffixation, they modify the meaning i.e. 'emphatic meaning'. In other words they express 'superlative degree'.

1. -trik

mun-trik	munbə	'very ripe'
ripe	ripe	
səŋ-trik	səŋ-bə	'deep green'
green	green-NZR.	(not still ripe)
tum-trik	tum-bə	'very pointed'
pointed	pointed -NZR.	

35. məhak-nə səŋ-trik səŋ-bə phurit pam-mi
he-NZR. green green-NZR. shirt like -asp
'He wants very dark green shirt'

2. - throk

law	-	throk laω-bə	'very loose'
loose	-	loose-NZR	
pak-throk		pak-pə	'very wide'
wide	-	wide-NZR.	
caω	-	throkcaω-bə	'very big'
big	-	big-NZR.	

37. məhak-ti caω-throk caω-bə phurititə lit-li
he -def. big - big-NZR. shirt -only put on-asp
'He wears only big shirt'

3. -droŋ

saŋ-droŋ		saŋ-bə	'very long'
long	-	long-NZR	

38. saŋ-droŋ saŋ-bə cəy-nə ya-roy
long- long-NZR stick-inst. do-neg. asp
'The very long stick cannot do it'

4. -suk / -sin

mu-suk/sin mu-ʋə phi
black black -NZR. cloth

39. məhak-nə mu-suk mu-bə phurit əma ləy
he-NZR. black black-NZR. shirt one buy
'He buys very deep black shirt'

5. - səŋ

ŋaŋ-səŋ ŋaŋ-bə ləy
red- red-NZR flower

40. əy ŋaŋ-səŋ ŋaŋ-bə ləy pam-mi
I red- red flower like-asp
'I want a very deep red flower'

6. - driŋ

cum-driŋ cum-bə 'very straight'

41. cum-driŋ cum-bə ləy-yi əma ciŋ-ŋu
straight straight line one draw-comd.
'Draw a very straight line'

7. -sit

kut-sit kut-pə 'very low / very deep'

42. mi-bu kutsit kut-nə ŋaŋbə phə-te
people-acc. deep deep-adv. speak good-neg.-asp
'To speak very badly of others is bad'.

8. - thrəŋ or - drəŋ

waŋ-thrəŋ ωaŋbə
ωaŋ-drəŋ ωaŋbə 'very tall'
tall tall

43. u-si məsa əmətə pan-de , ωaŋ-drəŋ ωaŋ-ŋi
tree -det. branches but very very tall
'The tree has no branches, but it is very tall'

9. - srok

ŋəω-srok ŋəω-bə phi
white- white cloth

44. əy-nə ŋəω-srok ŋəωbə un-nə kup-pə ciŋdol uy
I -NZR. white -white -NZR. cover hill see
'I see a very white snow -capped mountain top'.

9.6.5 Double Reduplication

There are some prefixes and suffixes which forces the root to occur thrice in a sentence, at the time the prefix or suffix is also repeated in the first and second successively, in the third the prefix or suffix is neither occurred.

9.6.5.1 Prefix

i-mun i-mun munbə həynəω
-ripe -ripe ripe mango
puŋ-mun puŋ-mun munbə həynəω
- ripe -ripe ripe mango
'Many many ripe mangoes'
suk-khəŋ suk-khəŋ-dəbə ωahəŋ
-know -know know-neg. -NZR. question
'Many many unknown questions' (difficult questions)

Semantically, these thrice repetition do not express any meaning of 'degree', i.e. 'degree of ripeness of the mango' or 'degree of difficulty of the question' but they give the meaning of 'plurality'

9.6.5.2 Suffixes

There are suffixes occurred twice with the root on the same way as the previous prefixes.

Examples are given below :

ŋaŋ-səŋ ŋaŋ-səŋ ŋaŋbə həytup
red - red- red apple
'Very very red apples'
səŋ-trik səŋ-trik səŋəbə həytup
green - green- green apple
'Very very green apples'
ŋəω-srok ŋəω-srok ŋəωbə thebə
white - white- white rabbit
'Very very white rabbits'

These indicates the 'degree of ripneness of apple' or whiteness of rabbit' at the same time it also indicate plurality of the objects.

9.6.6. Semantic Reduplication

Mentioned already that Manipuri is very rich in reduplication and also discussed many aspects of reduplication. There is still another aspect, that is, semantic reduplication. Moravcsik in his paper, Reduplicative Construction (1978) expresses his opinion that semantic reduplication words belong to different languages. This is true in the case of Manipuri also[2]. Because one word belong to one clan while another word belong to another clan.

1. nembi - siŋŋaŋ : 'weeds'
   - [Meitei clan]
   - [Khuman clan](Ningthourol Lamuba , 17)

2. ucek-səωa : 'birds'
   - [Moirang Clan]
   - [Meitei Clan] (Moirang Kangleirol, p. 9)

3. ərak-əkhəŋ : 'a sudden danger'
   - [Meitei Clan]
   - [Moirang Clan] (Ningthourol Lambuba, p.54)

4. pamba-kəy : tiger'
   - [Khuman]
   - [Meitei] (Khuman Kangleirol, p. 52)

---

2. It is accepted that the Modern Manipuri is the mixture of 9 gruops. viz. Chenlei, Luwang, Khuman, moirang (Kege), Angom, Khaba, Mangang, Heireni, and Khuman. During the process of state formation all the groups merged into one and become the Meitei. The language of the Meitei is Meiteilon (locally) and officially named as Manipuri. Each group has its own tongue. A few lexical items can be mentioned though a large number is not traceable.

5. taωtek-nəω : 'oar'
[Meitei Clan]
[Khuman Clan] (Khuman Kangleirol, p. 12)

6. həl-ləkpə - tərəkpə 'return'
[Seloy]
[Meitei Clan] (Ningthourol Lambuba p. 15)

7. yambi-loŋ 'spear'
[Meitei Clan]
[Luwang Clan] (Moirang Ningthourol Lambuba, p. 46)

The order of the words will remain as it is and semantic reduplication is mostly used in formal speech or in literature.

There are a few words which are formed by complete reduplication otherwise it does not indicate a meaning

They are :

məm məm	=	cak	;	kuku	= isiŋ
rice (cooked)		rice (cooked)		water	water
cu cu	=	khom			
breast milk		breast milk			

These three words are used to baby. There are other words also without reduplication it has no meaning. They are :

moli moli ; ŋaωri ŋaωri
very slowly slightly mad
ŋaŋli ŋaŋli ; ŋəωri ŋəωri
reddish in colour whitist in colour
(slightly red in colour) (slightly white in color)
silli sil-li
slightly sour ;

As they occur in sentence :

45. əy [silli sil-li / ŋaŋli ŋaŋ-li / nəωri ŋəωri] təωbə həytup pam-mi
I to be apple like-asp

'I want slightly [sour / reddish / whitist] apple'

From this, it is evident that reduplication is one of the major linguistic features of Meitielon and it is known that it has many aspects of reduplication.

CHAPTER–X

SOCIAL GRAMMAR

10.1 Taboo

Taboo in Manipuri is denoted by 'namu ›ba'. Taboos, here, are primarily concerned with the linguistic prohibition. Here it is more appropriate to say as **hay-hšy-de**. It is **hay-hšy-de** to mention **sšna** 'gold' or **lil** 'snake' at night, for example. In general, in a society certain words are not allowed to be uttered under certain condition and at certain time. In place of such forbidden words, it is necessary to use some kind of figurative paraphrases, euphemisms, circumlocutions and other linguistic devices, so as to render the speech more polite and acceptable. The taboo words reflect the values and beliefs of a society. They are determined by some factors like religion, belief, social condition and psychology of the people. The taboo words of Manipuri can be categorised into as follows : 1. Taboo on personal names 2. Taboo on kin terms 3. Taboo on certain animals 4. Taboo on diseases 5. Taboo on certain items at night 6. Taboo on certain words connected with spirit. 7. Taboo words related with sex.

10.1.1 Categories of Taboo Words.

10.1.1.1 Taboo on Personal Name :

It is prohibited to utter the name of a dead person under the normal circumstances in the presence of the relatives of the deceased. When it is compelled it is used some circumlocation such as **lšykhidršbš** 'the person (male) who is dead' along with appropriate kin term and the name of the decease person, e.g.

lšykhidršbš ibu ›o	'male'	'has become God'
lšykhidršbi	(female)	

Another case is that, generally wife is not allowed to use the name of her husband which is in Manipuri is **ipuroybš** derived from **šybu loybš** 'the one who owns me' (literally a woman is owned by her husband). The **ipuroybš < šybu loybš** is a compound word — **šy** 'I' bu 'accusative marker' + loy 'own' + bš 'NZR'. As a taboo a wife does not pronounce her husband's name but calls him by some ejaculations or teknonyms. She may address her husband by taking her eldest son's or daughter's name or the name of a person closely related to him (his sister's or brother's) e.g. **may pabu›** 'his father'. **mškhoy tacšω**' their eldest brother' etc. Besides it, she can generally draws her husband's attention by uttering **'tabiribra'** do you hear' (**ta** 'hear', **bi** honorific marker', **-ri** 'progressive aspect', bš 'NZR' **ra** 'question marker'). Even a husband also can use this term without the honorific marker **-bi** as **taribra**.

In Manipuri Meitei custom, it is not permitted to address older people by their personal names. The kinship addressing terms are extended and used the appropriate one, as given in the followings :

Male		Female	
tadš tamo	elder brother	ice	'elder sister'

pabu ›	'daddy'	ima	'mummy'
khura	'uncle'	indon	'aunty'
ibay	'brother-in-law'	ine	'father's sister'
mama	'mother's brother	itšyma	'elder brother's wife' etc.

10.1.1.2 Taboo on Kin Terms

In Meitei society, there is a very strict avoidance relationship between elder brother-in-law (husband's elder brother) and younger sister-in law (younger brother's wife). They cannot talk directly face to face. The elder brother-in-law can call her by name but the younger sister-in-law cannot call him (elder-brother-in-law) by name.

10.1.1.3 Taboo on Certain Animal Names

Taboo on the names of some dangerous animals are given below :

Words	Gloss	Euphemism	Gloss
samu	'elephant'	šωa ›bš	'the tall one'
kšy	'tiger'	ibudhšω	'grand-father'
lin	'snake'	napi	'grass'

The name of some these dangerous animals — **samu** 'elephant' **kšy** 'tiger' and **lin** 'snake' are not allowed to be mentioned specially at night. In place of those animal names displaced words such as **šωa›bš** 'the tall one' **ibudhšω** 'grand father' and **napi** 'grass' are used respectively.

10.1.1.4 Taboo on the Use of some Words at Night :

It is also prohibited to utter the words, namely, **yetum** 'needle' and **yay›š›** 'turmeric' at night. In place of **yetum**, displaced word, **phigi maybi** 'physician of cloth' and **mšcu** 'colour' for **yay›a›** 'turmeric' are found to be in use at night. In ceremonies **sanš** 'gold' is replaced by **yay›š›** 'turmeric'.

10.1.1.5 Taboo on Certain Diseases

It was also forbidden to mention the name of some dreaded diseases in Meitei custom. People were not allowed to utter dreaded diseases, such as **pukcštpš** 'cholera', **layjaω thokpš** 'small pox', **tibi** 'TB' and **š›šωbš pškpš** 'leprosy' in normal situation. Even today people are afraid of mentioning these and other dreaded diseases. Before mentioning, under some circumstances, the diseases people use a phrase **haybšdi hayhšy-de** 'it is not proper to mention, however.....'

10.1.1.6 Taboo on Certain Words Connected with Evil Spirit :

To utter unnatural deaths, namely, **thšωri-yanbš** 'hang' and premature deaths, namely **š›a›-yšythšbš** 'abortion' and **lšyyšy-cštpš** 'miscarriage 'were tabooed as such acts were believed to be associated with evil spirits. But now it gradually becomes light to mention.

It is also a taboo to say **haω** 'yes' as a respond to a stranger's call at night. Instead of saying **haω** 'yes' one is advised to say **kšri haybš-ge** 'what are you saying' or **kšna-no** 'who are you'.

10.1.1.7 Taboo items Connected with Sex

Generally words which are connected to sex, body parts and their functions are forbidden to be mentioned in public places. People find it extremely ill-mannered to use such words. Euphemistic words are used e.g. **š>a> unšbš** (lit.) 'to meet a child' for **š>a> pokpš** 'to give birth', **mironbš**'conceived' for **puk kš>bš.**

There is psychological notion that people felt use of the native words — items connected with sex — quite vulgar and impolite, so English words are being used mostly among the educated circle. More and above, the dreaded diseases such as Chorera, small pox, etc. are also used in place of native words.

KINSHIP TERMINOLOGY

10.2 Kinship Terminology

In Meitei society, kinship terminology normally operates over a span of seven generations — three above and three below that of ego (**ipu** 'grand father', **iben** 'grand -mother' and **isu** 'grandson'). In this society, the kinship relation is still strong among the kins; and people rightly used the kinship terms among the kins. Some kinship terms are given below : (**i**-1st PP, **nš** -2nd PP, **mš**-3rd PP).

Addressing terms		***Gloss***	***Reference***
šbok	'grand mother	**mš-ben**	'his grand mother'
i-dhšω **pupu**	'grand father'	**mš-pu**	'his grand father'
pabu> **paji** **baba**	'daddy'	**mš-pa**	'his father'
i-ma	'mummy'	**mš-ma**	'his mother'
mama			
khura **kška~**	'uncle'	-------	
kaka			
mamš	'maternal uncle'	-------	
i-maybema	'MoEl Sis'	-------	
i-mabok	'Fa El Bro Wi'	-------	
i-ne	'paternal aunt'	-------	
i-ce **i-cema**	'elder sister'	-------	
tadš	'elder brother'	-------	
tamo			
i-bay	'elder Bro-in law'(male ego)	------	
i-tšy	'elder Bro-in law	(female ego)	------
i-nšmš	'elder Sis-in law	(female ego)	------
i-tšymš	'elder Sis-in Law'	(male ego)	------

There are some qualifying words. They are **-hšn<šhšn** 'eldest', **-caω<šcaωbš** 'big',-**yay<yaymš** 'middle one', **ton<štonbš** 'last one', or youngest and **-ca<mšca** 'small'. These -

hšn, **-caω**, **-yay** and **-ca** are bound roots, and they can be suffixed to the above kinship terms to indicate, e.g. the order of elder brother or elder sister.

Example

ice-hšn ice-cšωbi	'eldest sister'
ice-yaymš ice-ton	'2nd elder sister' 'the youngest sister'
tamo-hšn tamo-cšω	'the eldest brother'
tamo-yaymš	'2nd elder brother'
tamo-tombš tamo-ca	'the youngest brother'

10.2.1 Variables Determining the Usage of Kin Terms

The structure of Meitei kinship terms involves (1) difference of generation (2) difference of age (3) marital affiliation and (4) difference of sexes. They are discussed in the followings :

10.2.1.1 Generation as a Determinant

Since the generation is the connecting relatives in the classification of relations, generation is one of the basic structuring characteristics of the terminology and it pay a major role in the composite seniority variable of the behavioural analysis of the Meitei kinship terms.

The Meitei kinship system is based upon a generational classification of relations (a) Members of the first ascending generation are referred to as **ima-ipa** 'parents'; **khura** or **kška** 'paternal uncle' ; **indonca** 'maternal aunt' and **ine** 'paternal aunt' ; (b) Members of Ego's generation are referred to as **icin-inaω** 'siblings and cousins' (only parallel cousin). Cross-cousin are termed as **i-bay** 'elder male cross cousin 'for a male ego while **i-tšy** is a female ego while **i-tšymš** 'elder female cross-cousin is for a male ego **inšmš** for a female ego. Others are **i-naω-nupi** 'younger' male cross-cousin for a female ego, **inawnupi** 'younger male cross-cousin 'for a male ego, and **i-cšn-nupi**' younger female cross-cousin 'for a female ego'. (c) Members of the first descending generation as **ica** 'child' (my), **i-mak** 'nephew' for a male ego, **iya** 'nephew' of the second ascending generation as **isu** 'grand-child and (e) Second ascending generation as **-ipu-iben** 'grand -parents' etc.

10.2.1.2 Relative Age as a Determinant

In Meitei kinship system, relative age is a deciding factor within a generation only but not across generations. In the case of ego's generation relative age is of important in respect of the immediate relatives of ego, specially to those referred to as brothers and sisters, whether real or classificatory, and to a lesser extent to the distant affinal kins of ego's generation such as wife's elder brother's wife's brother or sisters husband's sister in-law.

Relative age cannot be accountable to reference to ego in the case of lineal relatives since the age of ego cannot function as the reference point. That is relative age cannot play a role in deciding the kin terms of address within the kins. For instance, in the first ascending generation, the relative age of uncle and aunt is reckoned with respect to ego of the connecting parent and in the second ascending generation with respect to the ego of the connecting grand-parent.

10.2.1.3 Marital Affiliation

Regarding some of the affinal kins, the relative age may not be significant in deciding the kin terms of address. For example, although wife's elder brother younger than the ego, he commands respect being the elder brother of the ego's wife. Therefore, ego will call his wife's elder brother-in-law by the kin terms **i-bay** irrespective of the relative age of the two. In return, wife's elder brother will address ego by his personal name as he is considered to be junior (being younger sister's husband).

It is a fact that relative age becomes significant in the case of distant affinal kins such as brother-in-law's brothers and sisters and sister-in-laws sister and brothers, their husbands and wifes etc., and rather significant among the non-kins.

10.2.1.4 Sex as Determinant

Meitei kinship system vividly shows the significance laid upon sex of the person addressed or referred to, sex of the linking relative and sex of the ego.

Some of the kinship terms are decided by the sex of the ego: some of the terms are used by male ego while some only by female ego. So these terms can be regarded as designating the ego's sex. For instance, in order to refer ones elder brother, a male ego will use the kin term **iyam-bš** whereas a female ego will use the term **ibu›**. More examples are given below :

Reference Male ego	*Gloss*	*Reference Female ego*
i-mak	son-in-law	i-ya
i-naω	younger brother	i-pωa
i-bay	elder brother-in-law	i-tšy
i-tšymš	elder sister-in-law	i-nšmš

10.2.2 Influence of Social Structure in the Kinship Terms

It is a fact that the social structure of the Meitei society makes a great influence in the use of kinship terms. There is a large distinct sets of variable corresponding to the two distinct layers—Royal (Ninthemca, royal bloods locally known as Raj Kumar=R.K.) and commoners. The kinship terms used by the R.K's differ from those by the commoners. The honorific suffix **-si** is suffixed when addressed to elder persons of R.K. or among the R.Ks given in the following examples :

RK's terms	*Gloss*	*Commoner's terms*
i-ma-si	'mother'	i-ma
i-ne-si~inemsi	'paternal'	i-ne
indon-si	'maternal aunt'	indon
icem-si	'elder sister'	i-ce~icemš~cece
man-si	'maternal uncle'	ma-mš
inšm-si	'elder sister-in-law'	inšmš~inšmbem
iku-si	'father-in-law'	iku

There are some other royal kinship terms which do not have this honorific suffix **-si** . They are given below

Examples

Royal's terms	*Gloss*	*Commoner's terms*
pabu ›/sš̆nakhwa	'father'	pabš, baba, paji~baji
sš̆mkhwa	'father'	pabš, baba, paji~baji
sš̆mkhwa-puren	'grand father'	ipu-bok
yambu ›	'elder brother'	tadš, dada, tamo
khura-ibu ›o	'paternal uncle'	khura
sš̆na-ibema	'elder sister-in-law'	itšymš

In compare with the ancient time (during the kingdom), the kinship terms are strictly observed. But at present day, there are many flexibility and becoming more literal in the use of kinship terms. There have been some borrowings of kin terms from the Indo-Aryan languages through specially Bengali and Assamese due to long history of language contact. With the increase of the western education or with the popularity of English language, some kinship terms are becoming used, for instance, uncle, aunty, mummy, daddy. More other social rules can be seen in the next section, terms of Address.

TERMS OF ADDRESS

10.3 Terms of Address

The terms of address in the Meitei society is very complicated. Because they are determined by various parameters like religion, economy, social status and parameter like group membership of interlocuters. It is also a fact that there is a great distinction in the use of forms of address between interlocuters who are friends and acquaintances and ones who are strangers.

In Meitei society' there is a distinction in some of the kin terms between addresses and reference, for example, mš̆bu › 'elder brother' (female ego) is a reference term whereas **tadš** or **tamo** or **dada** is the addressing term both for male and female ego; **ipa** 'father' is a reference term whereas **pabu ›** or **baba** or **paji** or **papa** is an addressing term

10.3.1 Deciding Parameters for Terms of Address

Terms of address in Meitei society is decided by many parameters, such as (1) age difference, (2) hereditary group membership (3) sex difference (4) occupational rank (5) economic status and (6) educational status.

10.3.1.1 Age Difference

Age is an important deciding factor for terms of address in Meitei society among the non - kins and also among the kins of the same generation. Even one day old is taken into consideration. In some South Asian systems also, even 'one day' makes a person socially older. The kinship terms (mentioned in the previous section) are extended to address and choose the appropriate terms according to his relative age.

Examples

Age group	*Address terms*	
fatherly old	mamš mamo knura	'mother's brother'
motherly old	i-ma	'mummy'

	— ine —	'father's sister'
brotherly old	tadš /tamo/dada	'elder brother'
sisterly old	ice	'elder sister'

That age is a deciding factor for terms of address can be exemplified, for instance, in case the 'orderly' is senior in age, he should be addressed with an appropriate address term, mentioned above, mentioned above, with his personal name.

Example

[khura / tadš / mamš / ice / ine] + Name (middle)

e.g. **khura tomba** 'uncle Tomba' **ice meri'** 'elder sister Mary' **tadš caωbš** 'elder brother **caωbš**'

10.3.1.2 Sex Differences

The extended use of kinship terms of address involves the distinctions of sex — sex of the addressee and sex of the speaker. That is while addressing a male acquaintance (say elder brother's friend) who is in the age group of one's elder brother, the address term to be used is **tadš** or tamo or **dada** 'elder brother'. While addressing a female acquaintance who is the age group of one's elder sister, she should be addressed as ice 'elder sister'.

Regarding the sex of the speaker, there is also a distinction between male ego and female ego. For example, when a female speaker addresses her elder sister-in-law (elder brother's wife) she must address her (sister-in-law) as **inšmš** 'elder sister-in-law' whereas a male speaker must address her (elder sister-in-law) as **itšymš** 'elder- sister-in-law'.

10.3.1.3 Occupational Rank

This can be divided into two groups : (i) officers and (ii) non-officers. Here also use of kinship term in extended and makes a distinction between the two groups in the use of extended kinship terms depending upon the relative age of the speaker and addressee, as given in the following :

(i) Official Ranks (Addressed by Juniors)

pabu ›	-	'fatherly old'
tamo	-	'elder brotherly old'
icemš~ice-bemš	-	'elder sisterly old'
imay-bemš	-	'motherly old'

(ii) Non-Official Rank (Addressed by Juniors)

This group includes namely, clerks, peons, attendants and orderlies. When they are addressed by the juniors in age, the following terms of address are used.

khura] ' to fatherly old'
mamš

tadš 'to elder brotherly old'
ima 'to motherly old'

ice
ine] 'to elder sisterly old'
indon

'to motherly old' or 'to woman junior to one's mother's age.

10.3.1.4 Economic Status

This may also be divided into two groups: (I) high economic group and (ii) low economic group. The distinction in the use of extended kinship terms has made a similarity with that of occupational rank, that is, official rank and high economic group belong to the same category while non-official rank and low economic group in one category. In other words, the speaker uses the same extended kinship terms to both the official and high economic group; in the same way the speaker uses the same extended kinship terms to both the non-official and low group.

(iii) Names and Various Combinations

Full name can be written in various patterns, as given in the followings :

a. Surname + Middle Name + Last Name
b. Surname + Middle Name
c. Middle Name + Surname
d. Surname + Ningol + Middle Name [Ningol 'bride/Ms]
e. Surname + Last Name + Middle Name

In general, in Meitei Society surname is not used for addressing ; what the people regarded as 'name' is the middle name (MN). As concerned the structure in this society, it has its own tradition that surname should precede the name (MN) and the last name /part is 'Singh'/'Meitei' for male while 'Devi'/'Chanu' for female. The last name for both male and female are optional - some can use and some can drop. Dropping of the last name for both male and female is a new trend. It is shown here how a full name is written.

Surname	***Middle Name***	***Last Name***
Chungkham	Yashawanta	singh/Meitei
Nahakpam	Aruna	Devi/Chanu

It is more complicated in the case of married woman; it has two varieties :

a. Chungkham **Ongbi** Nahakpam Aruna Devi
b. Nhakpam **Ningol** Chungkham Aruna Devi

The underlined words 'Ongbi' and 'Ningol' in this syntagm indicates the social status of a female, i.e. she is a married woman (married to Chungkham Yashawanta, Nahakpam is her surname). But in the case of 'Miss'. 'Ongbi' and 'Ningol' do not occur.

10.3.2 Address by Professional Titles

It is a general norm to address person of higher status as nobles or ministers by their respective titles, while persons of lower ranks such as 'orderly', peon or watchman are not addressed by their professional specialities. They are addressed by extended kin terms of address, according to their relative age if the addressee is older than the speaker. Followings are the common professional titles :

Address terms	*Gloss*
daktšr babu	'doctor'
inginišr saheb	'engineer'
ukil saheb	'advocate'
thikadar	'contractor'
oja	'teacher'

10.3.3 Titles Used for Scholars

There are some terms of address for addressing scholars in Meitei society. They are given below :

Address terms	*Gloss*
maycšω	'scholar ' or 'learned man'
guru	'scholar' or 'learned man'
pšndit	'scholar 'or learned man'
oja	'scholar' or 'learned man'

The address term **oja** 'teacher' is very interesting. Because the address term **oja** is very simple, easy and is a palatable linguistic item in this society: it can be used by any speaker to any unknown addressee (in symmetrical or assymetrical relationship). By using this term **'oja'** the speaker felt more accessible to the addressec and felt giving honour to the addressee irrespective of age.

10.3.4 Expressive Terms or Endearment Terms

There are three very common expressive terms. They are :

a. ibemš 'my dear/Miss (female)
b. memš 'my dear'
c. ibu >o 'my dear' (male)

These two address terms (for female) are used by both the sexes in addressing to their female juniors - intimate as well as stranger. There are also affectionate terms used in different linguistic situations. In one situation, the parents preferably address their daughter as **ibema** rather than **memš** in lieu of the school name. In another situation, both the sexes can use these address terms **ibemš** or **memš** to any stranger. The term **memš** 'my dear' has another connotation. It is very often used by young boys for teasing young girls. In this context the term means 'darling'. The expressive term for male is **ibu >o** 'my dear'. Senior male as well as senior female can use this term **'ibu >o'** to any known or unknown (male) person.

In Meitei society, the term of address is just like a syntactic rule : one is to know to whom one is talking, what is the sex of the addressee. Use of honorific marker in speech is regarded as a refine one.

APPENDIX–I

MEITEI MAYEK MAPEE
(Manipuri Script)

ꯀ	ꯁ	ꯂ	ꯃ	ꯄ	ꯅ
kok	**səm**	**lay**	**mit**	**pa**	**na**
k	**s**	**l**	**m**	**p**	**n**

ꯆ	ꯇ	ꯈ	ꯉ	ꯊ	ꯋ
cil	**til**	**khəw**	**ŋəw**	**thəw**	**way**
ch	**t**	**kh**	**ŋ**	**th**	**w**

ꯌ	ꯍ	ꯎ	ꯏ	ꯐ	ꯑ
yaŋ	**huk**	**un**	**i**	**phəm**	**ətiya**
y	**h**	**u**	**i**	p^h	**ə**

Borrowed Sounds (Found in Loan Words)

ꯒ	ꯘ	ꯕ	ꯚ
g	**gh**	**b**	**bh**

ꯖ	ꯓ	ꯗ	ꯙ
j	**jh**	**d**	**dh**

ꯔ
r

Close Consonants (Occurred Finally)

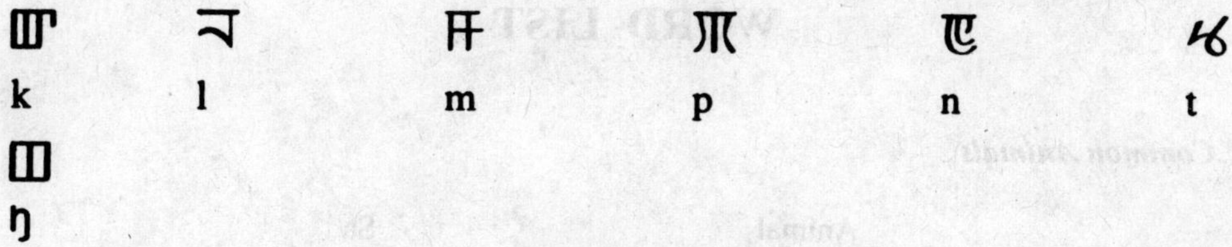

Vowel Matra

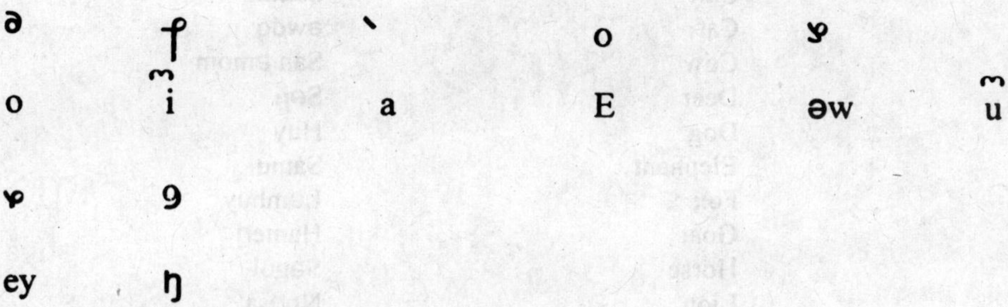

Numerals

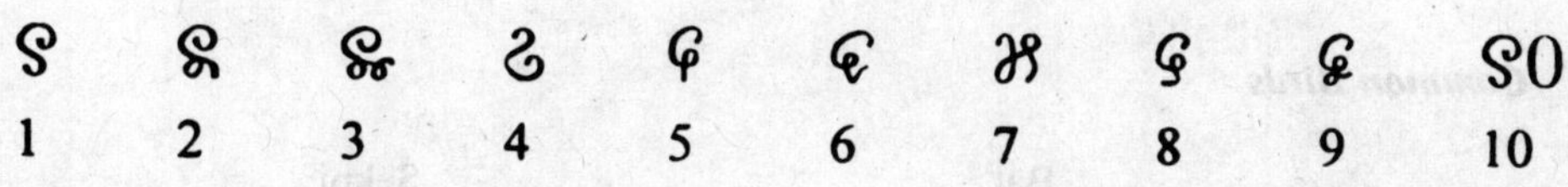

APPENDIX–II

WORD LIST

Common Animals

Animal	Sa
Ass	Gədha
Bear	Səwom
Buffalo	Iroy
Bull	San laba
Calf	Sanaw
Cat	əwdo
Cow	San əmom
Deer	Səji
Dog	Huy
Elephant	Samu
Fox	Ləmhuy
Goat	Hameŋ
Horse	Səgol
Lion	Noŋsa
Monkey	Yoŋ
Pig	Ok
Rat	Uci
Sheep	Yaw
Tiger	Kəy
Wild hoar	Ləm-ok

Common Birds

Bat	Sekpi
Bird	Ucek
Cock	Yenba
Crow	Kwak
Cuckoo	Kokil
Duck	ŋanu
Goose	Kaŋŋə
Hen	Yenbi
King-fisher	ŋərakpi
Nightingale	Khoyniŋ
Owl	Məku
Parrot	Tenəwa
Peacock	Wahoŋ
Pigeon	Khunu
Sparrow	Sendraŋ

Vulcher	Ləŋja
Wild-duck	Ləm ŋanu

Vegetables

Bean	Həway
Brinjal	Khamen
Cabbage	Kobi
Cauliflower	Kobi thəmcetmanbi
Garlic	Cənəm
Ginger	Siŋ
Gourd	Khoŋdrum
Green chilli	Morok ətekpə
Lady's finger	Bhelendri
Mustard plant (leaf)	Həŋgam
Onion	Tilhəw
Peas	Həway thərak
Potato	əlu
Pumkin	Mayren
Soyabean	Nuŋ həway
Sweet potato	Məŋgra
Tomato	Khamen əsinbə

Fruits

Apple	Həytup
Banana	Ləphoy
Berry	Boroy
Grape	əŋgur
Guava	Puŋdon
Lemon	Cəmpra
Mango	Həynəw
Orange	Komla
Papaya	əwathəbi
Pear	Naspati
Pomegranate	Kəmphoy

Common Insects

Bug	Ma
Butter-fly	Kurak
Fly	Həyiŋ
Grass-hopper	Kəwjeŋ
Honey-bee	Həyiŋ khoy
Insect	Tin-kaŋ
Mosquito	Kaŋ

Kinship Terms and Form of Address

Aunt	Indon
Brother's wife	I-təyma/i-nəmma
Brother (e)	Tamo/tadə/dada
Brother (y)	I-naw/mə-naw
Brother-in-law	Itəy/ibay
Daddy (father)	Pabuŋ/papa/paji
Father's brother (e)	Ipən
Father's brother (y)	Khura
Father's sister	I-ne
Father-in-law	I-kubok
Mother's sister	Indomca
Mother's brother	Mammə
Mother's brother's daughter (e)	I-təyma
Mother's brother's son (e)	I-bay
Mother's sister's daughter (e)	I-təyma
Mother's sister's son	I-bay
Mother-in-law	I-nembok
Mummy (mother)	Ima/mama
Name	Miŋ
Sister (e)	I-ce/cece
Sister-in-law	I-təyma/i-nəmma
Surname	Yumnak

Common Diseases

Blind	Mit taŋbə
Cholera	Pukcətpə
Common cold	Lok thuŋba
Deaf	Na-pəŋbə
Diabetes	Isiŋ pukcətpə
Diarrhoea	Khoŋ hambə
Dumb	Lon thoktəbə
Fever	Layhəw
Handicap	Nammə soybə
Headache	Kokcikpə
Hospital	əna layeŋsəŋ
Itching	Hagəjəbə
Lame	Khoŋ tekpə
Leprosy	əŋəwbə pək-pə
Local physician	Maybə
Medicine	Hidak
Midwife	Maybi
Operation	Thaŋ thabə
Patient	ənabə mi
Swelling	əpombə
Tablets	guli

Treatment	Layeŋbə
Vomiting	Obə

Name of the Days

Day	Numit
Sunday	Noŋmayjiŋ
Monday	Niŋthəwkabə
Tuesday	Ləypakpokpə
Wednesday	Yumsəkəysə
Thursday	Səgolsen
Friday	Iray
Saturday	Thaŋja
Yesterday	ŋəraŋ
Day before yesterday	Nəhan
Today	ŋəsi
Tomorrow	Həyeŋ
Day after tomorrow	Həŋcit
Last month	Məməŋgi tha
Next month	Məthəŋgi tha
Last year	Hakum
Next year	Noŋməy
Morning	əyuk
Midday	Numit yuŋbə
Evening	Numidaŋ wayrəm
Midnight	əhiŋ noŋyay

Common Goods of Daily Use

Air	Nuŋsit
Autumn	Naken tha
Axe	Siŋjəŋ
Bamboo	Wa
Basket	Thumok
Bed	Phəmuŋ
Bed sheet	Mompak phidək
Beef	Sən-sa
Bell	Sərik
Bloating Paper	Muk cabi
Book	Layrik
Bottle	Likli
Box	Upu
Bread	Təl
Bucket	Baltin
Chair	Cəwkri
Cigarette	Curup
Cloth	Phi
Coconut	Yubi

Court yard	Sumaŋ
Cow dung	Sənthi
Cow-shed	Səngon
Current	Icen/icel
Curry	Yensəŋ/insəŋ
Dagger	Thaŋjəw
Door	Thoŋ
Dry	əkəŋbə
Earth	Prithibi
East	Noŋpok
Egg	Yerum
Fire	Məy
Fire-wood	Siŋ
Fish	ŋa
Flesh	Sədoŋ
Frying pan	Khaŋ
Full moon	Purnima
Glass	Likli
Grainery store	Kəy/kot
Grass	Napi
Gun	Noŋməy
Hearth	Phuŋga
Hill	Ciŋ
Ink	Muk
Key	Sojəy
Kitchen	Cakhum/cakkhum
Knife	Həyjraŋ
Ladle	Khabəy
Light (N)	Məŋal
Liquor	Yu
Lock	Waykhu
Looking glass	Miŋsel
Market	Kəythel
Mat	Phək
Mattress	Mompak
Meat	Sa
Milk	Səŋgom
Mustard oil	Həŋgam thaw
Moon	Tha
Mosquito net	Kaŋkhəl
New moon	Thasi
New year	ənəwbə cəhi
North	əwaŋ
Ocean	Səmudrə
Oil	Thaw
Paper	Ce
Pen	Kolom
Pillar	Yumbi

Pillow	Mon
Plate	Pukhəm
Pond	Pukhri
Pork	Oksa
Pot	Cəphu
Quilt	Kanthə
Rainy season	Noŋju tha
Reed	Siŋnaŋ
Rice	Ceŋ/cak
River	Turel/turen
Road	Ləmbi
Roof	Yumthək
Room	Ka
Salt	Thum
Shield	Cuŋgoy
Shirt	Phurit
Shocks	Khoŋ moja
Shoe	Khoŋup/ khoŋ ŋup
Shop	Dukan
Sky	ətiya
Sliced bambo	Wacet
Song	Isəy
South	Kha
Spear	Ta
Spoon	Caməs
Spring	Məyon coŋbə tha
Star	Thəwanmicak
Stream	Khoŋ
Sugar	Cini
Summer	Kalentha
Sun	Numit
Sword	Thaŋsaŋ
Tea	Ca
Tree	Upambi
Trouser	Khoŋgraw
Tumbler	Khujay
Wall	Phəklaŋ
Wave	Ithək
West	Noŋcup
Wet	əcotpə
Window	Thoŋnaw
Winter	Niŋthəmtha
Woollan-cloths	Samtu

Colour (s)

Black	əmubə

Colour	Məcu
Green	əsəŋbə
Red	əŋaŋbə
White	əŋəwbə
Yellow	Napu

Pronouns

I	əy
We	əykhoy
you (sg)	Nəŋ
you (pl)	Nəkhoy
He	Məhak
They	Məkhoy
Me	əy-bu
My	əy-gi
Your	Nəŋ-gi
His	Məhak-ki
Him	Məhak-pu
Their	Məkhoy-gi
Them	Məkhoy-bu
Our	əykhoy-gi

Question Words

Who	Kəna
What	Kəri
Which	Kərəmbə
Where	Kəday-də
When	Kəydəwŋəy
How	Kərəm-nə
Why	Kərigi

Body Parts

Back bone	Yaŋlen səru
Belly	Puk
Blood	I
Body hair	Tu
Bone	Səru
Brain	Thop
Breast	Khom
Cheek	Khəjay
Chest	Thəbak
Chin	Khədaŋ
Ear	Na
Elbow	Khuniŋ(of hand)
Eye	Mit

Eye-brow	Pisum
Eye-lash	Pa
Face	May
Forehead	Laybək
Gold finger	Khuniŋthəw
Gum	Yari
Hair	Səm
Hand	Khut
Head	Kok
Heart	Thəmoy
Heel	Khuniŋ(of leg)
Hip	Niŋ
Intestine	Thirin
Iron finger	Khudomɔi
Joints	Taŋ
Knee	Khu
Leg	Khoŋ
Lip (s)	Cinban
Liver	Phirak
Lung	Thəbombi
Mouth	Cin
Nail	Khujin
Naval	Khoydəw
Neck	ŋəksəm
Nerve	Siŋli
Nose	Naton
Palm	Khubak
Shoulder	Leŋban
Skin	Unsa
Stomach	Cakkhaw/ cəkhaw
Teeth	Ya-siŋ
Thigh	Phəygən
Throat	Khanaw/khəwri
Thump	Khubi
Toe (s)	Khoŋsa
Tongue	Ləy
Waist	Khwaŋ
Wrist	Khudaŋ

Numerals

One	əma
Two	əni
Three	əhum
Four	Məri
Five	Məŋa
Six	Təruk
Seven	Təret
Eight	Nipan
Nine	Mapən
Ten	Təra
Eleven	Təramathoy
Twelve	Təranithoy
Twenty	Kun
Twenty-one	Kunmathoy
Twenty-two	Kunnithoy
Thirty	Kunthra
Thirty-one	Kunthramathoy
Thirty-two	Kunthra nithoy
Forty	Niphu
Forty-one	Niphumathoy
Forty-two	Niphunithoy
Fifty	Yaŋkhəy
Fifty-one	Yaŋkhəymathoy
Fifty-two	Yaŋkhəynithoy
Sixty	Humphu
Sixty-one	Humphumathoy
Seventy	Humphutəra
Seventy-one	Humphutəramathoy
Eighty	Məriphu
Eighty-one	Məriphumathoy
Ninety	Məriphutəra
Ninety-one	Məriphutəramathoy
One hundred	Camə
Two hundred	Cani
One thousand	Lisiŋ əma
Ten thousand	Lisiŋ təra

Ordinal Number

First	əhanbə
Second	ənisubə
Third	əhumsubə
Fourth	Mərisubə
Tenth	Təra subə

Other Lexical Items

A.

Able	ŋəmbə
Accuse	Məral sibə
Ache	Cikpə
Admit	Yabə
Again	əmuk hənnə
After	Tuŋdə(mətuŋdə)
Age	Cəhi(his age)
Agree	Yabə
All	Pumnəmək
Alone	Məthəntə
Also	-Su
Always	Mətəm pumnəməktə
Amend	Semdokpə
And	əmasuŋ
Anger	Sawbə
Annex	Hapcinbə/nəpsinbə
Answer	Pawkhum
Appetite	ərambə pokpə
Apple	Həytup
Appoint	Khənbə
Arrive	Thuŋbə
Arrow	Tenjəy
Ash	Ut
Ask	Həŋbə

B.

Bad	Phətəbə
Bake	Yaybə
Bald	Kok taŋbə
Ban	Thiŋbə
Bank	Turen-gi torban
Bark	Khoŋbə/uku
Bath	Irujəbə
Beak	Ucek-ki məcin
Beat	Phubə
Before	Məmaŋdə
Begin	Həwbə
Below	Məkha
Between	Mərək
Big	əcəwbə
Bind	Punbə
Bite	Cikpə
Bitter	Khabə
Blind	Mit taŋbə
Blow	Kambə

Blunt	Məcin pəŋbə
Blur	Məmi seŋdəbə
Boat	Hi
Body	Həkcaŋ
Boil	Səwbə
Bold	Thəwna phəbə
Bow	Liruŋ
Box	Upu
Boy	Nipa məca
Bracelet	Lik
Branch	Məsa
Break	Thugaybə
Breathe	Swor honbə
Breeze	Namibə nuŋsit
Brick	Cek
Bridge	Thoŋ
Bright	ŋanbə/ ləŋbə
Bring	Pubə
Bud	əpombə
Bunch	Cəbun
Burn	Məy-nə cakpə
Busy	Thəbək cinbə

C.

Cage	Sarəŋ
Calculate	Thibə/pabə
Calm	Iŋbə, cikpə
Cane	Li
Care	Ceksinbə
Carry	Thaŋ ləgə pubə
Catch	phabə
Chance	Tənja
Change	hoŋbə
Chapter	Taŋkək
Charm	Sumhətpə
Chase	Tanəbə
Cheap	hoŋbə
Cheat	nəmthak təwbə
Cheese	Səŋgom məpan
Child	əŋaŋ məca
Choice	Khənbə
Claw	Khubam
Clay	Ləykhom
Clear	məyek seŋbə
Climb	Kabə
Close	Thiŋbə
Cloud	Ləycin
Coarse	pəwbə

Cold	Iŋbə
Collide	Theŋgaynəbə
Colour	məcu
Combine	Punsinbə
Come	Lakpə
Commence	Həwbə
Compare	Caŋthəmnəbə
Condition	Phibəm
Consider	Khənnəbə
Console	Themjinbə
Conspire	Ləwtunəbə
Continue	Cətthəbə
Cook	Cakthoŋbə mi
Cottage	Khaŋpoksəŋ
Cotton	Ləsiŋ
Country	Ləypak
Courage	Thəwna
Coward	Məthəwna yawdəbə
Crab	Waykhu
Cradle	Nawsum
Cruel	Təmthibə
Cut	Kəkpə

D.

Dagger	Thaŋjəw
Damage	Maŋ-takhənbə
Dance	Jəgoy
Danger	Khudoŋthibə
Dark	əməmbə
Day	Numit
Deaf	Na peŋbə
Dear	Nuŋsibə
Debt	Sendon/ tonbə
Decide	Leppə
Delay	Theŋthəbə
Demand	Tanbə
Dense	Sukpə
Depend	Məkha ponbə
Desert (N)	Mərubhumi
Die	Sibə
Difficult	Khudoŋtnibə
Dig	Təwbə
Disease	Ləyna
Distance	Thappə
Divide	Khaydokpə
Divorce	Khaynəbə
Do	Thəbək təwbə
Door	Thoŋ

Dream	Məŋ
Dress	Phijol
Drink	Thəkpə
Drive	Thəwbə
Dust	Uphul
Duty	Məthəw

E.

Each	Khudiŋmək
Eager	Khəwraŋbə
Eat	Cabə
Eel	ŋaril
Elder	Ithək-ki əhəl
Empty	əhaŋbə/yaw-dəbə
End	əroybə
Enemy	Yeknəbə
Enough	Məraŋ kaybə
Enter	Mənuŋdə cəŋsinbə
Equal	Manəbə
Escape	Nanthokpə
Event	Thəwdok
Evil	Phət-təbə
Express	Phoŋdokpə
Extinguish	Muthətpə

F.

Fail	Maythibə
Fall	Məkha-də tabə
Famine	Caktaŋbə
Far	Thappə
Fat	Noybə
Fear	əkibə
Feed	Pithəkpə-pijəbə
Field	Ləwbuk
Fight	Khətnəbə /lantheŋnəbə
Find	Phəŋbə
Finish	Loysinbə
Flame	Məyri
Flat	Pakpə
Float	Tawbə
Fly	Paybə
Foam	Koŋgol
Fog	Ləycil
Fold	Thuppə
Food	Cinjak
Fool	əpəŋbə
Forget	Kawthokpə
Fort	Lanbən

Freeze	Phəmjinbə
Fresh	əseŋbə
Friend	Mərup
Frog	Həŋoy
Fun	Kuməy
Future	Tuŋ-gi mikup

G.

Gale	Noŋləy nuŋsit
Game	Məsannə
Garden	Ləykon
Gate	Thoŋgal
Gentle	Məpukcel təppə
Get	Phəŋbə
Gift	Khudol pot
Girl	Ləysabi
Give	Pibə
Glad	Hərawbə
Go	Cət-pə
God	Ishwor/lay
Gold	Səna
Good	əphəbə
Grave (N)	Moŋphəm
Great	əcəwbə
Group	Kaŋbu

H.

Habit	Həynəbi
Half	Təŋkhay
Hammer	Nuŋthəŋ
Hang	Yanbə
Hard	əkənbə
Harm	Maŋ-takpə
Hate	Tukəcəbə
Health	Həkcaŋ
Hear	Tabə
Heat	Məysa
Heavy	ərumbə /lumbə
Here	əphəm əsidə
Hide	Lotpə
Hit	Yəybə
Hoist	Ciŋkhətpə
Hole	Məkhun
Home	Yum
Honest	Pukcel seŋbə
Hop (V)	Coŋbə
Horn	Məci
Hot	Sabə

	Hour	Puŋsiŋ
	Humble	Nolukpə
	Hurt	Sokhənbə
I.		
	Ice	Un
	Idle	Tənbə
	Ill	Nabə
	Image	Məmi
	In	Mənuŋ
	Increase	Heŋgət-pə
	Inifinite	Loybə naydəbə
	Inquire	Həŋbə
	Insult	Ikaybə pibə
	Invent	Puthokpə
	Iron	Yot
	Island	Ithət
	It	Məsi
J.		
	Jar	Khəruŋ
	Jealous	Mihəw /kələkpə
	Journey	Khoŋcət
	Joy	Nuŋnaybə/hərawbə
	Juice	Məhi
	Jump	Coŋbə
	Jute	Limon
K.		
	Keep	Thəmbə
	Kick	Kawbə
	Kill	Hatpə
	King	Niŋthəw
	Kiss	Cuppə
	Kite	Teləŋga
	Know	Khəŋbə
L.		
	Ladder	Kəyrak
	Lap	Təmpak
	Large	əcəwbə
	Last	əroybə
	Late	ətheŋbə/theŋbə
	Laugh	Nokpə
	Leaf (N)	Una
	Leak	Yubə
	Learn	Təmbə
	Left (N)	Oy-nə

Length	Məyuŋ
Lick	Lekpə
Life	Punsi
Like	Pambə
Lily	Thəro
Line	Ləyyi
Liquid	Məhi
Little	əpikpə
Look	Yeŋbə
Loose	Kombə
Love	Nuŋsibə
Low	Nembə

M.

Mad	ŋawbə
Magnet	Yotcabi
Make	Sembə/sabə
Man	Nupa/nipa
Marriage	Luhoŋbə
Meal	Cəra
Medicine	Hidak
Meet	Unəbə
Melt	Səwdokpə
Modest	Nolukpə
Mole.	Səmbru
Morning	əyuk
Morsel	Cəkhom
Mother	Ima
Mourn	Teŋthabə
Mud	Ləykhom
Multiply	Puribə/məsiŋ yamhən-bə

N.

Nest	Ucek məkol
Net	Laŋ
New	ənəwbə
News	Paw
Next	Məthəŋ
Nice	Phəjəbə
Night	Numidaŋ
Noise	Laŋbə
Now	Həwjik

O.

Oath	Washək
Old	əhəl oybə
On	Məthək
Open	Haŋdokpa

Opium	Kani
Oppose	Mayyoknəbə
Origin	Həwrəkphəm
Ornament	Ləyteŋ
Other	ətopə

P.

Paddy	Phəw
Page	Cena
Pair	Jura
Paper	Ce
Picture	əyekpə lay
Piece	Məcet
Place	Məphə
Play	Sanəbə
Plenty	Məraŋ kaibə
Poor	Layrəbə
Pour	Həybə
Praise	Thagət-pə
Prepare	Sem-sabə
Prize	Məna
Property	Lən-thum
Prose	Wareŋ
Proud	Cawthok-pə
Pull	Ciŋ-bə
Pure	əseŋ-bə
Put	Thəm-bə

Q.

Quench	Khəwraŋbə kok-pə
Quiet	Cik-pə(iŋ-nə təp-nə)

R.

Race	Ləmjel
Rain	Noŋ
Read	Pa-bə
Reap	Ləw-khaw-bə
Reduce	Hənthə-bə
Repeat	Hən-nə hən-nə
Rest	Potha-bə
Return	Hələk-pə
Rich	Inak-khunbə
Riddle	Pawrəw
Ride	Toŋ-bə thəwbə
Right	Yetthəŋbə/cumbə
Ring	Khiŋ-bə khudop
Ripe	Mun-bə

Rise	Həwgət-pə
Road	Ləmbi
Rock	əcəwbə nuŋdum
Roof	Yumthək
Rotten	Pumbə
Round	əkoybə
Rub	Tək-pə
Run	Cen-bə
Rust	Kotliŋ

S.

Sale	Yonbə
Saline	Thumhi
Sand	Ləyŋoy
Save	Kən-bə
Saw (N)	Horay
Say	Hay-bə
Scold	Cey-bə
Score	Panjəl
See	U-bə
Seed	Məru
Seek	Thibə
Select	Khən-bə
Send	Tha-bə
Shadow	Məmi
Shame	Ikay-bə
Share	Səruk
Sharp	Thəw-bə
Shield	Cuŋgoy
Ship	Jəhaj
Shoot	Kap-pə
Shore	Səmudrə məpam
Show	Ut-pə
Shut	Thiŋ-bə
Sit	Phəm-bə
Sleep	Tum-bə
Slow	Təp-pə
Small	Pik-pə
Smell	Mənəm/mənəm nəm-bə
Smile	Nok-pə
Smoke	Məykhu
Snail	Thəroy
Sneeze	Hakthi khən-bə
Snow	Un
So	Mərəm əsinə
Soap	Sapon
Soft	Thot-pə
Soil	Ləypak

Soldier	Lanmi
Solid	Məpəŋ
Some	Khəra
Song	Isəy
Soon	Thunə
Sorrow	əwabə
Soul	Thəway
Sound	Khonjel
Source	Həwrək-pə
Space	əhaŋbə
Spade	Yopak
Speak	ŋaŋbə
Spend	Mətəm-lenbə
Spit (V)	Tin sit-pə
Spoil	Məŋhən-bə
Spoon	Caməs
Spread	Səndok-pə
Squeeze	Sumbə
Stand	Lep-pə
Starve	Cara-henbə
Steal	Huran-bə
Steam	Mənil
Step	Khoŋthaŋ
Stop	Lep-pə
Story	Wari
Strength	Paŋgəl
Suck	Çiŋ-bə
Surface	Ləymay/məmay
Swim	Iroy-bə

Taboo	Namuŋbə/pəlhəy-də-bə
Tail (N)	Məməy
Tailor (N)	Phurit tubə
Take	Ləw-bə
Tall	əwaŋ-bə
Tame	Te-bə
Tank	Pukhri
Taste	Məhaw
Teach	Təmbi-bə
Tear (N)	Pi
Tear (V)	Segay-bə
Tease	Ləknəbə
Test	Caŋyeŋ
Thank	Thagət-pə
Thatch	I
There	Məphəm ədudə

Thick	Tha-bə
Thief	Huranbə
Thin	əpa-bə
Thing	Pot
Thorn	Tiŋkhəŋ
Thought	Wakhəl/khən-bə
Thread	Ləŋla
Threat	Kihən-bə
Throw	Ləŋ-bə
Thunder	Noŋ khoŋ-bə
Tie	Pun-bə
Time	Mətəm
Tire	Cokthəbə
Today	ŋəsi
Top	Məton
Tortoise	Theŋgu
Touch	Sok-pə
Town	Səhər
Toy	Sanəpot
Trap	Laŋ
Travel	Koy-bə
Tremble	Nik-pə
True	əchumbə
Try	Hotnəbə
Turn	Ləy-bə
Twin	Phaybok
Twist	Ləythekpə

U.

Ugly	əthibə
Umbrella	Satin
Unite	Punsinbə
Use	Sijinnəbə

V.

Vacant	əhaŋbə
Vain	ərembə-də maŋbə
Vast	əpak-pə
Very	Yam-nə
Vibrate	Nik-pə
Village	Khuŋgəŋ
Voice	Khonthaŋ

W.

Wedge	Siŋcep
Wait	ŋaybə
Wake	Həwgət-pə
Walk	Cət-pə

	Want	Pam-bə
	War	Lan
	Warm	Lumbu lumbu sa-bə
	Wash	Sudok-pə
	Wave	Ithək
	Wax	Khoyru
	Wealth	Lən-thum
	Wet	Cot-pə
	Wheat	Gehu
	Wheel	Cəka
	Wide	Pak-pə
	Win	Thoy-bə
	Wing	Məsa
	Witch	Heloy
	Woman	Nupi
	Word	Wahəy
	Write	i-bə
	Wrong	əranbə
Y.		
	Year	Cəhi
	Young	Nəha
Z.		
	Zealous	Kələkpə
	Zero	Suyno

BIBLIOGRAPHY

Abbi, Anvita, 1980 : Semantic Grammar of Hindi. A Study in Reduplication. Bahri Publication Private Ltd., New Delhi

Adam, Valerie, 1973 : An Introduction to Modern English Word-Formation. Longman

Aissen, Judith, 1972 : 'Where do Relative Clause come form ?' In Syntax and Semantics (ed) John P. Kumbell. Vol 1. Academic Press.

Aronoff, Mark, 1976 : Word-formation Generative Grammar. MIT Press. Cambridge Massachussette.

Bauer, Laurie, 1983 : English Word-formation. Cambridge University Press. Cambridge, England.

Bhat, D.N.S., 1991 : Grammatical Relations : The Evidence against their Necessity and University. Routledge. London and New York.

Boschra, Peter, 1983 : Agreement and Anaphor : A Study of the Role of Pronoun in Syntax and Discourse. Academic Press. London , New York.

Bradle, David, 1995 : 'Reflexive in Burmese'. In Papers in South - East Asian Linguistics No. 13. Pacific Linguistics Series A-83. (ed) David Bradley.

Chafe, W.L., 1970. : Meaning and Structure of Language. University of Chicago Press. Chicago and London.

Chao, Yuan Ren, 1968. : A Grammar of Spoken Chinese. University of California Press., Berkeley.

Chhangte, Lalnunthangi, 1986 : (i.) A Preliminary Grammar of Mizo Language. (Unpublished M.A. Dissertation). University of Texas at Arlington.

(ii) 1989 : The Grammar of Simple Clauses in Mizo'. In Papers I South East Asian Linguistics No. 11: South-East Asian Syntax . 93-174. Pacific Linguistics . A-77 (ed) David Bradley.

— **1989** : Complementation in Mizo. In LTBA Spring Vol. 12:1 Berkeley.

Comrie, and Sandra A. Thomson, 1985 : 'Lexical Nominalization'. In Language Typology and Syntic Description. ed. Timothy Shopen Cambridge University Press. Cambridge.

Cornyn, W.S. and H.D. Roof, 1968 : Beginning Burmese. Yale University Press.

Devi, Nameirakpam Pramodini, (1989) : Social Grammar of Meiteilon. (Unpublished Doctoral Dessertation) . Manipur University. Imphal.

Dixon, R.M.W., 1994 : Ergetivity. Cambridge University Press. Cambridge.

Downing, Bruce T., 1978 : 'Some Universals of Relative Clause Structure' In Universals of Human Language. Vol. 4. ed. Joseph H. Greenberg. Standford University Press.

Fillmore, C., 1968 : 'The Case for Case' In Universals of Linguistic Theory eds. Bach and Harms Holt, Rinehart and Winston, New York.

Herring, Susan C., 1991 : 'Nominalization, Relativilization and Attribution in Lotha, Angami and Burmese'. In LTBA. Vol 14 : 1 Spring.

Jensen, Sohn T., 1990 : Morphology : Word Structure in Generative Grammar. John Company Amsterdam.

Larson, Rechard K., 1983 Restrictive Modification : Relative Clause and Adverbs (Unpublished Ph. D. Thesis) The University of Wisconsin Madison.

Koptjevskaja, Tamm Maria, 1993 : Nominalizations, Routledge London and New York 23. Kosule, Sanjukta, A Grammar of Ladhaki.

Masica, Colin, 1972 : 'Relative Clause and South Asia'. In Papers from the Relative Clause Festival, Chicago Linguistic Society (April 13, 1972).

Masica, Colin P., 1976 : Defining a Linguistic Area : South Asia Chicago : University of Chicago Press.

—1972 : 'Lahu Nominalization, Relativization, Genitivization'. In Syntax Kimbell Vol. 1. Academic Press.

Matisoff, James A., 1973 : The Grammar of Lahu , University of California Press, Berkeley.

Matthews, P.H., 1991 : Morphology, Cambridge University Press.

Moravcsik, Julius, 1978 : 'Reduplicative Construction in Universal of Human Language Vol. 4. ed. Joseph H. Greenberg. Standford University Press.

Ningomba, M.S., 1993 : Deitics in Manipuri. In LTBA Vol. 16.1. Spring, California Berkeley.

Nonigopal, 1987 : A Meitei Grammar of Roots and Affixes (Unpublished Thesis) Manipur University, Imphal.

Okell, John, 1969 : A Reference Grammar Colloquial Burmese Vol. I and II. Oxford University Press, London

Palmer, F.R., 1994 : Grammatical Roles and Relations, Cambridge University Press.

Payne, John. 1985 : 'Negation'. In Language Typology and Syntactic Description. Vol. I (ed.) by Timothy Shopen. Cambridge University Press. Cambridge.

Ranson, Evelyn N., 1986 : Complementation : It Meanings and Forms. John Bejamins Publishing Company, Amsterdam.

Scachter, Paul, 1973 : 'Focus and Relativlization' In Language, Vol. 49.

Selkirk, Elisabeth O., 1982 : The Syntax of Word, MIT Press, Cambridge , Massachussetts.

Sharma, D. D., 1988 : A Descriptive Grammar of Kinnauri. Mittal Publications. Delhi.

— **1990** : Pronominalization in Tibeto Himalayan Languages IJDL. Vol. 19. No. 1

Singh, Chungkhan Yashawanta, 1984 : Some Aspects of Manipuri Syntax, (Unpublished Ph. D. Thesis) J.N.U, New Delhi.

— "Word Order in Meiteilon" in Monograph on Modern Linguistics, Ed. Chauncey Chu, W. South Coblin and Feng-Fu Tsao. Students Book Co. Ltd. Taipei, Taiwan, 1983, p. 323-341.

— "Gender in Meiteilon" in South-East Asian Linguistics Studies Ed. Ratnakul, David Thomas and Suwilai Premsrirat, Mahidol University, Thailand, 1985, p. 113-123.

— "Reduplication of Meiteilon" in Archive Orientalni, Vol. 3 : 56/1988. Prague, p. 230-242.

— "Affixes in Meiteilon (Manipuri)" in International Journal of Dravidian Linguistics (IJDL). Vol. 18, No. 2, June 1989.

— "Terms of Address in Meiteilon" in Linguistics of Tibeto-Burman Areas, Vol. 12:2 Fall 1989, California, Berkeley.

— "Causativisation in Meiteilon" in Language of Tibeto-Burman Area, 14.2 Fall 1992, p. 133-144, California, Berkeley.

— Negation in Meiteilon" in Journal of Asian and African Studies, No. 44, 1992, p. 179-188, Tokyo University of Foreign Studies, Tokyo.

— "Tense or Aspects in Manipuri in New Horizons in Tibeto-Burman Morphosyntax (Semri Ethnological Studies No. 41), Eds, Yoshio Nishi, James A. Matisoff and Yasuhiko Nagano, National Museum of Ethnology, Asaka, Japan, 1995.

— "Tag-Question in Meiteilon " in Monkhmer Studies No. 25, 1996. A Journal of South-East Asian Languages, Ed. Pattiya Jimreivat and others, Institute of Language and Culture for Rural Development, Mahidol University at Salaya, Thailand.

— 'Negation in Kuki Languages' In Languages of Tribal and Indigenous Peoples of India, Ed. Anvita, Motilal Banarsidas, Delhi, 1997.

Thomson, Laurence C., 1965 : A Vietnamese Grammar. University of Washington Press Seattle.

Manipuri Grammar (in Manipuri)

Ningomba, M.S., 1992 : Meitei Lonmit. Saraswati Book House, Imphal.

Sharma, Dwijmani Dev., 1969 : Manipuri Byakaran. Imphal.

Sharma, Ibomcha, 1968 : Meiteil Byakaran, Imphal.

Sharma, Nawalal, 1965 : Meiteilon, Orient Book Depot, Imphal.

Sharma, L. Narayan : Meiteilon Byakaran, Waheng Leikai, Imphal.

Shastri, Kalachand, 1971: Manipuri Vyakaran Kaumudi. Abir Singh, O.K. Store, Imphal.

Thoudam P.C., 1991 : Remedial Manipur. Aman Interprise, Imphal.

INDEX

Language Index

Author's Index